The Ethics and Efficacy of the Global War on Terrorism

TWENTY-FIRST CENTURY PERSPECTIVES ON WAR, PEACE, AND HUMAN CONFLICT
Charles P. Webel, Series Editor

Terror, Terrorism, and the Human Condition
Charles P. Webel

*The Ethics and Efficacy of the Global War on Terrorism:
Fighting Terror with Terror*
Edited by Charles P. Webel and John A. Arnaldi

THE ETHICS AND EFFICACY OF THE GLOBAL WAR ON TERRORISM

FIGHTING TERROR WITH TERROR

Edited by

Charles P. Webel and John A. Arnaldi

THE ETHICS AND EFFICACY OF THE GLOBAL WAR ON TERRORISM
Copyright © Charles P. Webel and John A. Arnaldi, 2011

First published in 2011 by
PALGRAVE MACMILLAN®
in the United States—a division of St. Martin's Press LLC,
175 Fifth Avenue, New York, NY 10010.

Where this book is distributed in the UK, Europe and the rest of the world,
this is by Palgrave Macmillan, a division of Macmillan Publishers Limited,
registered in England, company number 785998, of Houndmills,
Basingstoke, Hampshire RG21 6XS.

Palgrave Macmillan is the global academic imprint of the above companies
and has companies and representatives throughout the world.

Palgrave® and Macmillan® are registered trademarks in the United States,
the United Kingdom, Europe and other countries.

ISBN: 978–0–230–11098–4

Library of Congress Cataloging-in-Publication Data

The ethics and efficacy of the global war on terrorism : fighting terror
with terror / edited by Charles P. Webel and John A. Arnaldi.
p. cm.—(Twenty-first century perspectives on war, peace, and
human conflict)
ISBN 978–0–230–11098–4
1. War on Terrorism, 2001–2009—Moral and ethical aspects.
2. Terrorism—Prevention—Evaluation. I. Webel, Charles. II. Arnaldi,
John A., 1951–
HV6431.E84 2011
363.3250973—dc23   2011020095

A catalogue record of the book is available from the British Library.

Design by Newgen Imaging Systems (P) Ltd., Chennai, India.

First edition: December 2011

10 9 8 7 6 5 4 3 2 1

Printed in the United States of America.

CONTENTS

Introduction: Applied Ethics, Human Security, and the War on Terrorism

John A. Arnaldi

> The history of modern war is also, in part, the history of the means by which war has been brought home to noncombatants.
> —*New York Times*, April 15, 2011

On September 11, 2001, nineteen men hijacked four passenger jets to carry out attacks that killed more than 3,000 people in the United States, demonstrating the vulnerability of powerful nations to massive attacks by groups of violent extremists. This shocking example of "asymmetric warfare" between powerful nations and adversaries unwilling to confront them directly served as a warning that national security had to be reexamined and an effective, multilateral antiterrorism strategy made a top priority. However, rather than waiting for a full accounting of facts and for debate of dissenting views, in the "global war on terrorism" (GWOT) the U.S.-led coalition has fought violence with more violence and terrorism with massive state terrorism.

After nearly a decade of costly warfare and the erosion of human rights, a comprehensive, fact-based understanding of these extremely important challenges is still urgently needed. The aim of the present volume is to critically examine the West's efforts to deter and counter nonstate terrorism from the perspectives of applied ethics, efficacy, and human security.

This volume begins with a section that explores the controversies of terrorism, counterterrorism, and antiterrorism. The articles in part one challenge widely promoted views that have favored the national security interests of states above other actors. The second part identifies ethical and legal concerns from a human security perspective and challenges arguments used by the coalition to justify its policies and conduct. The third part explores information warfare: how political rhetoric and media dynamics have shaped public understanding of the GWOT. The fourth part focuses on specific controversies in the conduct of the GWOT, including the use of drone aircraft, disregard for the sovereignty of allies, extraordinary rendition, extralegal detentions, torture, unreliable paid informants, and sham trials and tribunals. The book concludes with a discussion of research findings on how terrorist groups end and recommendations for effective anti-terrorism strategies that prioritize the long-term "vital interests of human beings"[1] above short-term national self-interests.

> The language of counter-terrorism incorporates a series of assumptions, beliefs and knowledge about the nature of terrorism and terrorists. These beliefs then determine what kinds of counter-terrorism practices are reasonable or unreasonable, appropriate or inappropriate.[2]

The language used to frame a problem also shapes the solution. After the attacks of September 11, the dominant Western narrative for terrorism, promoted by many top U.S., British, and other coalition decision-makers, held that terrorism, especially extremist Islamic terrorism, was the front line in a clash of civilizations—a new and grave threat to the "civilized" world. Framing the problem as a global war against "evil" implied that the only solution to terrorist attacks had to be a massive military response. Existing national security policies had already proven ineffective against this new threat, and had failed to prevent the attacks of September 11, and, therefore, new, tougher methods were ostensibly needed. Some high-level Bush administration officials, believing that "just war" concerns would handicap counterterrorism efforts, replaced them with a preventive war doctrine derived largely from a neoconservative version of realpolitik. This frame also justified questionable legal changes, such as passage and renewal of the *USA Patriot Act*, which grants U.S. government agencies greater powers to investigate, prosecute, or detain *potential* terrorists—but at the cost of limiting the civil rights of all citizens.

If a different narrative had been used, different solutions might have been prescribed. For example, if the attacks of September 11 had been framed as crimes perpetrated by a small group of violent extremists, a law enforcement narrative would have been more appropriate. This narrative would have explained that terrorism is an old problem, not limited to Muslim extremists, that is presenting a new ideological face, which might be fought effectively with methods that protect civil and human rights. Most significantly, a law enforcement model might neither have disregarded domestic and international laws nor conducted the bombings and occupations of sovereign nations, which, in disregard for proportionality, have caused hundreds of thousands of casualties to date, far exceeding the small number of suspected terrorists. By combining law enforcement and human security models, strong multilateral antiterrorism strategies might still be developed and implemented at much lower financial and human costs than required for the "GWOT."

Given the powerful influence of language in setting the parameters of discourse,[3] we offer brief definitions for these key terms:

- *War* is the use of lethal force to "settle" political conflicts between two or more adversarial groups or nations. There are many forms, including: civil war, revolution/insurrection, terrorist and counterterrorist campaigns, genocide, and blockades resulting in dehydration, starvation, disease, or death for civilians and others.
- *Terrorism* is a tactic for violent conflict between unequal adversaries that employs shocking attacks (or threatened attacks) on civilian, government/military, and symbolic targets in order to generate terror, which then is used to attempt to influence key persons (i.e., leaders) otherwise unreachable. Although states commonly limit this term to attacks by nonstate extremist groups, it also applies to such attacks when conducted or supported by states.[4] Both lethal and nonlethal actions can be used to systematically terrify targeted groups, for example, actual or threatened torture, disappearance, extrajudicial detention/imprisonment, seizure of property, and other violations of human rights.
- *Counterterrorism* employs methods of war to "fight fire with greater fire" to stop attacks by nonstate terrorists. The "GWOT" initiated by former president George W. Bush's administration and continued by President Barack Obama's as "Overseas Contingency Operations"[5] is a notable example of recent U.S.-led counterterrorism campaigns that employ long-term warfare and the restriction of civil and human rights as principal methods.
- *Antiterrorism* is a multilateral approach to human security that ideally uses ethical, legally sanctioned methods for establishing effective communication and just relations between adversaries, resolving conflicts peacefully, and bringing terrorists to justice.

Conceptulizations of security as defined by the vital interests of human beings rather than of the state are long overdue—and still virtually absent from mainstream political and media deliberations.[6]

National security and human security are not equivalent terms. Within the traditional paradigm of national security, the nation-state arrogates to itself the principal authority for protecting the collective health and welfare of its citizens. In contrast, "human security" is an emerging paradigm that challenges "the traditional notion of national security by arguing that the proper referent for security should be the individual rather than the state. Human security holds that a people-centered view of security is necessary for national, regional and global stability."[7]

From the perspective of human security, the costs of the war on terrorism have been unacceptably high: U.S. financial costs may exceed three trillion dollars just for the war in Iraq[8]; as of August 2011, 7,461 coalition troops have been killed in the wars in Afghanistan and Iraq[9]; and at least 100,000 civilians have been killed in Iraq alone.[10] In Afghanistan, Iraq, Pakistan, and Somalia, millions of persons have been rendered homeless and additional millions continue to suffer from shortages of food, clean water, medicine, and electricity. Drone, missile, bombing attacks, and other state-sponsored military actions continue to take a toll on civilians. Globally, tens of thousands of innocent persons have been detained by coalition military and security forces, usually without charges and without legal representation. Increased security measures within the United States have by-passed constitutional rights and judicial processes, as in the case of domestic spying.

Promises that costly national security actions will save unknown numbers of hypothetical persons from potential threats at an unspecified future time sharply differ from the top human security priority to protect real persons from actual harms. Citing the interests of national security and self-defense, states make the utilitarian claim that the potential benefits of military violence outweigh the costs. However, as tempting as it may be to view the absence of successful terrorist attacks in the United States after September 11 as evidence that the war on terror has succeeded (at least in part) in its primary mission to protect the United States, there is no demonstrable causal relationship between the war on terrorism and the absence of attacks since it began—there may have been no additional attacks even if the war had never been waged—and nonmilitary reasons, such as good police work, may be responsible for this.

In the first nine years of the war on terrorism, the number of deaths on American soil due to terrorist attacks remain at the approximately 3,000 killed on September 11, 2001, averaging out to 333 deaths per year. From a utilitarian perspective of seeking the greatest good for the greatest number of persons, the high costs of the war on terrorism are hard to justify based on 333 terrorist-caused deaths per year when compared to examples of four possibly preventable causes of death that kill nearly half a million persons each year, but which are not afforded a level of national and global attention and resources proportionate to what have been devoted to fighting non-state terrorism. The four categories accounting for 531,000 deaths annually in the United States are: abuse and neglect causing the deaths of more than 1,740 children,[11] vehicle-related accidents causing at least 43,000 deaths,[12] medical errors causing a minimum of 44,000 deaths,[13] and the use of tobacco causing 443,000 deaths.[14]

One becomes a killer by killing.[15]

Morality is concerned with the nature of right and wrong, good and bad actions; and ethics (or moral philosophy) studies the groundwork of morality. *Applied ethics* seeks an understanding of the moral dimensions of specific, real-life controversies and their potential solutions.

A brief overview of general approaches to ethics may be helpful. *Deontology* argues that the morality of an act is determined by an actor's goodwill—the *intent* to fulfill a moral duty or obey an applicable moral rule. From a Kantian deontological perspective, a rule is ethical when: (1) it is *categorical*—there are no exceptions to its application; (2) it exhibits *universality*—when the rule is applied to one person or group, the resulting good must equal the good obtained when the same rule is applied to any other persons or groups; and (3) it does not use persons as the means to gain specific ends—it respects all persons as the specific end.[16]

Utilitarianism is a version of consequentialism in which morality is determined by an act's utility (efficacy) in producing the greatest good for the most people. Good ends justify the means. The efficacy of an act has greater moral significance than the actor's intentions. The morality of an act is dependent upon how the outcome criteria are defined; for example, a drone attack may be judged a success by the nation that launched it because it met its criterion for killing alleged enemy combatants, while the villagers where the attack took place may judge it an immoral act because civilians were killed. The same would be true for judging the ethics of using nuclear weapons and other weapons of mass destruction—the outcome might be judged a success by the attackers, but the survivors and other members of the global community probably won't agree. Additionally, judgment of results often depends upon the length of time between the act and the evaluation of its consequences. For example, in the case of the drone attack, immediately afterward it may be judged a success because it killed the targeted group of alleged terrorists, but over a period of several years it may be judged a failure because many of the family, friends, and community of those killed subsequently supported or joined terrorist groups, or failed to cooperate with the nation that launched the drone.

Specific applications of ethics to war usually encompass three ethical traditions: realism/realpolitik, just war, and pacifism, each relevant to ethical analysis of the GWOT. All three traditions presume that an individual has a "natural" right to life; however, they differ in the extent to which war is acceptable as a moral means of protecting lives designated as innocent and of preserving "national security."

Realism or *Realpolitik* argues that the political behavior of nations and their adversaries is based, not on civilian private morality, but on pragmatic considerations of national self-interest and power. An alternate version is that the moral duty to protect the greatest number of innocent persons from harm justifies using virtually any means necessary, including total war. In realism, it makes no sense to fight under rules that might give an advantage to the enemy and thereby prolong the war, when unrestricted military action might end the war more quickly and efficiently. Universality is not a consideration, as the only obligation is to the nation's defense of its own citizens and interests.

The ethical criteria of the *Just War Tradition* presume that it is in the interests of all nations to restrict war within certain limits that will minimize harm to persons, especially to civilians and other noncombatants. Two phases of warfare are considered: *Jus ad bellum* stipulates the criteria for initiating a just war, while *jus in bello* describes just conduct during war. Unfortunately, the just war criteria have failed to reduce the frequency or destructiveness of war, in part due to the ease with which nations can interpret the criteria in favor of their own interests.

Pacifism is an ethical system that tends to be absolutist about the inviolability of the sanctity of human life—war is never defensible as a moral exception to society's standard prohibition against killing. Designating groups of persons as innocent or guilty is irrelevant because all persons have a natural right to life that is not dependent upon the fallible determinations made by human authority.

The disheartening fact that each year brings hundreds of thousands more civilian war deaths worldwide[17] points to an urgent need to reconsider the efficacy of lethal military solutions. This applies particularly to the "Fourth World War," the GWOT.

Unfortunately, the dominant war narrative in much of the advanced industrial world today acts as a filter through which the frequency and severity of recent wars and "terrorist" threats tend to be narrowly construed as evidence of this narrative's validity. Without the influence of that narrative, past and ongoing wars might be regarded as evidence of the catastrophic failure of lethal force to save lives and resolve political conflicts. This recognition might free decision-makers to seek, and the public to demand, solutions that have demonstrated long-term efficacy in preventing, reducing, and resolving violent conflicts. In the conclusion of this book, we offer a possible alternative to the GWOT, a partial solution to the unresolved conflict underlying it.

NOTES

1. Heidi Ross, "Rethinking Human Vulnerability, Security, and Connection Through Relational Theorizing," in *Comparative Education, Terrorism, and Human Security: From Critical Pedagogy to Peacebuilding*, ed. Wayne Nelles (New York: Palgrave Macmillan, 2003), 38–39.
2. Richard Jackson, *Writing the War on Terrorism: Language, Politics and Counter-terrorism* (New York: Manchester University Press, 2007), 8–9.
3. See Stephen D. Reese and Seth C. Lewis, "Framing the War on Terror," chapter seven in this volume.
4. See Charles P. Webel, "The 'Ethics' of Terror and Terrorism," chapter two in this volume.
5. DoD FY 2010 Budget Request Summary Justification: http://comptroller.defense.gov/defbudget/fy2010/fy2010_SSJ_Overseas_Contingency_Operations.pdf.
6. Ross, "Rethinking Human Vulnerability," 38–39.
7. "Human Security," *Wikipedia*, December 28, 2010: http://en.wikipedia.org/wiki/Human_security.
8. Joseph E. Stiglitz and Linda J. Bilmes, "The True Cost of the Iraq War: $3 Trillion and Beyond," *The Washington Post*, September 5, 2010: http://www.washingtonpost.com/wp-dyn/content/article/2010/09/03/AR2010090302200.html.
9. *Icasualties.org*: http://icasualties.org/.
10. *Iraq Body Count*: http://www.iraqbodycount.org/.
11. U.S. Department of Health and Human Services, "Child Abuse and Neglect Fatalities" 2010: http://www.childwelfare.gov/pubs/factsheets/fatality.cfm#children.
12. U. S. Census, "Table 118. Deaths and Death Rates by Selected Causes: 2006 and 2007," 2011: http://www.census.gov/compendia/statab/2011/tables/11s0118.pdf.

13. U.S. Agency for Healthcare Research and Quality, "Twenty Tips to Prevent Medical Errors" February 2000: http://www.ahrq.gov /consumer/20tips.htm.

14. American Cancer Society, "Cancer Facts & Figures 2010," April 18, 2011: http://www.cancer.org/Cancer/CancerCauses/TobaccoCancer /tobacco-related-cancer-fact-sheet.

15. Laurie Calhoun, "Just War? Moral Soldiers?," *The Independent Review* IV.3 (2000): 325.

16. Robert Johnson, "Kant's Moral Philosophy," *Stanford Encyclopedia of Philosophy* April 2008: http://plato.stanford.edu/entries/kant-moral/.

17. Milton Leitenberg, "Deaths in Wars and Conflicts in the 20th Century," *Occasional Paper #29*, Cornell University, 2006.

PART I

UNDERSTANDING ETHICAL CHALLENGES IN THE WAR ON TERRORISM

OVERVIEW

Charles P. Webel and John A. Arnaldi

Terrorism is a vexing term. Any actual or threatened attack against civilian noncombatants, and, arguably, against soldiers, police, and political leaders, may be considered an act of "terrorism." "Terrorists" are people who typically feel unable to confront their perceived enemies directly and who accordingly use violence, or the threat of violence, usually against noncombatants, to achieve their political aims.

Placing "terrorist" in quotation marks may be jarring for some readers, who consider the designation self-evident. This is done, however, not to minimize the horror of such acts but to emphasize that often one person's "terrorist" is another's "freedom fighter." Thus, who is or is not a terrorist and what may or may not be acts of terrorism depend largely on the perspective of the person or group using these terms.

Although it is possibly the most contested concept in the contemporary political lexicon, "terrorism" has been used most often to denote politically motivated attacks by subnational agents (this part is virtually uncontested among Western scholars) and states (this is widely debated, but increasingly accepted outside the United States) on noncombatants, usually in the context of war, revolution, and struggles for national liberation. In this sense, "terrorism" is as old as violent human conflict.

"Terrorism" is also a contemporary variant of what has been described as guerrilla warfare, dating back at least to the anticolonialist and anti-imperialist struggles for national liberation conducted in North America and Western Europe during the late eighteenth and early nineteenth centuries and continuing after World War II in Africa and South Asia against such European empires as the British, French, Dutch, and Portuguese. Many attacks committed by insurgents against occupying forces in Afghanistan, Iraq, Palestine, and elsewhere are similarly considered as anti-imperialist, not "terrorist," by their perpetrators.

Hence, "terrorism" is at bottom a political construct: a histori-cally variable and ideologically useful way of branding those who may violently oppose a particular policy or government as beyond the moral pale, and hence "not worthy" of diplomacy and negotiations. Moreover, yesterday's "terrorist" may become today's or tomorrow's chief of state—if successful in seizing or otherwise gaining state power.

Terrifying acts of political violence, whether from above (state ter-rorism) or from below (nonstate terrorism), are usually "justified" by their perpetrators, and hence viewed as "ethical" by terrorist agents. Nonstate terrorists often claim they're responding to state oppres-sion and foreign occupation, or retaliating for violence perpetrated by states against their people. Governments defend terrorizing internal measures against their own citizens with appeals to national security. And they justify attacks on foreign nationals and the military occu-pation of other nations by claiming the right of self-defense. For the victims, though, such acts are prima facie unethical.

The "global war on terror," having just entered its second decade, presents special challenges for mainstream and heterodox ethical tra-ditions. Consequentialists, deontologists, and pacifists must all grap-ple with the dilemmas posed by terrorist violence in general, and by the uncertainties and tensions generated by responding to terrorist attacks, whether from below or from above.

In this section, Noam Chomsky situates the current war on terror-ism in an historical context. Chomsky argues that the current "war on terror" is a redeclaration of a "war," or a "particularly virulent form of international state terrorism" initially declared 20 years ear-lier by the Reagan administration, against "the evil scourge of terror-ism." Chomsky claims that U.S. administration policy has inspired, not defeated, radical Islamist terrorism, and continues to violate such elementary moral principles as universality.

Charles Webel explores the links between the politics of terrify-ing political violence—perpetrated both by states and their agents (TFA, or "Terrorism from Above") and by nonstate terrorists (TFB, or "Terrorism from Below")—and the subjective experiences of the victims of terrorism. He focuses on terror, the root of terror-ism, which has been widely neglected. Webel argues that state and state-supported acts of terrorism (TFA) are more, not less, unethi-cal than what the mass media equate with terrorism—namely, the violence committed by non- and antistate agents—and that there are more ethical means to address the roots of all forms of terrorism. One possibility is to replace counterterrorist violence with antiterrorist prevention and interception measures. Another is negotiation with members or representatives of antistate terrorist groups. And finally, there are changes in state political policy. These include ending the occupation(s) of territories nonstate terrorists are dedicated to "liberating," and incorporating representatives of these groups into the political process.

Scott Atran examines and criticizes some prevailing theories of terrorism, especially the "mistaken premise" that assumes correlations with economic status, educational level, and the degree of civil liberties can predict who become terrorists. Based largely on his interviews with members of the families of suicide bombers and his visits to the breeding grounds of Islamist terrorists, Atran argues it is the social networks and group dynamics of these networks that are crucial for understanding how terrorists come together and why they are dedicated to "Takfiri" causes involving murder and suicide.

In this section, official mainstream constructions of "terrorists" and "terrorism" are challenged, as are the justifications for initiating and continuing a "global war on terror." This dominant discourse also cloaks numerous ethical assumptions—attempts to justify the morality of killing in "war"—which are called into question. And the contributors offer alternative frames for understanding the roots of terrorism from above and from below, and for responding to terrifying acts of political violence without escalating the conflict.

1

THE EVIL SCOURGE OF TERRORISM: REALITY, CONSTRUCTION, REMEDY

Noam Chomsky

The president could not have been more justified when he condemned "the evil scourge of terrorism." I am quoting Ronald Reagan, who came into office in 1981 declaring that a focus of his foreign policy would be state-directed international terrorism, "the plague of the modern age" and "a return to barbarism in our time," to sample some of the rhetoric of his administration.

When George W. Bush declared a "war on terror" 20 years later, he was *re*declaring the war, an important fact that is worth exhuming from Orwell's memory hole if we hope to understand the nature of the evil scourge of terrorism, or more importantly, if we hope to understand ourselves. We do not need the famous Delphi inscription to recognize that there can be no more important task. Just as a personal aside, that critical necessity was forcefully brought home to me almost 70 years ago in my first encounter with Erich Fromm's work, in his classic essay on the escape to freedom in the modern world, and the grim paths that the modern free individual was tempted to choose in the effort to escape the loneliness and anguish that accompanied the newly discovered freedom—matters all too pertinent today, unfortunately.

The reasons why Reagan's war on terror has been dispatched to the repository of unwelcome facts are understandable and informative—about ourselves. Instantly, Reagan's war on terror became a savage terrorist war, leaving hundreds of thousands of tortured and mutilated corpses in the wreckage of Central America, tens of thousands more in the Middle East, and an estimated 1.5 million killed by South African terror that was strongly supported by the Reagan administration in violation of congressional sanctions. All of these murderous exercises of course had pretexts. The resort to violence always does. In the Middle East, Reagan's decisive support for Israel's 1982 invasion of Lebanon, which killed some 15,000–20,000 people and destroyed much of southern Lebanon and Beirut, was based on the pretense that it was in self-defense against PLO rocketing of the Galilee, a brazen fabrication: Israel recognized at once that the threat was PLO diplomacy, which might have undermined Israel's illegal takeover of the occupied territories. In Africa, support for the marauding of the apartheid state was officially justified within the framework of the war on terror: it was necessary to protect white South Africa from one of the world's "more notorious terrorist groups," Nelson Mandela's African National Congress, so Washington determined in 1988. The pretexts in the other cases were no more impressive.

For the most part, the victims of Reaganite terror were defenseless civilians, but in one case the victim was a state, Nicaragua, which could respond through legal channels. Nicaragua brought its charges to the World Court, which condemned the United States for "unlawful use of force"—in lay terms, international terrorism—in its attack on Nicaragua from its Honduran bases, and ordered the United States to terminate the assault and pay substantial reparations. The aftermath is instructive.

Congress responded to the Court judgment by increasing aid to the U.S.-run mercenary army attacking Nicaragua, while the press condemned the Court as a "hostile forum" and therefore irrelevant. The same Court had been highly relevant a few years earlier when it ruled in favor of the United States against Iran. Washington dismissed the Court judgment with contempt. In doing so, it joined the distinguished company of Libya's Qaddafi and Albania's Enver Hoxha. Libya and Albania have since joined the world of law-abiding states in this respect, so now the United States stands in splendid isolation. Nicaragua then brought the matter to the UN Security Council, which passed two resolutions calling on all states to observe international law. The resolutions were vetoed by the United States, with the assistance of Britain and France, which abstained. All of this passed virtually without notice, and has been expunged from history.

Also forgotten—or rather, never noticed—is the fact that the "hostile forum" had bent over backward to accommodate Washington. The Court rejected almost all of Nicaragua's case, presented by a distinguished Harvard University international lawyer, on the grounds that when the United States had accepted World Court jurisdiction in 1946, it added a reservation exempting itself from charges under international treaties, specifically the Charters of the United Nations and the Organization of American States. Accordingly, the United States is self-entitled to carry out aggression and other crimes that are far more serious than international terrorism. The Court correctly recognized this exemption, one aspect of much broader issues of sovereignty and global dominance that I will put aside.

Such thoughts as these should be uppermost in our minds when we consider the evil scourge of terrorism. We should also recall that although the Reagan years do constitute a chapter of unusual extremism in the annals of terrorism, they are not some strange departure from the norm. We find much the same at the opposite end of the political spectrum as well: the Kennedy administration. One illustration is Cuba. According to long-standing myth, thoroughly dismantled by recent scholarship, the United States intervened in Cuba in 1898 to secure its liberation from Spain. In reality, the intervention was designed to *prevent* Cuba's imminent liberation from Spain, turning it into a virtual colony of the United States. In 1959, Cuba finally did liberate itself, causing consternation in Washington. Within months, the Eisenhower administration planned in secret to overthrow the government, and initiated bombing and economic sanctions. The basic thinking was expressed by a high State Department official: Castro would be removed "through disenchantment and disaffection based on economic dissatisfaction and hardship [so] every possible means should be undertaken promptly to weaken the economic life of Cuba [in order to] bring about hunger, desperation and [the] overthrow of the government."

The incoming Kennedy administration took over and escalated these programs. The reasons are frankly explained in the internal record, since declassified. Violence and economic strangulation were undertaken in response to Cuba's "successful defiance" of U.S. policies going back 150 years; no Russians, but rather the Monroe Doctrine, which established Washington's right to dominate the hemisphere.

The concerns of the Kennedy administration went beyond the need to punish successful defiance. The administration feared that the Cuban example might infect others with the thought of "taking matters into their own hands," an idea with great appeal throughout the continent because "the distribution of land and other forms of national wealth greatly favors the propertied classes and the poor and underprivileged, stimulated by the example of the Cuban revolution, are now demanding opportunities for a decent living." That was the warning conveyed to incoming president Kennedy by his Latin

America advisor, liberal historian Arthur Schlesinger. The analysis was soon confirmed by the CIA, which observed that "Castro's shadow looms large because social and economic conditions throughout Latin America invite opposition to ruling authority and encourage agitation for radical change," for which Castro's Cuba might provide a model.

Ongoing plans for invasion were soon implemented. When the invasion failed at the Bay of Pigs, Washington turned to a major terrorist war. The president assigned responsibility for the war to his brother Robert Kennedy, whose highest priority was to bring "the terrors of the earth" to Cuba, in the words of his biographer, Arthur Schlesinger. The terrorist war was no slight affair; it was also a major factor in bringing the world to the verge of nuclear war in 1962, and was resumed as soon as the missile crisis ended. The terrorist war continued through the century from U.S. territory, though in later years Washington no longer undertook terrorist attacks against Cuba, but only provided the base for them, and continues to provide a haven to some of the most notorious international terrorists, with a long record of these and other crimes: Orlando Bosch, Luis Posada Carriles, and numerous others whose names would be well-known in the West if the concerns about terrorism were principled. Commentators are polite enough not to recall what the Bush doctrine declared when he attacked Afghanistan: those who harbor terrorists are as guilty as the terrorists themselves, and must be treated accordingly, by bombing and invasion.

Perhaps this is enough to illustrate that state-directed international terrorism is considered an appropriate tool of diplomacy across the political spectrum. Nevertheless, Reagan was the first modern president to employ the audacious device of concealing his resort to "the evil scourge of terrorism" under the cloak of a "war on terror."

The audacity of Reaganite terrorism was as impressive as its scale. To select only one example, for which events in Germany provided a pretext, in April 1986 the U.S. Air Force bombed Libya, killing dozens of civilians. To add a personal note, on the day of the bombing, at about 6:30 P.M., I received a phone call from Tripoli from the Mideast correspondent of ABC TV, Charles Glass, an old friend. He advised me to watch the 7 P.M. TV news. In 1986, all the TV channels ran their major news programs at 7 P.M. I did so, and exactly at 7, agitated news anchors switched to their facilities in Libya so that they could present, live, the U.S. bombing of Tripoli and Benghazi, the first bombing in history enacted for prime time TV—no slight logistical feat: the bombers were denied the right to cross France and had to take a long detour over the Atlantic to arrive just in time for the evening news. After showing the exciting scenes of the cities in flames, the TV channels switched to Washington, for sober discussion of how the United States was defending itself from Libyan terror, under the newly devised doctrine of "self-defense against future attack." Officials informed the country that they had certain knowledge that Libya had carried out a bombing of a disco in Berlin a few days earlier in which a U.S. soldier had been killed. Soon after this bombing, this "certainty" was reduced to zero, as these officials quietly conceded well after their purpose had been served. And it would have been hard to find even a raised eyebrow about the idea that the disco bombing would have justified the murderous assault on Libyan civilians.

The media were also polite enough not to notice the curious timing. Commentators were entranced by the solidity of the nonexistent evidence and Washington's dedication to law. In a typical reaction, the *New York Times* editors explained that "even the most scrupulous citizen can only approve and applaud the American attacks on Libya…the United States has prosecuted [Qaddafi] carefully, proportionately—and justly," the evidence for Libyan responsibility for the disco bombing has been "now laid out clearly to the public," and "then came the jury, the European governments to which the United States went out of its way to send emissaries to share evidence and urge concerted action against the Libyan leader." Entirely irrelevant is that no credible evidence was laid out and that the "jury" was quite skeptical, particularly in Germany itself, where intensive investigation had found no evidence at all; or that the jury was calling on the executioner to refrain from any action.

The bombing of Libya was neatly timed for a congressional vote on aid to the U.S.-run terrorist force attacking Nicaragua. To ensure that the timing would not be missed, Reagan made the connection explicit. In an address the day after the bombing Reagan said: "I would remind the House [of Representatives] voting this week that this arch-terrorist [Qaddafi] has sent $400 million and an arsenal of weapons and advisers into Nicaragua to bring his war home to the United States. He has bragged that he is helping the Nicaraguans because they fight America on its own ground"—namely, America's own ground in Nicaragua. The idea that the "mad dog" was bringing his war home to us by providing arms to a country we were attacking with a CIA-run terrorist army based in our Honduran dependency was a nice touch, which did not go unnoticed. As the national press explained, the bombing of Libya should "strengthen President Reagan's hand in dealing with Congress on issues like the military budget and aid to Nicaraguan 'contras.'"

This is only a small sample of Reagan's contributions to international terrorism. The most lasting among them was his enthusiastic organization of the jihadi movement in Afghanistan. The reasons were explained by the CIA station chief in Islamabad, who directed the project. In his words, the goal was to "kill Soviet Soldiers," a "noble goal" that he "loved," as did his boss in Washington. He also emphasized that "the mission was not to liberate Afghanistan"—and in fact it may have delayed Soviet withdrawal, some specialists believe. With his unerring instinct for favoring the most violent criminals, Reagan selected for lavish aid Gulbuddin Hekmatyar, famous for throwing acid in the faces of young women in Kabul and now a leader of the insurgents in Afghanistan, though perhaps he may soon join the other warlords of the Western-backed government, current reports suggest. Reagan also lent strong support to the worst of Pakistan's dictators, Zia ul-Haq, helping him to develop his nuclear weapons program and to carry out his Saudi-funded project of radical Islamization of Pakistan. There is no need to dwell on the legacy for these tortured countries and the world.

Apart from Cuba, the plague of state terror in the Western hemisphere was initiated with the Brazilian coup in 1964, installing the first of a series of neo-Nazi National Security States and initiating a plague of repression without precedent in the hemisphere, always strongly backed by Washington, hence a particularly violent form of state-directed international terrorism. The campaign was in substantial measure a war against the Church. It was more than symbolic that it culminated in the assassination of six leading Latin American intellectuals, Jesuit priests, in November 1989, a few days after the fall of the Berlin wall. They were murdered by an elite Salvadoran battalion, fresh from renewed training at the John F. Kennedy Special Forces School in North Carolina. As was learned in November 2008, but apparently aroused no interest, the order for the assassination was signed by the chief of staff and his associates, all of them so closely connected to the Pentagon and the U.S. Embassy that it becomes even harder to imagine that Washington was unaware of the plans of its model battalion. This elite force had already left a trail of blood of the usual victims through the hideous decade of the 1980s in El Salvador, which opened with the assassination of Archbishop Romero, "the voice of the voiceless," by much the same hands.

The murder of the Jesuit priests was a crushing blow to liberation theology, the remarkable revival of Christianity initiated by Pope John XXIII at Vatican II, which he opened in 1962, an event that "ushered in a new era in the history of the Catholic Church," in the words of the distinguished theologian and historian of Christianity Hans Küng. Inspired by Vatican II, Latin American Bishops adopted "the preferential option for the poor," renewing the radical pacifism of the Gospels that had been put to rest when the Emperor Constantine established Christianity as the religion of the Roman Empire—"a revolution" that converted "the persecuted church" to a "persecuting church," in Küng's words. In the post-Vatican II attempt to revive the Christianity of the pre-Constantine period, priests, nuns, and laypersons took the message of the Gospels to the poor and the persecuted, brought them together in "base communities," and encouraged them to take their fate into their own hands and to work together to overcome the misery of survival in brutal realms of U.S. power.

The reaction to this grave heresy was not long in coming. The first salvo was the Kennedy-initiated military coup in Brazil in 1964, overthrowing a mildly social democratic government and instituting a reign of torture and violence. The campaign ended with the murder of the Jesuit intellectuals 20 years ago. There has been much debate about who deserves credit for the fall of the Berlin Wall, but there is none about the responsibility for the brutal demolition of the attempt to revive the church of the Gospels. Washington's School of the Americas, famous for its training of Latin American killers, proudly announced as one of its "talking points" that liberation theology was "defeated with the assistance of the US army"—given a helping hand, to be sure by the Vatican, using the gentler means of expulsion and suppression.

November 2009 was dedicated to celebration of the 20th anniversary of the liberation of Eastern Europe from Russian tyranny, a victory of the forces of "love, tolerance, nonviolence, the human spirit and forgiveness," as Vaclav Havel declared. Less attention—in fact, virtually zero—was devoted to the brutal assassination of his Salvadoran counterparts a few days after the Berlin Wall fell. And I doubt that one could even find an allusion to what that brutal assassination signified: the end of a decade of vicious terror in Central America, and the final triumph of the "return to barbarism in our time" that opened with the 1964 Brazilian coup, leaving many religious martyrs in its wake and ending the heresy initiated in Vatican II—not exactly an era of "love, tolerance, nonviolence, the human spirit and forgiveness."

We can wait until tomorrow to see how much attention will be given to the 30th anniversary of the assassination of the Voice of the Voiceless while he was reading mass, a few days after he wrote a letter to President Carter pleading with him—in vain—not to send aid to the military junta, who "know only how to repress the people and defend the interests of the Salvadorean oligarchy" and will use the aid "to destroy the people's organizations fighting to defend their fundamental human rights." As happened. And we can learn a good bit from what we are unlikely to see tomorrow.

The contrast between the celebration in November 2009 of the fall of the tyranny of the enemy, and the silence about the culmination of the hideous atrocities in our own domains is so glaring that it takes real dedication to miss it. It sheds a somber light on our moral and intellectual culture. The same is true of the retrospective assessments of the Reagan era. We can put aside the mythology about his achievements, which would have impressed Kim il-Sung. What he actually did has virtually disappeared. President Obama hails him as a "transformative figure." At Stanford University's prestigious Hoover Institution Reagan is revered as a colossus whose "spirit seems to stride the country, watching us like a warm and friendly ghost." We arrive by plane in Washington at Reagan international airport—or if we prefer, at John Foster Dulles international airport, honoring another prominent terrorist commander, whose exploits include overthrowing Iranian and Guatemalan democracy, installing the terror and torture state of the Shah and the most vicious of the terrorist states of Central America. The terrorist exploits of Washington's Guatemalan clients reached true genocide in the highlands in the 1980s while Reagan praised the worst of the killers, Rioss Montt, as "a man of great personal integrity" who was "totally dedicated to democracy" and was receiving a "bum rap" from human rights organizations.

I have been writing about international terrorism ever since Reagan declared a war on terror in 1981. In doing so, I have kept to the official definitions of "terrorism" in U.S. and British law and in army manuals, all approximately the same. To take one succinct official definition, terrorism is "the calculated use of violence or threat of violence to attain goals that are political, religious, or ideological in nature...through intimidation, coercion, or instilling fear." Everything I have just described, and a great deal more like it, falls within the category of terrorism, in fact state-directed international terrorism, in the technical sense of U.S.-British law.

For exactly that reason, the official definitions are unusable. They fail to make a crucial distinction: the concept of "terrorism" must somehow be crafted to include *their* terrorism against *us*, while excluding *our* terrorism against *them*, often far more extreme. To devise such a definition is a challenging task. Accordingly, from the 1980s there have been many scholarly conferences, academic publications, and international symposia devoted to the task of defining "terrorism." In public discourse the problem does not arise. Well-educated circles have internalized the special sense of "terrorism" required for justification of state action and control of domestic populations, and departure from the canon is generally ignored, or if noticed, elicits impressive tantrums.

Let us keep, then, to convention, and restrict attention to the terror *they* commit against *us*. It is no laughing matter, and it sometimes reaches extreme levels. Probably the most egregious single crime of international terrorism in the modern era was the destruction of the World Trade Center on 9/11, killing almost 3,000 people, a "crime against humanity" carried out with "wickedness and awesome cruelty," as Robert Fisk reported. It is widely agreed that 9/11 changed the world.

Awful as the crime was, one can imagine worse. Suppose that al-Qaeda had been supported by an awesome superpower intent on overthrowing the government of the United States. Suppose that the attack had succeeded: al-Qaeda had bombed the White House, killed the president, and installed a vicious military dictatorship, which killed some 50,000–100,000 people, brutally tortured 700,000, set up a major center of terror and subversion that carried out assassinations throughout the world and helped establish "National Security States" elsewhere that tortured and murdered with abandon. Suppose further that the dictator brought in economic advisers who within a few years drove the economy to one of the worst disasters in its history while their proud mentors collected Nobel Prizes and received other accolades. That would have been vastly more horrendous even than 9/11.

And as we all should know, it is not necessary to imagine, because it in fact did happen: in Chile, on the date that Latin Americans sometimes call "the first 9/11," September 11, 1973. The only change I have made is to per capita equivalents, an appropriate measure. But the first 9/11 did not change history, for good reasons: the events were too normal. In fact the installation of the Pinochet regime was just one event in the plague that began with the military coup in Brazil in 1964, spreading with similar or even worse horrors in other countries and reaching Central America in the 1980s under Reagan—whose South American favorite was the regime of the Argentine generals, the most savage of them all, consistent with his general stance on state violence.

Putting all of this inconvenient reality aside, let us continue to follow convention and imagine that the war on terror redeclared by George W. Bush on 9/11 2001 was directed to ending the plague of international terrorism, properly restricted in scope to satisfy doctrinal needs. There were sensible steps that could have been undertaken to achieve that goal. The murderous acts of 9/11 were bitterly condemned even within the jihadi movements. One constructive step would have been to isolate al-Qaeda, and unify opposition to it even among those attracted to its project. Nothing of the sort ever seems to have been considered. Instead, the Bush administration and its allies chose to unify the jihadi movement in support of bin Laden and to mobilize many others to his cause by confirming his charge that the West is at war with Islam: invading Afghanistan and then Iraq, resorting to torture and rendition, and in general, choosing violence for the purposes of state power. With good reason, the hawkish Michael Scheuer, who was in charge of tracking bin Laden for the CIA for many years, concludes that "the United States of America remains bin Laden's only indispensable ally."

The same conclusion was drawn by U.S. major Matthew Alexander, perhaps the most respected of U.S. interrogators, who elicited the information that led to the capture of Abu Musab al-Zarqawi, the head of al-Qaeda in Iraq. Alexander has only contempt for the harsh interrogation methods demanded by the Bush administration. Like FBI interrogators, he believes that the Rumsfeld-Cheney preference for torture elicits no useful information, in contrast with more humane forms of interrogation that have even succeeded in converting the targets and enlisting them as reliable informants and collaborators. He singles out Indonesia for its successes in civilized forms of interrogation, and urges the United States to follow its methods. Not only does Rumsfeld-Cheney torture elicit no useful information, it also creates terrorists. From hundreds of interrogations, Alexander discovered that many foreign fighters came to Iraq in reaction to the abuses at Guantánamo and Abu Ghraib, and that they and their domestic allies turned to suicide bombing and other terrorist acts for the same reason. He believes that the use of torture may have led to the death of more U.S. soldiers than the toll of the 9/11 terrorist attack. The most significant revelation in the released Torture Memos is that interrogators were under "relentless pressure" from Cheney and Rumsfeld to resort to harsher methods to find evidence for their fantastic claim that Saddam Hussein was cooperating with al-Qaeda.

The attack on Afghanistan in October 2001 is called "the good war," no questions asked, a justifiable act of self-defense with the noble aim of protecting human rights from the evil Taliban. There are a few problems with that near-universal contention. For one thing, the goal was not to remove the Taliban. Rather, Bush informed the people of Afghanistan that they would be bombed unless the Taliban turned bin Laden over to the United States, as they might have done had the United States agreed to their request to provide some evidence of his responsibility for 9/11. The request was dismissed with contempt, for good reasons. As the head of the FBI conceded eight months later, after the most intensive international investigation in history they still had no evidence, and certainly had none the preceding October. The most he could say is that the FBI "believed" that the plot had been hatched in Afghanistan and had been implemented in the Gulf Emirates and Germany.

Three weeks after the bombing began, war aims shifted to overthrow of the regime. British Admiral Sir Michael Boyce announced that the bombing would continue until "the people of the country...get the leadership changed"—a textbook case of international terrorism.

It is also not true that there were no objections to the attack. With virtual unanimity, international aid organizations vociferously objected because it terminated their aid efforts, which were desperately needed. At the time it was estimated that some 5 million people were relying on aid for survival, and that an additional 2.5 million would be put at risk of starvation by the U.S.-U.K. attack. The bombing was therefore an example of extreme criminality, whether or not the anticipated consequences took place.

Furthermore, the bombing was bitterly condemned by leading anti-Taliban Afghans, including the U.S. favorite Abdul Haq, who was given special praise as a martyr after the war by President Hamid Karzai. Just before he entered Afghanistan, and was captured and killed, he condemned the bombing that was then underway and criticized the United States for refusing to support efforts of his and others "to create a revolt within the Taliban." The bombing was "a big setback for these efforts," he said, outlining them and calling on the United States to assist them with funding and other support instead of undermining them with bombs. The United States, he said, "is trying to show its muscle, score a victory and scare everyone in the world. They don't care about the suffering of the Afghans or how many people we will lose."

Shortly after, 1,000 Afghan leaders gathered in Peshawar, some of them exiles, some coming from within Afghanistan, all committed to overthrowing the Taliban regime. It was "a rare display of unity among tribal elders, Islamic scholars, fractious politicians, and former guerrilla commanders," the press reported. They had many disagreements, but unanimously "urged the US to stop the air raids" and appealed to the international media to call for an end to the "bombing of innocent people." They urged that other means be adopted to overthrow the hated Taliban regime, a goal they believed could be achieved without further death and destruction. The bombing was also harshly condemned by the prominent women's organization RAWA—which received some belated recognition when it became ideologically serviceable to express concern (briefly) about the fate of women in Afghanistan.

In short, the unquestionably "good war" does not look so good when we pay some attention to unacceptable facts.

It should not be necessary to tarry on the invasion of Iraq. Keeping solely to the effect on jihadi terror, the invasion was undertaken with the expectation that it would lead to an increase in terrorism, as it did, far beyond what was anticipated. It caused a sevenfold increase in terror, according to analyses by U.S. terrorism experts.

One may ask why these attacks were undertaken, but it is reasonably clear that confronting the evil scourge of terrorism was not a high priority, if it was even a consideration.

If that had been the goal, there were options to pursue. Some I have already mentioned. More generally, the United States and Britain could have followed the proper procedures for dealing with a major crime: determine who is responsible, apprehend the suspects (with international cooperation if necessary, easy to obtain), and bring them to a fair trial. Furthermore, attention would be paid to the roots of terror. That can be extremely effective, as the United States and the United Kingdom had just learned in Northern Ireland. IRA terror was a very serious matter. As long as London reacted by violence, terror, and torture, it was the "indispensable ally" of the more violent elements of the IRA, and the cycle of terror escalated. By the late 1990s, London began to attend to the grievances that lay at the roots of the terror, and to deal with those that were legitimate—as should be done irrespective of terror. Within a few years terror virtually disappeared. I happened to be in Belfast in 1993. It was a war zone. I was there again last fall. There are tensions, but at a level that is barely detectable to a visitor. There are important lessons here. Even without this experience we should know that violence engenders violence, while sympathy and concern cool passions and can evoke cooperation and empathy.

If we seriously want to end the plague of terrorism, we know how to do it. First, end our own role as perpetrators. That alone will have a substantial effect. Second, attend to the grievances that are typically in the background, and if they are legitimate, do something about them. Third, if an act of terror occurs, deal with it as a criminal act: identify and apprehend the suspects and carry out an honest judicial process. That actually works. In contrast, the techniques that are employed enhance the threat of terror. The evidence is fairly strong, and falls together with much else.

This is not the only case where the approaches that might well reduce a serious threat are systematically avoided, and those that are unlikely to do so are adopted instead. One such case is the so-called war on drugs. Over almost 40 years, the war has failed to curtail drug use or even street price of drugs. It has been established by many studies, including those of the U.S. government, that by far the most cost-effective approach to drug abuse is prevention and treatment. But that approach is consistently avoided in state policy, which prefers far more expensive violent measures that have barely any impact on drug use, though they have other consistent consequences.

In cases such as these, the only rational conclusion is that the declared goals are not the real ones, and that if we want to learn about the real goals, we should adopt an approach that is familiar in the law: relying on predictable outcome as evidence for intent. I think the approach leads to quite plausible conclusions, for the "war on drugs," the "war on terror," and much else. That, however, is work for another day.

NOTE

2

THE "ETHICS" OF TERROR
AND TERRORISM

Charles P. Webel

We are determined to answer the call of history and we will defeat
terror.

—Former U.S. president George W. Bush

There is no war against terrorism being waged or being prepared for
waging. What we have been witnessing since 2001 and what we are
going to witness in the near future are not wars against terrorism, but
wars, period.

—Rüdiger Bittner,
Ethics of Terrorism and Counterterrorism

Throwing a bomb is bad,
Dropping a bomb is good,
Terror, no need to add,
Depends on who's wearing the hood.

—Roger Woddis in Coady,
Morality and Political Violence

THE SETTING

Over two millennia ago, during the waning days of the Roman
Republic, the great orator and statesman Cicero asked, "What can be
done against force, without force?" Cicero was rewarded for his effort
to pose a possibly nonviolent solution to Rome's internal political
struggles—with summary assassination.

About a century later, shortly after the turn of the first millennium
of what is now called our Common Era (CE), Roman legions were
ruthlessly putting down rebellions throughout their newly christened
Empire. One such insurrection was conducted by a group of religious

Jews known as the sicarii ("short swords"), also labeled "Zealots," who have been deemed one of history's first officially labeled "terrorist" movements.[1] The Roman response to violence from below was to use greater violence from above, a strategy that has rarely worked in eliminating threats to occupations and dominion over subjugated peoples. The Empire struck back against its foes, but did not defeat them, because its use of superior force was ultimately ineffective in quelling mass popular resistance to its rule.

Approximately two millennia later, on September 11, 2001, during the first year of this new millennium, the cities of New York and Washington D.C.—the centers of the American homeland and Empire in the eyes of its adversaries—were attacked by terrorists.[2] The loss of life—approximately 3,000 civilians—was exceeded in American history only by battles during the Civil War, although cities in other countries experienced far greater civilian casualties during World War II.

A number of factors make the events of 9/11 and their aftermath unprecedented in American history: First, the attacks were perpetrated by foreign terrorists on American soil. Second, U.S. civilian airplanes were transformed into weapons of mass destruction. Third, the United States was not in a declared state of war at the time. Fourth, the identities of the perpetrators were unknown at the time of the attack, and no one claimed official responsibility for the events of 9/11, in contrast to most other terrorist attacks and acts of violence committed against civilian populations during wartime and since 1945. Finally, millions of Americans, as well as many civilians in other countries, have felt unprecedented levels of stress, anxiety, trauma, and related feelings of having been "terrorized" by these attacks.

How might we try to account for the usage of "terrorism" as a political tactic and of terror as a predictable human response to the violence, and threats of violence, employed by terrorists against innocent people? And what might we all learn about terror from the experiences of people around the world who underwent and survived terrifying acts of political violence during the twentieth century?

The events of 9/11 and their aftermath constitute a unique variation on an all-too-common historical theme, one played out in terrifying variations in Europe during the twentieth century. These historical events offer us the opportunity to explore and to try to come to terms with our most basic needs, feelings, thoughts, and desires—including vulnerability, rage, meaninglessness, dread, revenge, hostility, conviction, hope, fortitude, courage, faith, and solidarity.

My methods for approaching terror and terrorism are multidisciplinary. They are drawn from phenomenological and trauma psychology, psychoanalytic and political theory, comparative politics, ethnography, and oral history. They are informed by a conviction that the kinds of nonviolent theory and practices articulated and exemplified by Gandhi and Martin Luther King, as well as by the peace movements of the early 1980s and by the "Velvet Revolutions" in Germany and Eastern Europe in the late 1980s and early 1990s and possibly by the recent wave of popular uprisings by peoples in Muslim countries, offer us today a practicable model both for confronting the terrorist "wars" outside our persons, and for understanding the inner experiences of terror evoked by terrifying political events.

WHAT IS "TERRORISM?"

The term "terrorism" means premeditated, politically motivated violence perpetrated against noncombatant targets by subnational groups or clandestine agents, usually intended to influence an audience.
——U.S. Central Intelligence Agency and State Department

It (terrorism) is distinguished from all other kinds of violence by its "bifocal" character; namely, by the fact that the immediate acts of terrorist violence, such as shootings, bombings, kidnappings, and hostage-taking, are intended as means to certain goals.., which vary with the particular terrorist acts or series of such acts...the concept of terrorism is a "family resemblance" concept...Consequently, the concept as a whole is an "open" or "open-textured" concept, non-sharply demarcated from other types/forms of individual or collective violence. The major types of terrorism are: predatory, retaliatory, political, and political-moralistic/religious. The terrorism may be domestic or international, "from above"—i.e., state or state-sponsored terrorism, or "from below."
——Haig Khatchadourian, *The Morality of Terrorism*

Terrorism is fundamentally a form of psychological warfare. Terrorism is designed, as it has always been, to have profound psychological repercussions on a target audience. Fear and intimidation are precisely the terrorists' timeless stock-in-trade...It is used to create unbridled fear, dark insecurity, and reverberating panic. Terrorists seek to elicit and irrational, emotional response.
——Bruce Hoffman, "Lessons of 9/11"

Etymologically, "terrorism" derives from "terror." Originally the word meant a system, or regime, of terror: at first imposed by the Jacobins, who applied the word to themselves without any negative connotations; subsequently it came to be applied to any policy or regime of the sort and to suggest a strongly negative attitude, as it generally does

today...Terrorism is meant to cause terror (extreme fear) and, when
successful, does so. Terrorism is intimidation with a purpose: the terror is meant to cause others to do things they would otherwise not do.
Terrorism is coercive intimidation.
                                    —Igor Primoratz, "What is Terrorism?"

All wars are terrorism!
                                                        —Political Slogan

THE LANGUAGE GAME(S) OF TERRORISM

In searching for a universal definition of "terrorism," a concept
that is as contested ("one man's terrorist is another man's freedom
fighter...") as it is "open," I found that "terrorism" has been used
most often to denote politically motivated attacks by subnational
agents (this part is virtually uncontested in the relevant scholarly literature) or states (this is widely debated, but increasingly accepted)
on noncombatants, usually in the context of war, revolution, and
struggles for national liberation.[3] In this sense, "terrorism" is as old
as human conflict.

However, "terrorism," and "terrorists" have become relativized in
recent times, since there is very little consensus on who, precisely, is,
or is not, a "terrorist," or what is, or is not, an act of "terrorism."[4]
Thus, who is or is not a "terrorist," and what may or may not be "acts
of terrorism," depend largely on the perspective of the group or the
person using (or abusing) those terms.[5]

"Terrorism" is clearly a subcategory of political violence in particular and of violence in general. Almost all current definitions
of terrorism known to me focus on the violent acts committed (or
threatened) by "terrorists," and neglect the effects of those acts on
their victims. *Hence they are agent (or perpetrator)-centered, not vic-
tim-centered*. Nonetheless, for functional purposes, I propose the
following definition of "terrorism": "Terrorism is a premeditated,
usually politically motivated, use, or threatened use, of violence, in
order to induce a state of terror in its immediate victims, usually for
the purpose of influencing another, less reachable audience, such
as a government." Note that under this definition, states—which
commit "terrorism from above" (TFA)—and subnational entities,
individuals and groups alike—which engage in "terrorism from
below" (TFB)—may commit acts of terrorism.[6] States may also
directly or indirectly sponsor terrorist violence, via death squads,
paramilitaries, and contractors. So there may be state-sponsored as
well as state terrorism. Note as well that the somewhat artificial

distinction between "combatants" and "noncombatants" does not come into play here, since both groups may be terrorized by acts of political violence, and since terrorists from below may target police and government officials as well as soldiers, civilians, and other noncombatants.

WHAT IS TERROR?

The idea that you can purchase security from terror by saying nothing about terror is not only morally bankrupt but it is also inaccurate.
—Former Australian prime minister John Howard

Unfortunately, despite the Australian prime minister's assertion, virtually no one has talked in a meaningful way about the root of terrorism—terror.[7] This is an omission that stands out amid the endless talk of fighting a "war against terrorism/terror." It is also a glaring lacuna in current scholarly investigations (at least in such major Western languages as English, German, and French), which focus either on trauma (post-traumatic stress disorder, PTSD) and anxiety (the clinical literature), or on terrorism, terrorists, and counterterrorism (the social scientific/policy-oriented literature). But there is virtually no serious analysis of terror in the major Western scholarly discourses, with the glaring exception of Spanish (mostly Latin American) accounts of political terror from above and below.

How do we behave when we feel terrified? Do we seek immediately and automatically to rid ourselves of terror? Do we then transmit this emotionally intolerable condition to others, whom we then brand as "terrorists," the alleged cause and source of our unease? Is terror contagious, spreading uncontrollably among panic-stricken people? Does the unbearable heaviness of being in terror compel us to expel, split off, and dissociate terror, as quickly as possible and by any means necessary?

Are "terrorists" really "criminals," "fanatics," and "zealots," wholly "other" to us? Or are they to a remarkable degree the "shadow side" of "civilized peoples," the unleashed and unrepressed violence lurking in virtually all of us? Do many "terrorists," especially those with deep ideological or religious convictions, have a way of facing death from which we might learn, even if we deplore their taking of human life?

Based on my reading of the extant psychological, psychoanalytic, historical, and social-scientific literature, as well as on a content analysis of 52 interviews I have conducted with survivors of terrifying political violence in 13 nations (ranging from Denmark to Chile, but mostly in Germany, the United States, Spain, and the former Soviet Union), *it seems clear that we have no scientific answers to these questions.*[8] But to initiate a broad-based, multidisciplinary inquiry into terror and its "family resemblances," I offer the following provisional definition: "The term 'terror' denotes both a phenomenological experience of paralyzing, overwhelming, and ineffable mental anguish, as well as a behavioral response to a real or perceived life-threatening danger." Ex post facto (sometimes as much as 80 years after the events occurred) descriptions of terrifying experiences by people I have interviewed cluster around the following themes:

- First, the experience is described as having been overwhelming. The people felt helpless and completely vulnerable during the time of the assault (mostly bombings by airplanes during war).
- Second, they described the situation as uncontrollable, a time of loss of autonomy and surrender of self-control to an often unseen, and always menacing, "other."
- Third, the outcome of the event is universally depicted as unknowable and unpredictable—possibly leading to bodily injury or death—and the terror is of indefinite if not infinite duration.
- Fourth, the salient subjective feeling is that of acute anxiety, sometimes panic, and the cognitive orientation is of profound spatial/temporal disorientation.
- Fifth, the person feels his/her body as frozen, immobilized, and often paralyzed, incapable of self-direction and mobility.
- Finally, the intensity of the experience of terror is so great that most people find themselves unable to speak, and later are left wordless when they attempt verbally to describe it.

Terror is profoundly sensory (often auditory) and is pre- or postverbal. The ineffability of terror is a complement to, and often a result of, the unspeakable horror(s) of war(s). I do not (yet) know if the sample of people I have interviewed is representative of the victims of politically terrifying events (ranging from sniper to aerial attacks) in their own countries, much less globally. Perhaps we will never know. But I do know that to *expose anyone to any of the terrors these people have lived through is to commit a significant transgression of human rights and an inexcusable assault on personal dignity. Accordingly, terrorism in all it forms is deeply unethical.*[9]

THE "ETHICS" OF TERRORISM FROM ABOVE AND FROM BELOW

Unless necessary and sufficient conditions can be provided by perpetrators of TFA (i.e., state actors using "terror bombing" to attempt to break the morale of a civilian population and its government, as has been done numerous times since the Italians bombed Tripoli in 1911) and TFB (ranging from the Russian revolutionaries and defenders of "Red Terror" during the late nineteenth and early twentieth centuries to al-Qaeda) to justify their bloody deeds, *any act that deliberately inculcates terror is, more or less, unethical. However, there are of course degrees of moral culpability.*

For example, the decisions by Churchill to target the civilian populations (especially the working-class neighborhoods of industrial cities) of Germany for "terror bombings" during World War II and by Truman to "nuke" Hiroshima and Nagasaki (which had no military significance) are, by this criterion, acts of TFA. But they are not morally equivalent to such acts of TFB as the terrorist attacks of 9/11 on the United States, or of the acts of other terrorist groups (such as the "Red Army Faction") during the late twentieth century who targeted civilians as means to achieving perceived political ends. This is not because they are "less unethical," but, on the contrary, because they are *more unethical*, for both consequentialist and deontological reasons.

From a consequentialist perspective, terror bombings of civilians during wartime have resulted in many more casualties (millions of dead and wounded) than all acts of TFB combined. Furthermore, they have rarely resulted in achieving their declared political objectives: The fire-bombings of German and Japanese cities did not by themselves significantly induce the German and Japanese governments to surrender, rather, they tended to harden the resolve of the indigenous populations to fight harder (as did the German Blitz of England during 1940). Even the nuclear bombings of Hiroshima and Nagasaki did not significantly influence, or accelerate, the outcome of the War in the Pacific, because the Japanese government seems willing to have surrendered before the bombings. On the other hand, the terror bombing of Rotterdam in 1940 (which, apparently, may not have been intended by the Luftwaffe) was followed almost immediately by the surrender of the Dutch to the Germans; and Serbia did withdraw from Kosovo soon after Belgrade and other Yugoslavian cities were bombed by NATO in 1999. But in these two cases, the bombing was brief and civilian casualties were probably in the hundreds, and not in the hundreds of thousands, as they were in Germany and Japan during World War II.

Accordingly, the terror bombings committed by Great Britain and the United States, as well as by Nazi Germany and by Japan (principally in China), are classic examples of TFA or "state terrorism" (ST), and they resulted in millions of civilian casualties, without accomplishing their most important political objectives, namely, the profound demoralization of the civilian populations and prompt surrender of their antagonists. But what these state terrorists did accomplish, like their TFB counterparts, was the terrorization of huge numbers of people, the use of persons as means to alleged political ends, and the dehumanization and denial of dignity to the objects of their terror bombings. And this is unethical by any known moral criterion.

To sum up the commonalities and differences between TFA and TFB in terms of their respective degrees of moral culpability for terrorizing or killing many innocent (and possibly a few "guilty") people, *while both are unethical*, TFA usually *exceeds* TFB in its moral reprehensibility in terms of the following:

- *Magnitude, or scale, of terror*: TFA, or ST, is immeasurably more pernicious than TFB, since nation-states under Hitler and Stalin killed and terrorized tens of millions of their own citizens in the 1930s and 1940s, and slaughtered millions of "enemies" during World War II. Japan, Great Britain, and the United States also killed and terrorized millions of "enemies" in Chinese and German cities during that war. Latin American, African, and Asian despots and dictators, many with American support, killed and terrorized many thousands of their own citizens during the twentieth century.[10] And the United States has used "precision bombing" and "counterinsurgency" campaigns to kill and terrorize millions of Vietnamese and other Southeast Asians, as well as civilians in countries ranging from Afghanistan to Somalia. In comparison, the collective efforts of TFB groups, ranging from the IRA and PFLP to al-Qaeda, have probably resulted in fewer than 10,000 casualties—a tragedy for all the victims and their families, but in scale not comparable to the TFA "collateral damage."
- *The culpability, or degree of legal and ethical responsibility* of the people who made the decisions to terrorize and kill people unfortunate enough to be living in states at war with their own is also disproportionately skewed toward TFA. Such decision-makers as Hitler, Stalin, Truman, Churchill, Pol Pot, and L. B. Johnson, who collectively issued orders resulting in the deaths of tens of millions of noncombatants and the terrorization of millions of their compatriots, rarely if ever engaged in personally overseeing

the soldiers, sailors, and bombardiers who "were just following" (their) "orders." On the contrary: they were distant and detached from the mass killings that resulted from their policies, and would probably have refused to acknowledge their culpability for any "war crimes" or "crimes against humanity"—had they ever been called before an institution such as the International Court of Justice. In contrast, most leaders of TFB subnational groups are themselves directly involved in the terrorist operations, and may even put their lives at risk "for the sake of the cause." They may rationalize what they do, and justify mass murder by appeals to political motives (as do TFA decision-makers), but they would be, and have been, held individually legally culpable for their "crimes against humanity," unlike their TFB counterparts (the trials of Serbian leaders may set a notable precedent for a TFA decision-maker to be held legally culpable for crimes against humanity, in this case Bosnians).

TFA and TFB *share comparable* degrees of moral culpability for the following reasons:

- *They instrumentalize the victims of their terrorist tactics.* Both TFA and TFB turn civilian noncombatants and combatants alike into disposable means to be used (or terrorized) in order to achieve perceived political ends.
- Along the way, *they dehumanize, objectify, and demonize* their real and perceived "enemies," including the leaders of other nations or groups ("The Great Satan," "The Evil One," etc.).
- They also frequently *polarize the conflicting parties,* esteeming themselves and their followers as "good and virtuous," with "God on our side," and denigrating their opponents as "wicked, evil," and frequently "in-(or sub-)human."
- Citizens of other states who are killed or terrorized by their subordinates' tactics are denoted as "*collateral damage,*" and "*body counts*" of those killed are often employed as quantitative measures of an "operation's" "success."
- They *use or threaten to use violence on a mass scale,* often disregarding or prematurely discarding nonviolent means of conflict resolution. From a crude utilitarian perspective, the "costs" of "inadvertent" or "unintentional"—but nevertheless predictable and foreseeable— "friendly fire" or "collateral damage" are reflexively seen by many decision-makers to be outweighed by the perceived "benefits" of "victory."

- Dialogue, negotiation, diplomacy, compromise, the use of nonviolent tactics or of nonlethal force, and the recourse to international institutions are *often regarded by both TFA and TFB* as futile at best and weak and defeatist at worst.
- *Weapons of mass destruction (WMD), including but not limited to chemical, biological, and nuclear weapons, are desirable "assets"* to both TFA and TFB, even though the use of such weapons on a significant scale may have global—even omnicidal and therefore suicidal—consequences. WMD terrorism is the logical extension of the "logic of deterrence" and the "ethics of retaliation" (a version of lex talionis).

Consequently, this "Age of Global Terrorism," dating from the early twentieth century, when "total war" and "strategic bombing" became acceptable components of military and diplomatic strategy, has culminated in the progressive obliteration of important previously held distinctions. *Most notably, there has been a gradual collapse of the distinction between "illegitimate" (i.e., civilian noncombatants) and "legitimate" (i.e., military) "targets," as well as of the distinction between "terrorists" and "the states" (and peoples...) who, allegedly, "support them."* In addition, *the very idea of a "just war," must be called into question because the colossal civilian casualties during virtually every major war since 1939, including the "Global War on Terror," the massive violations of the requirements of "jus in bello," vitiates the "principle of discrimination," aka "noncombatant immunity."* As Michael Walzer has stated, "The dualism of jus ad bellum and jus in bello is at the heart of all that is most problematic in the moral reality of war."[11]

But when violations of noncombatant "immunity" become an intrinsic part, and the foreseeable effect, of such strategic policies as the bombing of cities (resulting in hundreds of thousands of casualties during World War II) and the occupation of nations "that harbor terrorists" (also resulting in hundreds of thousands of civilian casualties and millions of displaced persons since the U.S.-led invasions of Afghanistan and Iraq), *the theoretical separation of "ends"* ("defeating totalitarianisms" and "vanquishing terrorists") *and "means"* (aerial bombings, "renditions," "targeted assassinations," "enhanced interrogation techniques," drone attacks, etc.) *collapses.*

Furthermore, the "Global War on Terror" has *not* been fought "as a last resort," with a realistic "goal of peace" and a reasonable" chance of success, thus violating the "principle of proportionality," a necessary condition for a "war to be just."[12] The ongoing "just war on terror(ism)," no matter how comprehensible as retaliation for TFB atrocities and mass murders, is unjust because the costs to civilians greatly exceed any perceived "benefits" in terms of revenge and "national security." Instead, the conflict endures and escalates, without an endpoint in sight or a clear means of achieving, or recognizing, "victory" or even "defeat."

Finally, this century-long process is leading to the erosion of the boundary between "terrorism" and "war," to such a degree that, since at least the early days of World War II, for the civilian populations of the affected states, war has, ipso facto, become indistinguishable from terrorism. Terror, or psychological warfare, has become a predictable tool to be employed by war planners and policymakers. This turn of events is on the one hand a regression to the kind of "barbarism" that preceded the rise of "civilization" about 5,000 years ago in the Ancient Near East, and on the other hand is a seemingly inevitable consequence of technological "progress" unaccompanied by a comparable "moral evolution" on the parts of the proponents, practitioners, and apologists for TFA and TFA alike.

CONCLUSION: THE FUTURE OF TERRORISM AND THE TERRORS OF THE FUTURE

This is terror against terror...No ideology, no cause, not even the Islamic cause—can account for the energy which fuels terror. The aim is no longer even to transform the world, but...to radicalize the world by sacrifice. Whereas the system aims to realize it by force...Terrorism, like all viruses, is everywhere. There is a global perfusion of terrorism, which accompanies any system of domination as though it were its shadow, ready to activate itself like a double agent...It is at the very heart of this culture which combats it, and the visible fracture (and the hatred) that pits the exploited and underdeveloped globally against the Western world secretly connects with the fracture internal to the dominant system...There is indeed a fundamental antagonism here, but one which points past the spectre of America...and the spectre of Islam..., to triumphant globalization battling against itself. In this sense, we can speak of a world war—not the Third World War, but the Fourth and the only really global one, since what is at stake is globalization itself...The repression of terrorism spirals around us as unpredictably as the terrorist act itself. No one knows where it will stop...And...that is terrorism's true victory...There is no remedy for this extreme situation, and war is certainly not a solution, since it merely offers a rehash of the past...

—Jean Baudrillard, *The Spirit of Terrorism*

Everyone has the right to life, liberty, and security of person.
—Universal Declaration of Human Rights,
Article 3, United Nations

Only by the elimination of terrorism's root causes can the world hope
to succeed in greatly reducing it if not putting an end to it.
—Khatchadourian, *The Morality of Terrorism*

The cardinal principles of humanitarian law are aimed at the protection
of the civilian and civilian objects. States must never make civilians the
objects of attack and must consequently never use weapons that are
incapable of distinguishing between civilian and military targets.
—The International Court of Justice, Paragraph 78,
Legality of the Threat or Use of Nuclear Weapons,
Advisory Opinion, July 8, 1996

Are terror and terrorism a portal into our common human condition?
What do the existence of terror and terrorism reveal about the world,
one in which our worst fears may indeed come true? Is the future of
terrorism to include an ever-escalating series of attacks and counterat-
tacks culminating in global annihilation? Or can such hypothetical,
but foreseeable, terrors be minimized by the judicious application of
self-restraint on the one hand, and of nonviolent means of conflict
avoidance and resolution on the other hand?

The answer is "maybe a great deal, maybe very little; it depends
on the situation." But to assume that the only, or best, "realistic"
response to the use of deadly force, or terror, is to reply either "in
kind" or with even greater force may guarantee that our common
future will be even more terrifying than has been our collective history. Is this the future we wish our descendants to have?

Or is there a less violent, or even a nonviolent, alternative to TFA—
sometimes called "*counter*terrorism"—which often deploys state-
sanctioned military and paramilitary forces against alleged terrorists
and the states and civilian populations alleged to support them?[13]
One possibility is to replace counterterrorist violence with antiterrorist prevention and interception measures. Another is negotiations
with members or representatives of antistate terrorist groups. And
finally, there are changes in state political policy. These include ending the occupation(s) of territories nonstate terrorists are dedicated to
"liberating," and incorporating representatives of these groups into
the political process (as has been done with Hamas in Palestine and
the IRA in Northern Ireland).

Consequently, there are viable alternatives to terrorism and ways
to mitigate if not eliminate terror. It is imperative that we pursue and

develop these alternatives before the vicious cycle of TFB and terrorism—of futilely countering lesser terror from below with greater terror from above—escalates to a war of the world in which weapons of mass destruction are employed.

To answer Cicero's question: It is possible to use force, without violence, against violent force. But it is difficult and it takes time and discipline. The future of life on earth may hinge on the political will, or lack of it, to respond forcefully—but nonviolently—to terror and terrorism.

NOTES

1. See Bruce Hoffman, *Inside Terrorism* (New York: Columbia University Press, 1998), 88–89; Walter Laqueur, *The Age of Terrorism* (Boston: Little, Brown & Company, 1987), 11–12; and James M. Lutz and Brenda J. Lutz, *Terrorism Origins and Evolution* (New York: Palgrave Macmillan, 2005), 22–23.

2. For an account of al-Qaeda's (Khaled Sheikh Mohammed's and Osama bin Laden's) rationale for the 9/11 attacks, see Lawrence Wright, *The Looming Tower Al-Qaeda and the Road to 9/11* (New York: Alfred A. Knopf, 2007), 307–308.

3. For contending definitions of "terrorism," see David Barash and Charles P. Webel, *Peace and Conflict Studies*, 2nd ed. (London: SAGE Publications, 2009), chapter 3, esp. 44–47; Charles P. Webel, *Terror, Terrorism and the Human Condition* (New York: Palgrave Macmillan, 2007), chapter 1, esp. 8–10; Trudy Govier, *A Delicate Balance What Philosophy Can Tell Us About Terrorism* (Boulder, Co: Westview Press, 2002), 86–92, who also focuses on victims while noting the "double standard" and "Our Side Bias" of decrying the "terrorism" of political violence directed against us while exonerating uniformed agents of our state's political violence; Robert F. Goodin, *What's Wrong Terrorism?* (Cambridge: Polity Press, 2006), 36–37, 46–49, and 54–55; J. Angelo Corlett, *Terrorism: A Philosophical Analysis* (Dordrecht: Kluwer Academic Publishers, 2003), 116; Jean Baudrillard, *The Spirit of Terrorism* (London: Verson, 2002); and Jacques Derrida in Giovanna Borradori, *Philosophy in a Time of Terror* (Chicago: University of Chicago Press, 2003), 102–109.

4. "Just about everybody claims to be against terrorism—but people disagree about whether some particular political violence amounts to terrorism. The term *terrorism* has a core of descriptive content; but, in addition, it is used to express value judgments—and because people disagree about those value judgments, they apply the term differently. Thus the familiar saying that one person's terrorist is another man's freedom fighter." Govier, *A Delicate Balance*, 87.

5. For "The Language Game, Semantics, Theatre, and Western Model of Terrorism," see Edward S. Herman and Gerry O' Sullivan, " 'Terrorism' as Ideology and Culture Industry," in *Western State Terrorism*, ed. Alexander George (Cambridge: Polity Press, 1992), 43–52. Hence, "terrorism...*is a social construction*...is not given in the real world but is instead an interpretation of events and their presumed causes...When people and events come to be regularly described in public as terrorists and terrorism, some governmental or other entity is succeeding in a war of words in which the opponent is promoting alternative designations such as 'martyr' and 'liberation struggle' " [Austin T. Turk, "Sociology of Terrorism," *Annual Review of Sociology*, XXX (2004): 273]. "It (terrorism) is as emotional a word as 'war'...(and) some governments, countries, or regimes...use the word as a political-psychological weapon in their fight against the perpetrators and their avowed causes..." (Khatchadourian, *The Morality of Terrorism*, 3). " 'Terrorism' is used by most people in a rather unfortunately hypocritical manner. It appears that politicians of various countries condemn as 'terrorist' acts of political violence...against their own countries, or those of their allies, while they fail to admit that their own governments sponsor actual terrorism. The U.S. is a clear instance of this" [J. Angelo Corlett, *Terrorism A Philosophical Analysis* (Dordrecht: Kluwer Academic Publishers, 2003), 48].

6. For a spectrum of views on TFA and TFB, see Webel, *Terror and Terrorism*; Barash and Webel, *Peace and Conflict Studies,* 44 and 48–50; Khatchadourian, *The Morality of Terrorism,* 11: "The terrorism may be domestic or international, 'from above'—i.e., state or state-sponsored terrorism—or 'from below.' "

"Those who wish to restrict terrorism usually claim it involves a *non-state* actor, or actors, as the perpetrators of the violence, the victims, or both...State to state violence is excluded even though some state actions directed against other states are designed to cause terror...(but) When governments support or condone the use of terror against their own citizens, it does constitute terrorism..." (Lutz and Lutz, *Terrorism Origins and Evolution,* 7 and 9). Also, "by definition, terrorism is the behavior of substate groups. This view is not universally shared" [Louise Richardson, *What Terrorists Want* (New York: Random House, 2007), 80].

"A layperson's instinctive understanding of Terrorism as: politically motivated violence,usually directed against 'soft targets,' and an intention to affect (terrorize) a larger audience"[Gus Martin, *Understanding Terrorism*, 3rd ed. (Thousand Oaks: SAGE Publications, 2010), 5].

The "common features of most formal definitions:the use of illegal force subnational actors unconventional methods political motives attacks against "soft" civilian and passive military targets acts aimed at purposefully affecting an audience..." (ibid., 43).

7. Some exceptions are Webel, *Terror and Terrorism*; Khatchadourian, *The Morality of Terrorism*, 8–9; Robert F. Goodin, "Fear is the Key," in *What's Wrong Terrorism?*, 45; and Derrida Borradori, *Philosophy in a Time of Terror*, 102–103.

8. For more details, see Webel, *Terror, Terrorism, and the Human Condition*, chapter 3.

9. "The moral problem with terrorism is that terrorists frighten and kill civilian people and societies who are caught in the middle of serious political conflicts when the terrorists resort to violence for political ends. The moral problem with war (just or otherwise) is that soldiers frighten and kill innocent people and societies who get caught in the middle...And the moral dilemmas of political violence arise if we want to argue that sometimes—but only sometimes—this killing of the innocent is justified. Appeals to the evil of terrorism won't make this thorny problem go away" (Govier, *A Delicate Balance*, 91–92).

10. For a statistical comparison of the victims of and killings by state and nonstate terrorists, see Herman and O'Sullivan, " 'Terrorism' as Ideology and Culture Industry," table 3.1, 41–42. The historical bottom line: TFA kills more than one hundred times as many people as TFB, at least from 1965 to 1990.

11. Michael Waltzer, *Just and Unjust Wars* (New York: Basic Books, 1977), 21.

12. Barash and Webel, *Peace and Conflict Studies*, 362–366.

13. "Antiterrorism" (not counterterrorism) "refer(s) to the 'administrative, police...psychological resources, tactics, equipments, security, judicial, and political measures' employed by governments...designed to prevent terrorist attacks...antiterrorist measures include the use of judicial and penal systems as a whole to bring terrorists to justice. Thus antiterrorism has both a deterrent and a punitive aspect: to deter and so as to prevent terrorism, to apprehend and bring to justice suspected terrorists, and to punish convicted terrorists...Therefore, antiterrorist measures and strategies are, ideally speaking, nonviolent and in accord...with extant international law..." (Khatchadourian, *The Morality of Terrorism*, 113–114).

3

WHO BECOMES A TERRORIST TODAY?

Scott Atran

INTRODUCTION: TAKFIRI TERRORISM

Since the invasion of Iraq, and with the rapid spread of Internet access, the world has witnessed a more egalitarian, less-educated and less materially well-off, and more socially marginalized wave of would-be jihadi martyrs. Although millions of people support violent jihad, very few are willing to do it. Those who do pursue violent jihad usually emerge in small groups of action-oriented friends. They come from the same neighborhood and interact during activities such as soccer or paintball. Often they become camping and hiking companions who learn to take care of one another under trying conditions, which causes them to become even more deeply attached. Increasingly, they may first meet in a chat room where the anonymity of the World Wide Web paradoxically helps to forge intimate emotional ties among people who might otherwise physically intimidate or put one another off. They learn to live in a parallel universe—a conceptually closed community of comrades bound to a cause—which they mistake for the world.

These young people self-mobilize to the tune of a simple, superficial, yet broadly appealing *takfiri* message of withdrawal from impure mainstream society and the need for violent action to cleanse it. It is a surprisingly flat but fluid message preadapted to any new event in the world, which is readily shared by young people I have interviewed from the remote Indonesian Island of Sulawesi, to the Spanish enclave of Ceuta (Septa) in North Africa, and in places scattered throughout Pakistan, Palestine, and the suburbs of Paris.

Takfiris (from *takfir*, "excommunication") are rejectionists who disdain other forms of Islam, including *wahabism* (an evangelical creed, which preaches Calvinist-like obedience to the state) and most fundamentalist, or *salafi*, creeds (which oppose fighting between coreligionists as sowing discord, or *fitna*, in the Muslim community). Salafi Islam is the host on which this viral Takfiri movement rides, much as Christian fundamentalism is the host upon which white supremacism rides. The host itself is not the cause of the virus and is, indeed, a primary victim. As one senior Saudi intelligence officer recently told me, "Often the first sign of someone becoming a Takfiri is that he stops praying where his family and tribe pray. He leaves the mosque and turns against his family, tribe and our Salafi way."

One telltale sign of radicalization in the move to Takfirism is when members of a neighborhood mosque or cultural center (or just an informal discussion group that meets at a bookstore or at picnics) gel into a militant faction that leaves, voluntarily or involuntarily. This is what happened, for example, when Ali al-Timimi and his group of paintball buddies were ejected from the Dar al-Arqam Cultural Center in Falls Church, Virginia, after they praised the 9/11 attacks (12 members of the group were later convicted for aiding Lashkar-e-Taiba, a Pakistani group allied to al-Qaeda). Another example is when the soccer-playing Salafi imam at the M-30 mosque in Madrid expelled Serhane Fakhet and friends (who continued to self-radicalize, playing soccer and picnicking together, in the lead-up to the Madrid train bombings).

Western politicians, pundits, and publics generally do not understand that the strict Salafi schools in Indonesia, Egypt, Saudi Arabia, Yemen, and elsewhere are the most vociferous and effective opponents of violent jihad. Most present-day Takfiris are "born again" in their late teens and early twenties and have little knowledge of religion beyond the fact that they consider themselves "true Muslims" who must fight enemies near and far to defend their friends and the faith that makes their friendship meaningful and enduring.

Soccer, paintball, camping, hiking, rafting, body building, martial arts training, and other forms of physically stimulating and intimate group action create a bunch of buddies (usually not less than four and not more than twelve, with a median of eight), who become a "band of brothers" in a glorious cause. It usually suffices that a few (usually at least two) of these action buddies come to believe in the cause, truly and uncompromisingly, for the rest to follow even unto death. Humans, like all primates, need to socially organize, lead, and be led; however, notions of "charismatic leaders" going out or sending recruiters to "brainwash" unwitting minds into joining well-structured organizations with command and control is grossly exaggerated. Standard counterterrorism notions of "cells" and "recruitment"—and to some degree even "leadership"—often reflect more the psychology and organization of people analyzing terrorist groups than terrorist groups themselves.

Such "bureaucratic mirroring" is also evident in misguided policies grounded in the premise that simply presenting people with rational arguments and material incentives will lead them down the correct or better path. Most human beings are more interested in persuading themselves that they are right, whatever the evidence against them, than in finding out that they are wrong. They are more interested in victory than in truth. And when was the last time rational argument or a buy-off offer convinced anyone you know to select the right (boy or girl) friend?

PROBLEMS WITH PREVAILING THEORIES OF TERRORISM: OUTDATED DATA AND INATTENTION TO DETAIL

Alan Krueger, in his new book *What Makes a Terrorist: Economics and the Roots of Terrorism*,[1] produces data for three general findings: (1) poverty and lack of education are uncorrelated, or slightly negatively correlated, with being a terrorist or with support for terrorism; (2) most terrorists stem from countries that are not poor, but that restrict civil liberties; and (3) terrorism is mostly directed against democratic rather than authoritarian regimes. He then infers causes from these broad correlations: (i) poverty and poor education do not produce terrorism, but denial of political freedom does; and (ii) terrorists target democratic regimes because they seek publicity and widespread panic and democracies are more responsive to public opinion. These conclusions echo the theories in Robert Pape's best-selling book *Dying to Win: The Strategic Logic of Suicide Terrorism*.[2]

A major problem with such works is that they assume correlations with economic status, education level, or degree of civil liberties usefully predict who or how people become terrorists. This mistaken premise misleads policymakers and researchers. It is the *social networks* and *group dynamics* of these networks that are critical to understanding how terrorist networks form and operate, not the demographic profiles of individuals and whole populations.

Consider Islamic terrorism, the main focus of Krueger's book. The significant correlation between the countries of origin of Islamic terrorists and countries that limit civil liberties is true, but uninformative. The same correlation holds for indefinitely many Muslim groups that have nothing to do with terrorism.

Only al-Qaeda is interested in attacking the "far enemy," that is, the United States and its allies. Isaac Ben Israel, an Israeli parliamentarian who currently heads his country's space agency, was former chief of air force operations and top military strategist in a successful campaign to stop Hamas suicide bombings. He told me that "al-Qaeda is a very different problem and is not ours; our operational problems with Hezbollah and Hamas involve regional networks with regional aims, although we are ready to help the United States with its global al-Qaeda problem whenever we can." More than 80 percent of people who have joined or expressed allegiance to al-Qaeda have done so outside their country of origin. This, of course, is not the case with Hezbollah or Hamas. Whether one joins jihad in the diaspora or in one's native country, and not country of origin per se, is the key factor in how one is willing to use terrorism and against whom.

The correlation between terrorist acts and target countries, indicating that democracies are victims more than autocracies, is spurious. It requires accepting that attacks on U.S. occupation forces in Iraq and Afghanistan are attacks upon U.S. democracy. In fact, there have been very few attacks carried out directly against Western democracies, and only three with significant casualties (United States—9/11; Spain—March 11, 2004; and United Kingdom—July 7, 2005). There have been no major attacks against the democracies of Israel or Indonesia in the last two years, and only one major attack in India outside the disputed territory of Jammu and Kashmir (November 26, 2008, in Mumbai). There have been 2,400 arrests related to Takfiri terrorist activities in Europe, where civil liberties are guaranteed.

Only in Iraq and Afghanistan has there been a continuing high rate of attacks against U.S.-led coalition forces, which are increasingly perceived as occupation forces by large segments of the populations of these two countries. It is doubtful the reaction would be much different if invasion and occupation forces were those of a dictatorship, as with Soviet forces in Afghanistan in the 1980s. The world's newest and most active areas for suicide attacks are Pakistan and North Africa, where civil liberties are restricted. Over 200 people were killed in North Africa in 2007, mostly in Algeria. In Pakistan, nearly 500 were killed in suicide attacks in the second half of 2007 (including former prime minister Benazir Bhutto), greater than the number of people killed in terrorist attacks in Europe over the last two decades. Local groups proclaiming allegiance or sympathy with al-Qaeda have claimed responsibility, but al-Qaeda does not appear to have direct operational command or control over any of these groups.

Consider, now, the relationship between socioeconomic status and terrorism. To independently confirm Krueger's findings on Hamas, my research group statistically regressed Palestinian support for suicide attacks against Israelis on education and income levels in three nationally representative surveys of Palestinians (West Bank and Gaza) during the years 1999, 2001, and 2005. We controlled for area of residence, refugee status, age, gender, and religion. Income and education levels were unrelated to support for suicide attacks. When there was a relationship between support for suicide attacks and economic variables, we found, like Krueger, that income and education levels were modestly, but *positively*, correlated with support. In the 1999 survey, wealthier Palestinians expressed greater support for attacks, while more educated Palestinians showed greater support for suicide attacks in the 2001 surveys.

But when we turn to al-Qaeda's most important Southeast Asian ally, *Jemaah Islamiyah* (JI), we find something different. We analyzed every attack by Southeast Asia's JI between 1999 and the second Bali bombing of 2005 (apart from the purely local conflicts of Poso and Ambon) and entered demographic details on all known operatives. Of about 180 people implicated in JI attacks, 78 percent worked in unskilled jobs, and only 23 percent had education beyond high school.

We also found that operational associations in JI are determined by four variables: (1) being a member of the self-styled "Afghan Alumni," that is, someone who went through training with the Indonesian volunteers in the Abu Sayyaf's Sadah training camp during the Soviet-Afghan War and its immediate aftermath; (2) continuing to work together (e.g., on Abdullah Sungkar's chicken farm in Malaysia) or to play soccer together after demobilization from Afghanistan (and before JI was officially established); (3) having studied or taught in at least one of the two religious schools established by JI's founders (Al-Mukmin in Java and Lukman Al-Hakiem in Malaysia); and (4) being related by kinship or marriage to someone else in the network (e.g., there are more than 30 marriages woven through 10 attacks). In contrast with these factors, we find that the knowledge of JI's "official" organizational structure is largely uninformative in helping us understand the networks involved in JI attacks.

Levels of education and skill are significantly higher for Hamas than for JI. Nevertheless, the main predictors for involvement in suicide attacks are, again, small-world aspects of social networks and local group dynamics rather than large-scale social, economic, and political indicators, such as education level and economic status.

For example, Hamas's most-sustained suicide bombing campaign in 2003–2004 involved several buddies from Hebron's Masjad (mosque) al-Jihad soccer team. Most lived in the Wad Abu Katila neighborhood and belonged to the al-Qawasmeh *hamula* (clan); several were classmates in the neighborhood's local branch of the Palestinian Polytechnic College. Their ages ranged from 18 to 22. At least eight team members were dispatched to suicide shooting and bombing operations by the Hamas military leader in Hebron Abdullah al-Qawasmeh (killed by Israeli forces in June 2003 and succeeded by his relatives Basel al-Qawasmeh, killed in September 2003, and Imad al-Qawasmeh, captured on October 13, 2004). A closer look at actual attacks reveals that almost all are rooted in local networks of preexisting social relationships.

In February 2008, I interviewed members of the families of suicide bombers Mohammed Herbawi and Shadi Zghayer, shortly after an attack in Dimona, Israel. This was the first suicide attack claimed by Hamas since December 2004, when it declared a unilateral truce on martyrdom actions across the Green Line. These two friends were members of the same Hamas neighborhood soccer group as several others who died in 2003: the Masjad al-Jihad team. Herbawi had been arrested as a 17-year-old on March 15, 2003, shortly after a suicide bombing on Haifa bus (by Mamoud al-Qawasmeh on March 5, 2003) and coordinated suicide shooting attacks on Israeli settlements by others on the team (March 7, 2003, Muhsein, Hazem al-Qawasmeh, Fadi Fahuri, and Sufian Hariz), and before another set of suicide bombings by team members in Hebron and Jerusalem on May 17–18, 2003 (Fuad al-Qawasmeh, Basem Takruri, and Mujahed al-Ja'abri). Herbawi's mother, Basma Harmoni (she is divorced), said her son loved all those boys.

The imam at Masjad al-Jihad Fellah Naser Ed-Din is also crazy about soccer (he showed me albums of his soccer team pictures since his boyhood days) and refereed the boys. He told us that the soccer buddies self-organized matches involving 15 mosque teams in the area, naming the matches after martyrs (a painted sign behind the goalpost at the Abu al-Dhabat school reads "Championship by Martyr Ra'ed Missak," in honor of the young man from Hebron who killed 23 people and wounded more than 130 on a Jerusalem bus on August 19, 2003). According to the imam, Muhsein Qawasmeh was the smartest and best of the 2003 team and he inspired the others. I received much the same message from Fawzi Qawasmeh, father of one of the young men who went on the mission with Muhsein. Hazem Qawasmeh, who went on the mission with Muhsein, stated that "without Muhsein, I doubt the other would have would have acted." At the house where Muhsein's family now lives, I found his mother and brother commiserating with Herbawi's uncle. Muhsein's mother said her son had been an exemplary student but left school after the Intifada broke out and focused on soccer and religion.

The Hamas leadership in Damascus later claimed responsibility for the Dimona attack (after Fatah's Al-Aqsa' Martyrs Brigades had claimed it) but the politburo clearly did not order it or even know about it (Usama Ham-dan, who handles external relations for Hamas in Beirut, initially said he didn't know who was responsible; and when I asked senior Hamas leaders in the West Bank if this meant that he didn't know about it, they said, "You can conclude that; we certainly didn't"). Sources close to Israeli intelligence told me at the Knesset that Mahmoud Zahar, the Hamas leader in Gaza, and Ahmed Al Ja'abri, the military commander of the Izz ad-Din al-Qassam Brigades, probably wanted to launch an operation across the Israel-Egypt border after Hamas breached the border wall between Gaza and Egypt but couldn't; so al-Ja'abri called upon his clan ally in Hebron Ayoub Qawasmeh to conduct an operation. Ayoub Qawasmeh then tapped into the young men on the soccer team who had been earnestly waiting to do something for their comrades and their cause.

The most complete data in Krueger's book concerns Hezbollah and Hamas. There is a secondary focus on al-Qaeda. For all three cases, the data is old and of questionable relevance to global terrorism today. Hezbollah ceased suicide bombings and attacks on civilians (outside of open war) by the 1990s. Hamas has claimed responsibility for only one attack since December 2004. Al-Qaeda central, the command set up by Osama bin Laden in the summer of 1988 and which was involved in the 9/11 attacks, has had no direct success in carrying out a terrorist operation since 2002 (the Djerba, Tunisia, bombings), though it had a hand in prior financing of operations carried out later (Istanbul bombings of 2003) and in training people implicated in subsequent attacks (about 50 suicide bombers involved in attacks in Saudi Arabia through April 2005).

The original al-Qaeda group around bin Laden (mostly Egyptians) has been decimated by about an order of magnitude. After bin Laden's death, al-Qaeda's surviving remnants may still be concentrated in a handful of small mobile camps in Pakistan's Federally Administered Tribal Areas. The largest remaining al-Qaeda camp in 2007, *Mir Ali* in North Waziristan, has had a few dozen trainees under the tutelage of Abu Ubaydah Al-Masri. Al-Masri instructed those responsible for the summer 2006 suicide bombing plot to smuggle liquid explosives aboard a number of passenger jets, and he has likely been involved in a few other dangerous but so-far unsuccessful plots.

For the most part, the "new wave" of terrorism that expresses allegiance to al-Qaeda tends to be poorer, less educated, and more marginal than the old al-Qaeda or its remnants. It relies to a greater extent for financing and personnel on preexisting petty criminal networks because large-scale financing is easily tracked (the 9/11 attacks cost some $400,000 followed by the 2002 Bali and 2004 bombings at about $50,000 each, with all others considerably less). The Saudi Ministry of Interior conducted a study of 639 detainees through 2004. Nearly two-thirds of those in the sample say they joined jihad through friends and about a quarter through family. A closer look at other terrorist groups reveals strikingly similar patterns of self-radicalization based on almost chance encounters within preexisting local circles of friends and kin. Former CIA case officer Marc Sageman analyzed al-Qaeda networks through 2003 and found that about 70 percent join through friends and 20 percent through kin. In his new book *Leaderless Jihad: Terror Networks in the 21st Century*[3] Sageman finds that more recent networks are also built up around friendship and kinship but members are more marginal relative to surrounding society.

The newer Saudi sample bears this out. Compared with the earlier sample, the newer wave tends to be somewhat younger (and more likely to be single), less educated and less financially well off, less ideological, and more prone to prior involvement in criminal activities unrelated to jihad, such as drugs, theft, and aggravated assault. They are much more likely to read jihadi literature in their daily lives than other forms of literature. They tend to look up to role models who stress violence in jihad, such as the late Abu Musab al-Zarqawi, than to those who justify and limit violence through moral reasoning, such as the late Abdullah Azzam. A majority come to religion later in life, especially in their early twenties. In the older cohort there was little traditional religious education; however, the newer cohort tends to be less ideologically sophisticated and especially motivated by desire to avenge perceived injustices in Iraq. (When I asked detainees in Saudi Arabia who had volunteered for Iraq why they had done so, some mentioned stories of women raped, the killing of innocents, and desecrations of the Koran, but all mentioned Abu Ghraib.)

This "new wave" pattern of increasingly marginality and "born-again" religion is reflected in European and North African groups that express allegiance to al-Qaeda, as well as foreign fighters in Iraq (41 percent from Saudi Arabia and 39 percent from North Africa since August 2006, many of whom come in bunches from the same town, e.g., the 50 or so volunteers from Darnah, Lybia, according to West Point's *Sinjar Report on Foreign Fighters in Iraq*).

Krueger and others repeatedly refer to predictive factors in "recruitment." It is important to understand that there is no, and has never been, clear evidence of "recruitment" into al-Qaeda. In its heyday, al-Qaeda operated more like a funding agency than a military organization. People would come to al-Qaeda with proposals for plots. Al-Qaeda would accept some 10–20 percent. Even the 9/11 suicide pilots were not "recruited" into al-Qaeda. They were Middle Eastern Arabs who lived in a middle-class German community (the Hamburg suburb of Harburg) and were seeking friendship and identity in an Islamic community that was mostly Moroccan. Our interviews with friends in their circle and investigators reveal that the plotters met in the dorms and started hanging out together, including going to mosque services and meeting in local restaurants. Three wound up living in the same apartment, where they self-radicalized. They first thought of going to Chechnya to do jihad (but getting there proved too difficult) then to Kosovo (but the Albanian jihadis didn't want them), and eventually wound up in an al-Qaeda training camp in Afghanistan as a distant third choice.

There is no clear evidence that al-Qaeda ever had a recruiting or training infrastructure in Europe, although there is increasing evidence that al-Qaeda and al-Qaeda-related groups in Pakistan's tribal areas maintain communication with Europeans after they train in Pakistan. This seems to be especially the case with those involved in recent plots in the United Kingdom. Generally, however, people go looking for al-Qaeda, not the other way around. Because there is very little of the old al-Qaeda left, many who go seeking al-Qaeda are caught. Those who seek out al-Qaeda do so in small groups of friends, and occasionally through kin. Almost all are schoolmates or workmates, and camp, soccer, or paintball buddies. Only a minority has gone beyond high school. Some have steady jobs and family, but many have only intermittent jobs and no families of their own. All have self-radicalized to some degree as friends before they go after al-Qaeda, although an encounter with someone who has been to an al-Qaeda training camp in Afghanistan is occasionally an added stimulant. The overwhelming majority have not had sustained prior religious education but become "born again" into radical Islam in their late teens and early twenties. About 10 percent are Christian converts.

For example, in the wake of the Iraq invasion in April 2003, a disciple of the radical Islamist preacher Sheikh Omar Bakri organized a barbecue in a London suburb for about 100 people, most from the immigrant Pakistani community. Guests were asked for donations to help send a few volunteers to Pakistan to train for jihad. Among those who used some of 3,500 euros collected to pay their way to Pakistan were Mohammed Sidique Kahn, one of the four suicide bombers in the July 2005 London Underground attack, and Omar Khyam, one of the conspirators convicted in the 2005 "Crevice" plot to plant fertilizer bombs around London. Their original intention was to do jihad in Kashmir, but after a quick course in bomb-making they were told to "go home" and do something there. Each joined up with a few friends to concoct a plot. Interviews by journalist Jason Burke with investigators and friends familiar with the Crevice case suggest that ten days of arduous hiking, camping, and training in Pakistan cemented commitment between buddies who learned to live together and care for one another. White-water rafting seems to have played a similar role in bonding the London Underground plotters. One of the four London suicide bombers was also a Jamaican Christian convert and pinball buddy.

Another telling example is the Madrid train bombing in March 2004. Five of the seven plotters who blew themselves when cornered by police grew up within a few blocks of one another in the tumble-down neighborhood of Jemaa Mezuak in Tetuan, Morocco: Jamal Ahmidan ("El Chino"), brothers Mohammed and Rachid Oulad Akcha, Abdennabi Kounjaa ("El Afghan"), and Rifaat Asrin ("El Niño). One, nicknamed the "Chinaman," fled Morocco in 1993 from a murder charge, joining his elder brother in Madrid in taking and dealing drugs. In 1995, with his teenage Christian girlfriend and fellow junkie five months pregnant, the Chinaman decided to kick his heroin habit. His wife says he did it cold turkey with the help of the religion he was getting in a local mosque. The Chinaman turned around to preach reform to his drug-dealing associates, three brothers from the Mezuak, convincing two to quit their habit. The brothers became devoted to the Chinaman, and were thereafter known in the barrio as his "bodyguards."

The fourth of Madrid's Moroccan suicide bombers was described to us by some of his friends as Mezuak's first "Afghan" (a religious militant who grows a full beard and dresses with an Afghan hat, coarse knee-length tunic, and sandals). He would preach jihad against "infidels" (*kuffar*) and Muslims who merit takfir because they refuse to follow "pure" Islamic ways. The father and friends of the fifth suicide bomber, a young gay man in his early twenties known as "The Kid," said that he had sold candies from a cart in Mezuak until 2000. He did not care much for religion until he was hooked up with The Afghan. By 2002, The Afghan and The Kid were in Madrid, the former as a part-time construction worker who dealt drugs with the Chinaman's "bodyguards," and the latter devoting himself to charity work helping out other young immigrants.

In the fall of 2003, just after the Chinaman returned from a prison stint in Morocco, he and his chums from the "old neighborhood" of Mezuak linked up with the economics-turned-religious student Serhane Fakhet and his buddies at a couple of apartment-mosques and soccer fields, and in daily dealings along Tribulete Street (at the *halal* butcher shop, the *Alhambra* restaurant, the barbershop, and the cell phone and Internet store) in the Lavapies neighborhood of central Madrid. The hands-on drug dealer and dreamy student bonded in an explosive combination. There was no al-Qaeda, or any other outside organization, involved.

From March to December 2007, I went to the Mezuak, and found that at least a dozen other young men had "gone Afghan" since the summer of 2006, according to local residents who knew them. Each would one day suddenly shave his beard, don Western clothes, and simply disappear; sometimes two vanished on the same day. Their friends and local Moroccan police say that they probably left for Iraq to become martyrs. The names and itineraries of five of them have been confirmed: Abdelmonim al-Amrani, Younes Achebak, Hamza Aklifa, and the brothers Bilal and Muncef Ben Aboud (DNA analysis has confirmed the suicide bombing death of Amrani in Baqubah, Iraq). All five attended a local elementary school (Abdelkrim Khattabi), the same one that Madrid's Moroccan bombers attended. And four of the five were in the same high school class (Kadi Ayadi, just outside Mezuak). The fifth, Bilal's brother Muncef, was a gifted mathematics student who went on to receive a scholarship to Morocco's prestigious air force academy, the *École Royale de l'Air*. But Muncef's mother said he was unsettled by what was happening around the world to Muslims and left his studies as he sought solace in religion.

All were soccer buddies who prayed at Masjad al-Rohban (the Dawa Tabligh mosque where Kounjaa had first gone "Afghan") and all hung out at the Chicago Café on Mamoun Street, Mezuak's main drag. The cousin of one of the Iraq-bound group (Hamza) was married to The Afghan, and all prayed in the same mosque where The Afghan first preached jihad (the mosque's Imam was arrested in 2006 for collecting *zaqat* charity money from local business men to help send young men to Iraq). Friends say the young men bound for Iraq all respected the courage of the Madrid plotters but disagreed about their civilian targets and believed that action in Iraq would be more just and "soldierly" than in Europe. Like the Madrid plotters (as well as the Hamburg and London plotters), they were buddies, hung out together at local cafés and restaurants, and mingled in the same barbershops (where young men gather and talk).

The boundaries of the newer-wave networks are very loose, and the Internet now allows anyone who wishes to become a terrorist to become one anywhere, anytime. For example, the "Al-Ansar" chat room network was involved in plots by young men in half-a-dozen countries (United States, United Kingdom, Canada, Sweden, Denmark, and Bosnia), and many of the men had never physically met. They would hack into Midwest media sites to post jihadi videos (e.g., of Zarqawi's beheading of Nick Berg) and recipes for making car bombs and suicide vests from scratch. From a basement apartment in Britain, a self-styled *Irhabi 007* ("Terrorist 007") helped in his spare time to coordinate plots with some high-school chums in Toronto to blow up the Canadian parliament, and with others to attack the U.S. embassy in Bosnia (three conspirators who did meet up physically in Bosnia were arrested with AK-47s, suicide belts, and thousands of rounds of ammunition).

A main problem in terrorism studies is that most "experts" have little field experience (for understandable but not insurmountable reasons) and otherwise lack the required level of details that statistical and trend analyses could properly mine. There are many millions of people who express sympathy with al-Qaeda or other forms of violent political expression that support terrorism. From a 2005–2006 survey of ten countries involving 50,000 interviews, a Gallup study projected that 7 percent of the world's 1.3 billion Muslims (some 90 million people) felt that the 9/11 attacks were "completely justified." There are, however, only a few thousands who show willingness to actually commit violence. They almost invariably go on to violence in small groups consisting mostly of friends and some kin (although friends tend to become kin as they marry one another's sisters and cousins; indeed, there are dozens of such marriages among members of Southeast Asia's JI).

CONCLUSIONS FROM THE FIELD

The causes that humans are most willing to kill and die for are not just about particular ideas; they are about particular groups of people, in particular places, at particular times. Terrorist groups that kill and die for the Takfiri cause arise within specific "scenes": neighborhoods, schools (classes, dorms), workplaces, common leisure activities (soccer, mosque, barbershop, cafés, etc.), and, increasingly, online chat rooms. The process of self-selection into terrorism occurs within these scenes. Takfiri terrorism is stimulated by a massive, media-driven transnational political awakening in which jihad is represented as the only the way to permanently resolve glaring problems of global injustice. This incites moral outrage against perceived attacks upon Islam. If moral outrage resonates with personal experience that reverberates among friends in a scene, and if aspects of the scene are already sufficiently action-oriented, such as group of soccer buddies or camp mates, then willingness to go out and do violence together is much more likely.

The publicity associated with spectacular acts of violence in the name of justice is the oxygen that currently fires terrorism. As Saudi Arabia's General Khaled Alhumaidan crisply said to me recently in Riyadh, "The front is in our neighborhoods but the battle is the silver screen. If it doesn't make it to the six o'clock news, then al-Qaeda is not interested." These young people constantly see and discuss among themselves images of war and injustice against "our people," become morally outraged (especially if injustice resonates personally, more a problem with immigrants in Europe than the United States), and dream a war for justice that gives their friendship cause. They mostly self-radicalize in cafés, barbershops, restaurants, and informal discussion groups (people mostly pray in mosques, not plot in them).

Most human violence is committed by young people seeking adventure, dreams of glory, and esteem in the eyes of their peers. Omar Nasiri's *Inside Jihad: My Life with Al Qaeda*[4] rings true in its picture of the highs the militants get from the sense of brotherhood and sense of purpose. They want to belong to something that is at once intimate, bigger, and more permanent than a person alone. They kill and die for faith and friendship, which is the foundation of all social and political union, that is, all enduring human associations of nonkin: shared faith reigns in self-interest and makes social life possible; friendship allows genetically unrelated individuals to cooperate to compete. The most heroic cause in the world today is jihad, where anyone from anywhere can hope to make a mark against the most powerful army in the history of the world. But they need their friends to give them courage, and it is as much or more for love of comrades than the cause that they will kill and die for in the end.

This new wave of Takfirism is about youth culture, not theology or ideology. It is mostly irrelevant to classic military and law enforcement programs that seek success by "imposing unsustainable costs" on enemies and criminals, as the U.S. Department of Defense *Quadrennial Defense Review* suggests. It is about sharing dreams, heroes, and hopes that are more enticing and empowering than any moral lessons or material offerings (although jobs that relieve the terrible boredom and inactivity of immigrant youth in Europe, and with underemployed throughout much of the Muslim world, can help offset the alluring stimulation of playing at war).

How you change youth culture is a difficult and fickle affair. Role models or small changes often have big effects on attitudes and fashions (gangster culture, skateboarding, post-Madonna belly-button exposure, Hush Puppies fad, etc.). Take the new comic book series of 99 Muslim superheroes, modeled on Marvel comics, which is rapidly catching the imagination of legions of Muslim youth in Southeast Asia and now the Middle East. The first issue of *The Ninety-Nine* (published in Arabic and English editions beginning in 2006) weaves together heroic slam-bang action in the "fight for peace" with clear messages "to provide services ranging from the distribution of food and medicine to impoverished parts of the world" and "to multicultural educational programs and housing initiatives."

It is also important to provide alternate local networks and chat rooms that speak to the inherent idealism, sense of risk and adventure, and need for peer approval that young people everywhere tend toward. It even could be a twenty-first-century version of what the Boy Scouts and high-school football teams did for immigrants and potentially troublesome youth as America urbanized a century ago. Ask any cop on the beat: these things work. It has to be done with the input and insight of local communities, however, or it will not work. Deradicalization, like radicalization itself, engages from the bottom up, not from the top down. This, of course, is not how you stop terrorism today, but how you help prevent it tomorrow.

NOTES

Originally published in *Perspectives on Terrorism*.

1. Alan Krueger, *What Makes a Terrorist: Economics and the Roots of Terrorism* (Princeton: Princeton University Press, 2007).
2. Robert Pape, *Dying to Win: The Strategic Logic of Suicide Terrorism* (Chicago: University of Chicago Press, 2005).
3. Marc Sageman, *Leaderless Jihad: Terror Networks in the 21st Century* (Pennsylvania: University of Pennsylvania Press, 2007).
4. Omar Nasiri, *Inside Jihad: My Life with Al Qaeda* (New York: Basic Books, 2006).

Part II

Applying Ethics to the Global War on Terrorism

OVERVIEW

Charles P. Webel and John A. Arnaldi

This section provides in-depth examinations of ethical, political, and legal rationales for and against war in general and the invasion of Iraq in particular. The contributors note the complexities and challenges posed by theoretical and practical efforts to come to terms with warfare and mass slaughter. And by analyzing the ongoing war on terrorism, they assess the advantages and disadvantages of violent and nonviolent means adopted to advance political goals.

Laurie L. Calhoun argues that wars in general and the war on terror in particular do vastly more harm than good, and the harm done to the countless victims of these violent conflicts greatly outweighs any perceived short-term political benefit. Viewing war from what Calhoun calls "the first-person perspective" entails a respect for everyone's, even terrorists' and "the enemy's," "moral personhood." State-based or prioritized "third-person" security policies unjustifiably tend to apply different moral standards to the peoples of other lands than to one's own citizens. Military policies that lead to the slaughter of innocent people and their characterization as "collateral damage" effectively negate the moral personhood of the victims no less than do the practices of officially designated terrorists. The aspersion of adversaries as "evil" is counterproductive to the aims of human security, effectively precluding the possibility of constructive dialogue and thereby increasing rather than decreasing the probability that a conflict will lead to deadly violence. Calhoun advocates dialogue and consideration of the viewpoints of others, even one's enemies, instead of modern war, which she claims runs the risk of annihilation.

William A. Cohn argues that law should be a beacon of virtue, but it often falls far short. For Cohn, law, at its best, enshrines ideals of fairness, dignity, autonomy, equality, and justice. But at its worst, law is a tool the rich and powerful use to maintain and further their advantage in society. Law rooted in sound moral principles commands respect; unprincipled law breeds fear and scorn. The ideal of a rule of law rooted in universal moral principles has been supplanted by the rule of men bent on fashioning their own version of justice.

Cohn argues that post-9/11 events have raised questions about established law and its applicability. Do we best combat terrorism by military might? Law enforcement? Intelligence-gathering? Diplomacy? Commerce? Charity? Investment? A combination of these? Does application of the rule of law in response to terrorism enhance or degrade our security? Some say we are now engaged in a new kind of war where the old rules no longer apply. Others claim it is not a war, and that established rules and norms are indispensable—they define who we are and we degrade them at our own peril. The post-9/11 U.S.-led global war on terror (GWOT) has been reframed by NATO as a worldwide armed conflict with al-Qaeda, the Taliban, and associated forces. This campaign prioritizes military action over law enforcement; thus the GWOT remains an apt description of policy—even if the British government has disavowed this name and the Obama administration has rebranded it as "overseas contingency operations."

Nine years of trial and error with settled norms of constitutional justice enable us to draw conclusions, according to Cohn. The GWOT is not meeting its stated objectives (to weaken militant jihadists, inter alia) because the methods used (kidnapping, indefinite detention, torture, hypersecrecy, illegitimate war, etc.) are wrong—unethical and ineffective. Cohn concludes that rather than enhancing security, the misguided policies of the GWOT have made us less secure.

Jørgen Johansen claims that there are four phases of action and decision-making for those who want to act against terrorism. These are: (1) prevention; (2) stopping ongoing terrorism; (3) reducing the effects of terrorism; and (4) healing and reconciliation. He explains the meanings and implications of these phases and focuses on current and potential actors. This general framework is then applied to the unfolding phases of the "war on terrorism."

Johansen also analyzes the similarities and differences between state and nonstate terrorism. And he describes possible future types of actions and the actors who ideally should be responsible for each of them. The argument is that actors are morally obliged to act when they are able to reduce the effects of terrorism. And in this context, sins of omission can be just as immoral as those of commission. Johansen also looks at why terrorism gets as much attention as it does. For him, it is not because terrorists kill so many people. But rather this may be due to the mass fear that is promoted by the mainstream media and state actors for their own purposes, namely, to profit from the public's fear of terrorism without taking responsibility for it.

The contributors raise important questions regarding the conduct of military, political, and (quasi- or il-) legal operations during periods of violent conflict in general and especially during the GWOT. Government rationales for national security and self-defense against nonstate terrorists, if accompanied by preemption, retaliation, invasion, and occupation, are shown to be ethically dubious at best. And they become morally repugnant, if not illegal, when operationalized by the day-to-day tactics of waging this "war."

4

MORAL PERSONHOOD, HUMAN SECURITY, AND THE WAR ON TERRORISM

Laurie L. Calhoun

THE PERSPECTIVE OF MORALITY

There are many different ways of thinking about the world in which we live, each of which represents a perspective, a point of view commencing from a set of values and interests. Sometimes we adopt an aesthetic stance, evaluating things in terms of concepts such as beauty and symmetry. At other times we prioritize economics, assessing things primarily in terms of monetary value and net efficiency. In some contexts we prefer to regard ourselves and others as objects of scientific study, which can be described in naturalistic terms. Within science, there are several different layers of description from which to choose. According to evolutionary biologists, we are but animals that evolved from primordial sludge into conscious beings. According to physiologists, we are collections of organ systems; according to biochemists, we are complex agglomerations of molecules. All of these different views represent the perspectives of conscious beings.

As conscious agents, we regard ourselves as *persons*, with perspectives, values, interests, and beliefs. The moral perspective, in contrast to aesthetic, economic, and scientific views, commences from the idea of moral worth and the entities that possess it. The fundamental premise of the moral perspective is that persons have a special sort of value or dignity which non-persons do not. To adopt a moral perspective toward other people requires that we regard them as having intrinsic, inviolable value, a moral worth equivalent to our own. The moral perspective forms the basis of civil societies, which are governed by laws established by moral persons precisely in order to protect such persons from harm.

To embrace a moral perspective is to accept what is sometimes referred to as the "overriding" nature of moral considerations. Convenience, prudence, economics, aesthetics, and all other perspectives must be set to one side when morality is at stake. Because the moral perspective commences from the ascription of consciousness and sentience to other persons, national security practices, which ignore these qualities, cannot with linguistic propriety be described as genuinely *moral*, although they are virtually always defended through the use of moral *rhetoric*. When the essential value of conscious and sentient personhood is flatly denied, or brushed aside as irrelevant, the policies in question have prioritized nonmoral interests and values.

Bombing campaigns abroad characterized as "humanitarian interventions" by their instigators routinely ignore the fact that the members of a society most vulnerable to the objectionable practices of their government are simultaneously those with the least access to the sources of protection—including effective shelters—so desperately needed during wartime. When such people are killed, the killers exonerate themselves by claiming that the offending regime needed to be toppled. But it cannot truly be said that the victims themselves are better off dead than they would have been under an oppressive regime during peacetime. What was the intrinsic, inviolable value of so-called collateral damage victims has been reduced to nothing.

The overriding nature of morality forms the basis for the widely articulated idea that wars may only be waged as a last resort, for nothing could justify war, which culminates in the annihilation of persons, but the direst of circumstances—a case, for example, in which the people are so miserable that they themselves would take up arms and risk death rather than continue in their current state. This condition has not been met in recent U.S. wars, for the people of the lands under bombing are typically not consulted before intervention, and some among them have even openly protested the attacks made in their name by what they regard as officious outsiders with ulterior motives.

An optional war, which does not need to be waged, could only be an immoral war; for if there is a pacific option, which can circumvent the slaughter of human beings, then it must, morally speaking, be pursued. Similarly, a war waged to protect economic interests could never be *moral*, for such considerations cannot compete with the moral perspective, which asserts the absolute value of conscious human life.

Wars waged for oil, to acquire new territory, or to protect the economic interests of a country do not reflect a moral perspective.

Nonetheless, at the political level, discussions of war among diplomats often prioritize an economic perspective. The representatives of nations bargain with one another, compromising and making concessions in exchange for economic benefits. On the one hand, this is entirely understandable, for the people charged with safeguarding and promoting the interests of a nation are generally focusing upon quasi-prudential as opposed to moral matters. Often prudence and morality become conflated, when the economic interests of a nation are assumed by government officials to coincide with the interests of the citizenry. But when governments are bribed or extorted to support a war they would have rejected of their own accord, a war that leads to the annihilation of human beings (albeit the inhabitants of another land), then there is a sense in which those who acquiesce have been corrupted, at least according to a moral assessment of what has transpired. In some cases, such as those of poor African nations faced with the specter of allowing even more of their own citizens to perish due to the withdrawal of aid from a wealthy nation courting their favor, morality appears to have been sacrificed for prudence, though the leaders of nations who succumb to bribery or extortion undoubtedly reason along quasi-utilitarian lines and under the assumption that their first priority must be the people of their own land, rather than the prospective victims of a war waged abroad.

The tendency of government officials to conflate economic and moral considerations, as though the productivity of a nation directly reflected the well-being of its citizens, is symptomatic of a more general trend among intellectuals. Throughout the twentieth and now in the twenty-first century, the ascendancy of science has directed many scholars involved in normative areas of human endeavor toward the goal of a quasi-scientific paradigm. In science, the perspective of individual subjects is an irrelevant "hurdle" to be cleared in order to arrive at objective knowledge about the state of the world. However, to disregard the subjective experience of individual centers of consciousness, to assimilate them with insentient, nonmoral things, is effectively to deny the very basis for morality, for the peculiar value of moral persons inheres precisely in their unique status as conscious agents, susceptible of pleasure and vulnerable to pain, and embodying a moral worth that transcends the purely physical sum of their parts.

The pervasive error of prioritizing the third-person perspective in theories of value, while disregarding the first-person perspective, leads directly to problems in distinguishing amoral policies defended through the use of moral rhetoric, which all leaders wield, from policies that genuinely support and promote morality. Policymakers and leaders—whether of nations or of factions—often speak in terms of good and evil or right and wrong, as though everything comes down to an objective truth to which they have privileged access. Yet they rarely, if ever, mention the intrinsic value of conscious life, though this forms the very basis for the idea that moral persons should be protected from harm. So, for example, if the first-person perspective is of paramount importance, morally speaking, then it is false and misleading to suggest that "collateral damage" is any less deplorable than intentional murder. For what matters above all is not the *aggressor's* but the *victim's* perspective on what is done to him or her, and the horrific consequences of the use of deadly force do not differ from an innocent victim's perspective whether it be brandished by governments, individuals, or factions.

Similarly, from the perspective of a casualty of the homicidal use of force, terrorism is terrorism, whether its vehicles wear uniforms or not. When the populace accepts the military's anodyne characterization of the consequences of its violent attacks as morally permissible without reflecting upon what was actually done to those harmed, they thereby acquiesce in the dismissal of the perspectives of "collateral damage" victims as irrelevant. The very concept of "collateral damage," assumed by military spokesmen to be morally innocuous, presupposes that victims are summarily expendable, as though the military had a right to its victims' lives, being required only to account for them in the data collected and disseminated in postmortem official reports, after which they are relegated forever to oblivion. By supposing that the plight of civilians slaughtered in war can be summed up in "collateral damage" statistics alone, the reigning military paradigm effectively denies the moral worth of those people. Moral persons have plans and projects, relationships and histories, all of which are erased from the face of the earth with the dropping of a bomb.

Soldiers are obviously reified and slaughtered during wartime as well, but throughout the twentieth century, innocent civilians were the primary victims of decisions on the part of leaders to embroil their nations and groups in warfare, despite the oft-recited rhetoric of "noncombatant immunity." To regard war from a moral, as opposed to a political or economic, vista requires that we consider the perspectives of all individuals, on both sides of the conflict, civilians and soldiers alike, for the moral worth of persons is a function of neither their place of birth, nor the particular role which they happen to play within their own society. It is often simply assumed that enemy soldiers may be slaughtered, even though many of them have been coerced—whether physically or economically—to serve in the military. From the vista of morality, the snuffing out of any center of consciousness is a cause not for celebration but for regret.

The moral perspective carries with it practical implications for the conduct of nations and their associated institutions. The policies adopted by a democratic nation are done so in the name of *the people*, who must, in consistency, own that the same policies are equally valid for the leaders of other nations acting in the name of their people. The most basic requirement of rationality, that of simple consistency, is expressed by the law of noncontradiction, that nothing can both be and not be in the same way at the same time [expressed symbolically by philosophers thus: $\sim (p \ \& \sim p)$]. This serves as a fundamental constraint upon all theories, including moral theories, which in order to be acceptable cannot be self-contradictory. Consider, for example, the formal principle of justice "treat equals equally" or "treat like cases alike." This content-free principle does not imply that any particular mode of conduct is morally required, but only that, *whatever practices and policies are decided upon by the community, they must be applied to all relevantly similar cases.*

The requirement of simple consistency or noncontradiction is sometimes referred to by philosophers as "universalizability," and is arguably an indispensable part of any truly *moral* perspective. In the view of Immanuel Kant, the requirement of universalizability takes the explicit form of the test for the "categorical imperative," that one act only upon those maxims which one can will all others to act upon as well. This would seem to imply that if the people of one nation deem the possession of nuclear weapons permissible for themselves, then they must, in consistency, admit the same for all others similarly situated. Conversely, to decry the development and stockpiling of nuclear arms in other lands should lead one, in consistency, to decry the same in one's own as well, barring any morally relevant distinction between the two cases.

The perspective of human rights, according to which all human beings possess an inalienable right to life, liberty, and the pursuit of happiness, also insists upon the equal worth of all people, whether they live within or outside one's own country. The reigning military paradigm conflicts with the concern of human rights advocates to protect all people from aggression; it assumes that "collateral damage" victims may be killed during war, though they are in no way responsible for the crimes that allegedly justify recourse to deadly military force. Consider, for example, the Iraqi civilians killed during the 1991 Gulf War and the 2003 invasion and subsequent occupation of Iraq.

While the U.S. administration often claimed that the people of Iraq would be better off after Saddam Hussein had been ousted from power, many thousands of Iraqis were summarily stripped of their lives not by Saddam Hussein, but by those who waged war against him. From the victims' perspective, their own demise, characterized by the U.S. military as "collateral damage," was a crime—indeed, the worst sort of injustice that can befall a human being, the theft of one's very life. The so-called collateral damage victims of the 1991 and 2003 Iraq wars were wronged no less than they would have been had they been killed by Saddam Hussein himself. Yet those deaths, albeit foreseeable consequences of the deliberate decision of U.S. officials to wage war, were characterized by the killers themselves as permissible, given what they claimed to be the necessity of achieving their military objectives. To say that the leader of one nation may with impunity obliterate the people of another is to confer upon him the status of a god who takes or spares human life for reasons all his own. There is a strange paradox embedded in the idea that people who never appointed (and thus conferred legitimacy upon) foreign leaders should be subject to their political will to the point of being literally sacrificed for their cause.

THE CONCEPT OF LEGITIMATE SELF-DEFENSE VERSUS THE CONDUCT OF WAR

Nothing could be more valuable to a person than his or her own life, the sine qua non of the possibility of valuing anything else. If there are any human rights whatsoever, then the most basic of them must be the right to defend oneself from the possibility of annihilation. This idea finds clear expression within civil society, where it is deemed illegal to harm other people, and the penalties for doing so are proportional to the degree of damage done. The worst crime that one can commit in civil society is intentionally to kill another human being, to strip someone of his or her own life. However, self-defense, the use of force to protect oneself from an aggressor, is considered an acceptable justification for harming another person, *if and only if* doing so is the only way to prevent harm to one's self. The concept of self-defense seems straightforward and relatively uncontroversial: an innocent person directly threatened with harm may defend him- or herself from such unjust attack.

Many people appear to assume that the military is analogous to a parent-protector figure, who would naturally defend his children in the very manner in which he would defend himself. Children are incapable of defending themselves from attack, and so it is the responsibility of their parents to protect them. The analogy, then, is supposed to be that the military similarly defends the civilian population from acts of aggression: just as helpless children have the right to be protected by their parents, so, too, do helpless civilians have the right to be protected by the military, which has been charged with this responsibility and armed to this end.

While superficially plausible, the assimilation of the military to the head of a household does not withstand scrutiny, most obviously because the military concept of "collateral damage" has no analogue whatsoever within civil society. No father would support the bombing of a school or playground where his children were located—even if there were a dangerous criminal on the premises. Although it is true that the police are empowered to use lethal force, if necessary in apprehending a dangerous criminal, they are not permitted foreseeably to kill innocent people in the process, not even when this might facilitate their ability to carry out their duty to protect the rest of the community. The bombing of city centers abroad, in contrast, condones such killing, perfunctorily written off as "collateral damage."

In fact, on closer examination it emerges that none of the features of legitimate self-defense are present in wars fought abroad. Arguably the most striking difference between war and literal self-defense inheres in the means deemed acceptable for achieving "defense" objectives. The weapons developed by modern military institutions supposedly for the purpose of protecting the populace differ significantly from those used in defending one's self and family from harm. While guns have "dual" usage for either offensive or defensive action, bombs are always and only used through *transporting them to other parts of the world and dropping them upon other people's property.* The gun wielded in self-defense by a person suddenly confronted by danger in his own home existed antecedently for a legitimate domestic purpose. In contrast, bombs have no purpose independent from that of war, for which they have been expressly developed and *premeditatedly* produced *only* for deployment *away* from one's own home.

The officials involved in planning and contracting for the production of weapons of mass destruction (WMD) under the rubric of national defense will retort that the aggressor against which the military defends the populace is far more dangerous than any individual, which is why formidable weapons must be developed and stockpiled in order to protect the nation, weapons which can indeed destroy large numbers of people in a small period of time. But the modern

weapons of war—not only nuclear warheads and chemical and biological weapons, but also "conventional" WMD—have the capacity
to devastate entire populations, and the environments in which they
and their descendants might live, without regard to the victims' roles
in society. Strikingly, weapons such as landmines, cluster bombs, and
uranium-tipped missiles effectively target civilian populations *long
after the war has officially ended*. Such weapons severely compromise
the human security of innocent people during *peacetime* and effectively constitute uncontrollable vehicles of aggression. The ongoing
production and use of such weapons does not cohere with the picture
according to which war is a form of self-defense, for noncombatant
civilians do not pose a clear and present threat to anyone, and legitimate cases of self-defense harm only violent aggressors.

While there can be little doubt that soldiers fighting a ground
war on their own territory view themselves as engaged in literal self-
defense when directly faced with attack by enemy troops, combat
soldiers fighting abroad do not simply *find themselves* on the battlefield. Rather, they have been *sent* by the commander-in-chief to meet
the enemy soldiers whom they fight. So another obvious distinction
between wars fought abroad and legitimate self-defense is that the
former involve an intention on the part of the commander-in-chief to
engage his troops in battle, while the latter always involves a person
who finds him- or herself in a dangerous situation by chance and,
in desperation, defends him- or herself from harm. But, to reiter-
ate, when a country has been invaded by enemy soldiers, then the
soldiers of the invaded land do find themselves in that situation by
chance. Their use of force to repel acts of aggression by the invaders is
much easier to construe in terms of self-defense, for they may reasonably regard themselves along the lines of a sleeping person suddenly
awakened in his own home by an armed trespasser. Viewed through
a moral lens, the activities of so-called insurgents fighting in their
homeland against aggressive invaders diverges rather radically from
the derogative depiction of them proffered by military spokesmen.
This way of looking at the situation furthermore explains the explosion of "terrorist activities" in Afghanistan and Iraq subsequent to
the 2001 and 2003 U.S. invasions.

WAR VIEWED FROM THE FIRST-PERSON PERSPECTIVE

In 2003, experts from all over the world predicted that the invasion
and occupation of the sovereign nation of Iraq would lead to a global

increase in terrorist activity—which, the U.S. State Department later confirmed, it did. Many warned before the invasion that waging an offensive war against a sovereign nation would be interpreted as an act of U.S. military aggression and that those who instigated the attacks upon the Pentagon and the World Trade Center on September 11, 2001, would point to this as further evidence of the United States' hegemonic aspirations. War critics warned that some of those who viewed U.S. military action as criminal would retaliate, causing the deaths of even more innocent people.

During the rhetorical build-up to the 2003 invasion, many were also dismayed by the U.S. administration's "shock and awe" plan to drop more bombs in the first 48 hours than were dropped during the entire 1991 Gulf War. A Pentagon official, whose words were publicly broadcast on CBS News, indicated the following:

> There will not be a safe place in Baghdad...The sheer size of this has never been seen before, never been contemplated before...We want them to quit, not to fight, so that you have this simultaneous effect— rather like the nuclear weapons at Hiroshima—not taking days or weeks but minutes.[1]

If terrorism is the threat of the use of deadly force against innocent people in arbitrary ways, then it is quite difficult to understand how else "shock and awe" might have been understood by the Iraqis themselves, and a fortiori given that the existence of the alleged WMD arsenals serving as the pretext for the war had not even been established, much less their location. We now know that there were none at all. While thousands (not millions) of innocent people were destroyed by U.S. military forces during the spring of 2003, millions were effectively terrorized by the administration's ominous threat of "shock and awe."

When people are terrorized, the phenomenological quality of their trauma is not a function of the identity of the persons threatening the use of deadly force against them. But the dominant military paradigm entirely ignores the perspective of the individual subjects victimized in war. Because most people simply assume that war is a form of legitimate self-defense, they rarely reflect upon the meaning of military proclamations such as "There will not be a safe place in Baghdad" from the perspective of a prospective victim. Were war supporters to take into consideration the perspective of the human beings at the receiving end of bombing campaigns, they might recognize that "collateral damage" reports leave out the very basis for morality and, there subsumed, self-defense.

Instead, one sometimes hears military supporters praising a mission abroad for having limited "collateral damage" to 50, 100, or 1,000 civilian deaths. These numbers may seem small when compared to the entire population potentially affected. But what has actually transpired in such cases is that the victims' lives have been prematurely terminated through the decision of a political leader to deploy deadly force beyond the boundaries of his proper political domain. In fact, the subjective experience of civilians trapped in lands undergoing bombing raids would seem to be phenomenologically indistinguishable from the threat of terrorism with which citizens of the United States became familiar on September 11, 2001. From the perspectives of those abroad threatened with the use of U.S. military force in their own homeland and in retaliation to other people's actions, they are being terrorized no less than were the victims of 9/11 and its survivors, who continued to live in fear for months subsequent to those attacks.

The psychological insecurity of the inhabitants of a nation under bombing results from the fact that these people, who happen to be located through no fault of their own in countries run by criminal regimes, have no way of knowing whether they will survive. All they really know is that some, perhaps many, people are bound to die when the military of another nation begins to drop bombs from on high. Before the 2003 invasion, the Iraqis certainly knew that mistakes would be made, given their experience of the 1991 Gulf War. Among many other cases, on February 13, 1991, the U.S. military had bombed a large neighborhood shelter in Baghdad's Amiriya district, killing more than 400 people, mostly women and children.

Even according to the early, most conservative estimates of the number of civilians killed in Iraq by the U.S. military during the 2003 invasion, the range was from 8,000 to 10,000. All of those people were terrorized before they died. Yet, because of the dominance of the military paradigm in contemporary society and the government's euphemistic characterization of wartime atrocities, most people manage to avoid ever having to process such harsh realities. If, viewed from a moral perspective according to which each person's life is inviolable, the slaughter of nearly 3,000 innocent Americans on September 11, 2001, was an abomination, one can only wonder how the slaughter of multiple times that number of innocent Iraqis could be anything but worse. In the absence of access to killers' true intentions, we are left only with the piles of dead bodies they leave in their wake. Different conscious agents will interpret those dead bodies in very different ways.

When on March 11, 2004, the simultaneous explosion of several trains in Madrid killed some 200 people and injured many more, the horror of the act was patent to all. Images of mangled, bloody bodies being carried out of the wrecked trains were widely broadcast. In contrast, no major media outlet in the United States transmitted any images of the thousands of dead civilians killed by U.S. bombs in 2003. In comparing the two cases, one notes that it would have taken dozens of such coordinated train attacks as occurred in Madrid to add up to the slaughter of Iraqi civilians by the U.S. military in March and April of 2003. In other words, even using simple utilitarian calculation, there is a serious moral problem with the reigning paradigm.

Military solutions to conflict assume the benevolence of the killers, provided that they are one's own allies, while dismissing the perspectives of the victims as irrelevant, and defining the intentions and perspectives of the enemy as evil. It is widely accepted that the distinction between political killing by factions and military killing by states (at least one's own state and allies) is based upon a "legitimacy" enjoyed by the latter but not by the former. However, it is unclear that this view can withstand scrutiny, given that the leaders of nations are conventionally appointed by contingent assemblages of human beings no less than are the leaders of subnational factions. Every nation began as an informally assembled group of people who staked a claim to a piece of land.

When civilians are erroneously targeted and destroyed (as often happened in Vietnam, during the 1999 NATO bombing of Kosovo, throughout the lengthy and ongoing campaign against the Taliban regime in Afghanistan, and in Iraq from 1991 to the present day), a thorough diffusion of responsibility ensues. The planners who mistakenly selected the targets exculpate themselves by reasoning that they never physically caused the death of anyone. For their part, soldiers may absolve themselves from any moral responsibility for the innocent lives they destroy on the grounds that they were merely doing their soldierly duty. It is the role of a soldier to obey, not to call into question the orders he receives from on high. Since soldiers most likely do not *intend* to harm innocent people, such "collateral damage" is an unfortunate consequence of human fallibility as it manifests itself in warfare. Philosophers of war who defend the received view have often explained the distinction between accidental killings and war crimes by appeal to the Catholic "doctrine of double effect," which assesses the moral rightness or wrongness of an action by considering the actor's intention. If a killer targets innocent life directly—whether as an end in itself or as a means to an end intentionally sought—then his act constitutes murder. If, in contrast, a killer physically causes the deaths of innocent people as a side effect of a legitimate military action, then those killings are said not to be cases of murder.

While this line of reasoning may help to console the people causally responsible for the killing of innocents during wartime, one must, in consistency, allow that it applies to *all* military strategists and soldiers, including those on the enemy side, whether they wear uniforms or not. And it is entirely unclear that any soldiers, whether ally or enemy, kill people with the express aim of destroying innocent life. Rather, soldiers typically do what they are told out of a sense of duty and in obedience to authority. As misguided as the soldiers on the enemy side may be, they probably do not have evil intentions, and their actions are unquestionably informed by a story told to them by their leader. Even when dissenting factional groups wreak havoc upon civilians, as happened on September 11, 2001, they are in all likelihood interpreting their victims as complicit in the crimes of the government, through their ongoing support of what the faction takes to be the evil regime in power.

BLIND SPOTS IN THE STATE SECURITY MODEL

Governments are erected by groups of people who band together in order to promote their own interests and protect themselves. The authority of a state is contingent upon its satisfaction of the needs of the populace, who alone can legitimate that authority. The details of those needs will differ from community to community, given variable geography, climate, and other factors, but the most fundamental purpose is generally assumed to be the protection of people from violence and the threat of violence. Because the state-centered paradigm of security that gained sway during the Cold War period continues to dominate discourse regarding national security, during times of perceived global instability such as in the aftermath of 9/11, the political leaders of powerful nations naturally assess the range of military responses available to them—of which there are many.

Most writers in the mainstream security community simply assume that "security" is synonymous with "state security," a tendency repeatedly reflected in each U.S. administration's version of the *National Security Strategy of the United States of America*. Notoriously, the Bush administration went even so far as to assert the right to deploy nuclear arms preemptively, should U.S. officials deem the use of such weapons necessary in "self-defense." As the vexing conflict with Iran reveals, U.S. security strategists remain intent upon maintaining

U.S. military supremacy by preventing other nations from developing the WMD that already form an important part of U.S. arsenals. Unfortunately, the stockpiling, development, and testing of WMD, the withdrawal from international treaties and conventions, the refusal to ratify human-security-focused agreements such as the Ottawa ban on landmines or the recent convention against cluster bombs, and the waging of preemptive war have all served as overt endorsements by the United States of the use of brute force as a means of conflict resolution.

In 2003, George W. Bush waged an offensive war, in violation of international law, against one of the members of what he had decried as the so-called axis of evil. A wide array of rationalizations for the war were offered, but the most frequently recited was that Saddam Hussein's regime needed to be toppled in order to prevent his future use of WMD or his transfer of the same to terrorists for their purposes. Against all objective evidence, a concerted effort was made by some of the war's most vociferous supporters—including George W. Bush and Dick Cheney—to link Saddam Hussein to the then relatively recent attacks on the World Trade Center, the insinuation being that more such crimes could be expected to follow, if Hussein were not toppled. U.S. national security advisor Condoleezza Rice went even so far as to invoke the frightening specter of nuclear holocaust, warning the American people on nationally broadcast television: "We don't want the smoking gun to be a mushroom cloud."

As a result of the U.S. unilateral decision to wage war on Iraq unprovoked, brazenly flouting the protocol of the United Nations established to minimize the commission of wars since 1945, other countries publicly denounced by the U.S. administration could harbor no further doubts as to the willingness of the self-proclaimed "good" U.S. government to deploy deadly force in unpredictable and offensive ways. In reflecting upon the global effects of the 2003 invasion, it should not be forgotten that the United States had been a party to the UN weapons inspection process for several months before abruptly opting to invade Iraq. During a comprehensive report to the UN assembly, Chief Weapons Inspector Hans Blix had requested that he be permitted to continue his work in Iraq, citing the need for more time, as his group had failed to unearth evidence confirmatory of the U.S. government's allegations about WMD. But, in defiance of the findings of those charged with assessing the danger of WMD in Iraq, the U.S. administration called a halt to the process already in motion in order to wage war. Tragically, for the thousands of victims of the U.S. invasion, Inspector Blix was right: Iraq had no WMD.

The United States attacked Iraq but not North Korea in 2003. But one clear difference between the two cases was that North Korea seems *already* to have possessed nuclear arms, which it was poised to use against its neighbors, while Iraq was said only to have a program for the *development* of nuclear weapons. This suggests that the United States' offensive approach to defense can only lead to global nuclear proliferation, as overtly threatened nations covertly scramble to protect themselves from unpredictable, offensive war waged by the U.S. administration. Unpredictability implies uncertainty, which undermines the psychological and emotional security of threatened leaders. The offensive behavior of the United States may also galvanize terrorist factions to develop further innovative methods of destruction, and the danger of nuclear recipes finding their way into the manuals of terrorist factions will naturally increase with the proliferation of those technologies among governments. Consider, for example, the case of Pakistani scientist Abdul Qadeer Khan, who confessed in early 2004 to having sold nuclear secrets around the world. Particularly baffling to those concerned with human security was the U.S. administration's decision to pursue the development of "suitcase nukes," which can obviously be carried just as easily in the suitcases of terrorists as in those of U.S. Marines.

Acts of military aggression, even on the part of coalitions with the best of intentions, may have the infelicitous effect of strengthening the popular support of criminal leaders and nonstate actors who wield deadly force. When armies invade nations, the people themselves personally witness the destruction and death wrought. For example, political consequences of the 1999 NATO bombing of Kosovo suggest that people probably cannot be bombed into changing their views, a point amply illustrated by the election to parliament in December 2003 of Slobodan Milosevic's Serbian Radical Party ally, Vojislav Seselj, though both men were at the time standing trial at The Hague for war crimes. In fact, the Serbian Radical Party fared better than the pro-Western groups supported by the NATO bombing. Even more disturbingly, the new (anti-Milosevic) Serbian prime minister, Zoran Djindjic, was assassinated on March 12, 2003.

Nowhere are the perilous blind spots of "military science" better illustrated than in the cases of Saddam Hussein and Osama bin Laden. By now people are generally aware of the role that the international community played in producing the tyrant that Saddam Hussein eventually became. The picture of U.S. defense secretary Donald Rumsfeld shaking hands with the former dictator in December 1983 tells a thousand words, but unfortunately U.S. security strategists have not read them. Today's ally may well become tomorrow's enemy, and there is no way to retract the technology, weapons, and training already bestowed upon what has transmogrified into a dictator such as Saddam Hussein or an international terrorist such as Osama bin Laden, who was trained and supported by the United States during the Soviet invasion and occupation of Afghanistan. Until the implications of such cases are taken seriously by administration officials, such blunders are bound to be repeated.

VIEWING "THE ENEMY" AS A LOCUS OF CONSCIOUSNESS AND AN INTERLOCUTOR

All people, including "evil" leaders, act on the basis of their own values and beliefs—misguided and confused though they may sometimes be. But conscious agents do not *themselves* regard their *own* intentions as evil, any more than the soldiers enlisted to kill for a leader's avowed "good" or "just" cause do so with evil intentions. The ascription of evil intentions to one's adversaries effectively precludes the possibility of dialogue, thereby undermining the goals of peace and security with which institutions of national defense are presumably concerned. Bear in mind that people who have nothing to lose are the most dangerous people of all, and when they are placed in desperate or impossible situations, we should expect them to react accordingly. For example, during the 1991 Gulf War, Saddam Hussein's troops set many oil wells on fire. This was a grotesque assault upon the environment and an obvious waste of the nation's resources. But what behavior can we realistically expect of leaders who have been cornered in such a way that they are left with the means neither for escape nor for saving face?

When people offer arguments for taking up arms, they invariably begin with the assumption that the enemy is evil and must be stopped through the use of military force. In cases such as that of Saddam Hussein, few would deny that the leader committed many serious crimes. But to summarily destroy entirely innocent human beings—the so-called collateral damage casualties—in contending with a tyrannical regime is, from the perspective of those who disagree, to make the same mistake that the enemy has already made. Should not, then, the United States' annihilation of innocent people lead others, who reject the U.S. administration's interpretation of its own acts of killing as morally innocuous while nonetheless sharing their meta-view regarding the permissibility of "collateral damage," to follow their example and attempt to *stop U.S. leaders*, whom they regard as "the evil enemy"?

The principle of simple consistency implies that if one may wield deadly force whenever one *believes* this to be justified, then the same holds true also for other conscious agents as well. This suggests that sending the military abroad to kill people on their own soil can only lead to more violence on the part of those who find themselves in social climates already conducive to the incubation of terrorists, who may well interpret their own actions as a form of legitimate self-defense.

The interpretations of other people matter, strategically speaking, because they base plans, policies, and actions upon *their* interpretations, not upon *ours*. If we are disturbed by those interpretations, then we must attempt to transform them. From the perspectives of the citizens of nations such as North Korea and Iran, persistent, ongoing, thinly veiled "warnings" by the U.S. administration that "all options remain on the table" are empirically indistinguishable from the threat of terrorist attack. Civilians abroad continually faced with the ominous specter of U.S. acts of military aggression—including the Predator Drone assassination of suspects, along with anyone who happens to be around them—are being terrorized, while the leaders of denounced nations are simultaneously placed in the psychologically perilous situation of not knowing whether they will be next in the line of fire. Again, far from promoting security, looming threats of possible military action by a nation with vast arsenals of WMD may well strengthen the domestic support even of criminal leaders. As has been amply illustrated in Iraq and Afghanistan, some fraction of those outraged by what they take to be U.S. hypocrisy and hegemony will decide to fight back, even sacrificing their own lives in the process.

The reigning military paradigm commences from the conception of outsiders as objects to be talked about, not as other persons with whom to communicate. Moreover, there seems to be a general tendency to regard as "strong leaders" those who embrace the "conviction" model of morality, according to which one's beliefs in the moment about a so-called evil adversary are not subject to revision and furthermore suffice to rationalize what is tantamount to the sacrifice of countless innocent victims, through the inevitable "collateral damage" of contemporary war. Such readiness to wage war at the slightest provocation conflicts with the basic recognition of one's own fallibility, which rationally requires one to acknowledge that others, too, are persons acting in accordance with their own beliefs, arrived at through historically unique pathways.

If individual centers of consciousness constitute the essence of moral value, a genuinely moral perspective will not simply issue edicts about objectively wrong actions and bad states of affairs. In circumstances of conflict, to engage in dialogue is to accord other persons the dignity of having their own opinions and perspectives on the situation. War supporters and war opponents alike can agree about the existence of threats to global security and peace. Having concurred on this point, we need to reflect seriously upon not only how to protect ourselves, but also how to avoid repeating the mistakes of history, which led to the current state of affairs.

Military supporters and leaders often speak in abstract terms of the future triumph of "freedom and democracy," rather than the concrete consequences, the maiming and death, psychological terror, and insecurity to which military campaigns invariably give rise. It is essential to recognize that people can be molded into and indeed are never *born as* terrorists, which implies that an effective strategy for confronting the threat posed by terrorist groups must address etiological factors ignored by advocates of preemptive defense and the "kill them before they reach our borders" approach. The Israeli-Palestinian, the Russian-Chechen, and the U.S.-Iraq and Afghanistan situations, among others, suggest that the last way to put an end to the use of deadly violence by subnational factions is to summarily execute suspects. When during their "antiterrorist" military initiatives governments perfunctorily dismiss innocent victims as irrelevant "collateral damage," they thereby effectively confirm the very theories promulgated by dissenting factional groups, some of whom decide to wield deadly force in response to what they regard as war crimes.

The people who hold in their hands the power to wage war are the very same people who hold the key to peace. Accordingly, pointing out what we take to be their moral and intellectual failures and deficiencies will probably not alter their views. Indeed, if we simply assume that an administration is incorrigibly corrupt or hopelessly incoherent, then we close off the avenues to dialogue and, with them, the possibility of transforming their policies in the future. When people assume that leaders and governments are evil, they adopt a perspective toward them that permits the rationalization of any number of acts of destruction in the name of what is claimed to be self-defense. In reality, people, leaders, and governments are all evolving entities whose attitudes and practices transform over time. We may believe a nation and its government to be our ally today, but in the future this may or may not be the case.

The United States treated Saddam Hussein with the utmost respect, as an international interlocutor, during the Iran-Iraq conflict. As a direct result of the provision of Western aid and technology, the Iraqi leader became in less than a decade a full-fledged tyrant. Such cases strongly suggest that the prevailing military paradigm of state security is ill equipped to deal effectively with the complex challenges of the contemporary world. Among other things, it has become increasingly obvious that, since we cannot now know who our allies and our enemies in the future will be, we should call a halt to the weapons export trade today.

Conclusion

Moral rhetoric is invariably deployed by spokesmen for nations, but to look at conflict from a moral perspective requires that we consider the viewpoints of individuals. A leader who wishes to conduct himself in conformity with the dictates of morality in his dealings with other nations must accord to other leaders the rights and responsibilities which he accords to himself. When a leader acts in ways that threaten the sought-after peace among nations, which undergirded the establishment of the United Nations, the worst manner in which to address the problem is to violate Articles of the very same Charter that the offending leader is alleged to have transgressed.

There is no room for unilateralists in international affairs any more than there is room for "free-riders" at the level of interpersonal morality. Can, for example, anyone rationally condone "preemptive war" or "offensive defense" as a heuristic principle for all nations? If it is wrong for some governments to develop and test nuclear warheads, then it is wrong for any to do so. If it is wrong for some to develop and stockpile biological and chemical WMD, then it is wrong for others to do so as well. The basis for a peaceful community of nations is the same as the basis for a peaceful community of persons: the members of the group in question must treat other members of the group with the same respect with which they expect to be treated, and they must accord to them the same rights which they accord to themselves.

Human beings are creatures of habit, and belief is conservative: we tend to accept "the received view" until a compelling case is made to reject it. This explains why it is so difficult to overturn deeply entrenched beliefs such as that national defense is no more and no less than a form of legitimate self-defense, even when upon inspection the two prove to be quite different in structure, content, and consequences. Given the new kinds of dangers we face in the twenty-first century, we need to examine etiological factors that lead to factional violence but are generally ignored by national security strategists, whose policies focus upon the current situation, not the history leading up to it, nor what may later ensue.

The adoption of policies that genuinely promote human security has been severely hindered by the relatively recent capitalization of the weapons industry. Extremely powerful economic forces conspire to perpetuate the reigning state security model and favor the incessant expansion of the military state. We need to be vigilant of such forces, acting behind the scenes of what may appear on the surface to be a debate about justice and morality. So long as weapons exports reap hefty profits for the associated corporate interests, the economic perspective will be a formidable enemy to the adoption of truly moral policies at the international level. But the situation is far from hopeless, as a glance at history reveals.

The United States and many other nations used to condone racial and sexual discrimination, and even slavery. These practices contradict the basic principle "treat equals equally," given that race and gender are not morally relevant properties. After many, many years of dissent by those who recognized the injustice of racist and sexist practices, the laws of civil society finally changed. This was not easy, but in the end reason prevailed, and while some racists and sexists persist, their views are no longer codified as law in modern Western democracies. In confronting the deeply entrenched racial and gender prejudices of millennia, promoters of civil rights insisted upon the status of racial minorities and women as moral persons.

The same strategy needs to be adopted in resisting modern war, which victimizes human beings in the name of a form of "security," which, far from protecting the subjects of morality, actually puts them at ongoing risk of annihilation. From a moral perspective, a person's citizenship (or lack thereof) should not be used as a basis for deciding whether or not he or she has rights to life, liberty, and the pursuit of happiness. But deeply entrenched patriotic traditions continue to prevent people from seeing that when they apply different moral standards to their compatriots and to "outsiders," this chauvinism is morally equivalent to racism and sexism. This does not mean that people are incapable, in principle, of recognizing the analogy of patriotism to racism and sexism. But it does mean that we have a long distance to travel before the paradigm of cosmopolitanism favored by those concerned with the future of the world and the species will be widely embraced.

While it is unfortunate that economic factors often persuade administrators to be more accommodating of unjust policies than they might otherwise be, the same problem occurred in the pre–Civil War United States. Slaveholders were always wary of abolitionists, and they had every economic reason in the world to be so. But eventually it became clear that race is not a moral basis for the differential treatment of human beings. The views of slaveholders were also obviously buoyed by extraordinarily powerful psychological and emotional forces, and those same forces help to explain the widespread approbation by the populace of the military. Stated starkly: citizens do not wish to believe that their federal taxes are being used to terrorize, maim, and slaughter innocent people. This is why they so readily accept the euphemistic "collateral damage" apologies proffered to them by military spokesmen. In order to arrive at informed beliefs about the deadly conflicts in which their governments become embroiled, the populace needs to be told the ugly facts. Though often filtered out by the mainstream media, ugly facts—such as what transpired at the Abu Ghraib prison in Iraq— are being covered more and more by independent outlets concerned with the fate of the moral persons destroyed during wars waged in the name of defense.

In a world in which one nation possesses and wields overwhelming military superiority, the prospects may seem dim for the role of morality at the international level. But the fact that leaders persistently offer *moral* interpretations of their actions, even as some of them violate international law, itself illustrates that the populace is moved by moral considerations. The challenge becomes to make graphic the contradictions inherent to the military practice of mass destruction, which annihilates moral persons, the very repositories of moral value for whom institutions of defense were initially established.

Democracy is founded upon and flourishes under conditions conducive to open dialogue and dissent. Ideas that survive in a democratic society do so because they make sense to the people. At any given point in time, some of the practices and policies of any government comprising fallible human beings will be wrong. But it is one of the crowning virtues of democracy that no policy is etched in stone for eternity.

NOTES

I would like to thank Ajume Wingo and John Arnaldi for their thoughtful comments on this essay, a lengthier version of which was first published in the *International Journal of Peace Studies* (2005).

1. Andrew West, "800 Missiles to Hit Iraq in First 48 Hours," *The Sun-Herald*, January 26, 2003, August 6, 2010: http://www.smh.com.au /articles/2003/01/25/1042911596206.html.

RECOMMENDED READING

Bush, George W. *State of the Union Address.* January 20, 2004. Washington, D.C.: United States Capitol: http://www.whitehouse.gov/news /releases/2004/01/20040120-7.html.

Calhoun, Laurie. "Regarding War Realism," *International Journal on World Peace,* XVIII. 4 (2001): 37–61.

———. "The Phenomenology of Paid Killing," *International Journal of Human Rights,* 6.1 (2002): 1–18.

———. "The Strange Case of Summary Execution by Predator Drone," *Peace Review,* 15.2 (2003): 209–214.

———. "Be All That You Can Be," *New Political Science,* 25.3 (2003): 5–17.

———. "Michael Walzer on Just War Theory's 'Critical Edge': More like a Spoon than a Knife," *Independent Review,* X.4 (2006): 419–424.

Charter of the United Nations. 1945. August 6, 2010: http://www.un.org /aboutun/charter/.

Grossman, Dave. *On Killing: The Psychological Cost of Learning to Kill in War and Society* (Boston: Little Brown and Company, 1995).

Harman, Gilbert. *Change in View* (Cambridge, MA: MIT Press, 1986).

Hartigan, Richard Shelly. *The Forgotten Victim: A History of the Civilian* (Chicago: Precedent Publishing, 1982).

Higgs, Robert, ed. *Arms, Politics, and the Economy: Historical and Contemporary Perspectives* (New York: Holmes & Meier, 1990).

Ikenberry, G. John. "America's Imperial Ambition," *Foreign Affairs,* 81.5 (2002): 44–60.

Kant, Immanuel. *Groundwork of the Metaphysic of Morals* [1797], trans. H. J. Paton (New York: Harper & Row, 1964).

Mill, John Stuart. *On Liberty* [1859], ed. Elizabeth Rapaport (Indianapolis: Hackett Publishing Company, 1978).

———. *Utilitarianism* [1863] (Indianapolis: ITT Bobbs-Merrill, 1985).

The National Security Strategy of the United States of America (NSSUSA), September 2002, March 22, 2005: http://www.whitehouse.gov/nsc /nss.pdf.

Sifray, Micah L., and Christopher Cerf, eds. *The Gulf War Reader* (New York: Random House, 1991).

West, Andrew. "800 Missiles to Hit Iraq in First 48 Hours," *The Sun-Herald,* January 26, 2003, August 6, 2010: http://www.smh.com.au /articles/2003/01/25/1042911596206.html.

Williams, Ian. "Kofi Annan: A 'Moral Voice,'" *The Nation,* 270.24 (June 19, 2000): 20–24.

5

DEGRADATION OF THE RULE OF LAW IN RESPONSE TO TERRORISM: A FAILED APPROACH

William A. Cohn

INTRODUCTION

Law should be a beacon of virtue, but it often falls far short. At its best, law enshrines ideals of fairness, dignity, autonomy, equality, and justice. At its worst, law is a tool the rich and powerful use to maintain and further their advantage in society. Law differs from ethics, which is why there exists civil disobedience.[1] Law rooted in sound moral principles commands respect; unprincipled law breeds fear and scorn. Does fear now bind us to law? Has the ideal of a rule of law rooted in universal moral principles been replaced by the rule of men bent on fashioning their own version of justice?

Post-9/11 events have raised questions about established law and its applicability. Do we best combat terrorism by military might? Law enforcement? Intelligence? Diplomacy? Commerce? Charity? Investment? A combination of these? Does application of the rule of law in response to terrorism enhance or degrade our security?

Some say we are now engaged in a new kind of war where the old rules no longer apply.[2] Some say it is not a war, and that established rules and norms are indispensable—they define who we are and we degrade them at our own peril.[3] The post-9/11 U.S.-led global war on terror (GWOT) has been reframed by NATO as a worldwide armed conflict with al-Qaeda, the Taliban, and associated forces. Still, the campaign prioritizes military action over law enforcement; thus GWOT remains an apt description of policy—even if the British government has disavowed this name and the Obama administration has rebranded it as "overseas contingency operations."

Nine years of trial and error with settled norms of constitutional justice enable us to draw conclusions. The GWOT is not meeting its stated objectives (to weaken militant jihadists) because the methods used (kidnapping, indefinite detention, torture, hypersecrecy, illegitimate war, etc.) are so wrong—unethical and ineffective. As shown herein, rather than enhancing security, the misguided policies of GWOT have made us less secure.

RULE OF LAW—HELP NOT HINDRANCE

The origins of the rule of law can be found in antiquity, namely, the writings of Aristotle and the development of Roman law. Aristotle developed the concept of natural law rooted in universal morality.[4] Natural law theorists use ethical principals to evaluate law. Cicero saw natural law as the necessary foundation for all valid law.

The Basic Rule of Law principles include:

- supremacy of law—all persons are subject to law; no one is above or below it
- limited government power; individual liberties
- due process[5] (basic fairness in legal proceedings)
- presumption of innocence (*writ of habeas corpus*; no coerced confessions)
- separation of powers; checks and balances ◊ oversight of state action
- an independent judiciary
- protection of minority rights against the "tyranny of the majority"/ mob rule
- access to information ◊ transparency
- blind justice ◊ accountability
- a concept of justice; an underlying moral basis for all law
- doctrine of judicial precedent; common law methodology
- restrictions on the exercise of discretionary power
- legislation is prospective, not retrospective
- a rational and proportionate approach to punishment

Post-9/11 responses by Western governments have brought to the fore the relationship between means and ends—can immoral acts be justified in pursuit of ostensibly virtuous aims? Can such acts bring good results? The international legal community has been shaken by state-sanctioned indefinite—and sometimes incommunicado—detention of terror suspects, extrajudicial abductions, secret prisons, and torture.[6]

For a millennium, Western secular rule of law principles have been the guiding light of establishing more just and prosperous communities.[7] Aristotle asserted, "The rule of law is better than that of any individual."[8] Unchecked power corrupts; thus, transparency and accountability are indispensible. Immanuel Kant taught that natural law is international law, which is needed for peace.[9]

War Mentality

In GWOT, the criminal justice response to acts of terrorism has given way to a military approach. The Bush administration's decision to cast 9/11 as an act of war rather than a criminal act has had foreseeable dire consequences.[10] It helped enable the Patriot Act, Homeland Security Act, Military Commissions Act, intelligence and defense authorization acts, the unprecedented use of executive signing statements, a unitary executive theory, and other measures to weaken individual rights and strengthen the powers of the national security state, greatly reducing transparency and accountability. Rampant corruption, ineffective policy, mayhem, massive loss of life, and loss of faith in democratic institutions have ensued.

The past nine years have seen a major expansion of the concept of armed conflict, stretching it to cover violent criminal acts such as terrorism. The transitory U.S. military rules of engagement are far more permissive of killing than human rights law or a state's domestic law, providing a rationale for assassinations of alleged terrorists and the killing of civilians in combat zones, and prompting the director-general of the International Committee of the Red Cross (ICRC) to ask whether international humanitarian law—regulating the conduct of hostilities and the protection of persons during armed conflict—was still relevant.[11] The Bush administration's GWOT approach was premised on the notion that the United States is at war with al-Qaeda and international terrorism in general, rather than targeting the people who commit acts of horrifying political violence as criminals who should be captured and prosecuted. Secret prisons in Romania, renditions to Syria, drone strikes in Yemen, illegal wiretapping, and the indefinite detention of prisoners at places such as Guantánamo all rest upon the war construct. The Obama administration has reformed but not rejected this construct.[12] President Obama stated in early 2010 "Our nation is at war" and "We are at war."[13] The success the legal system has had in dealing with criminal acts of terror has been disregarded.[14]

The construct of a war without end against a nebulous enemy has grave historical implications.[15] Emergency war powers end when the war ends. When do emergency powers end in GWOT? Because terrorism is not aligned with particular states or governments, against which war may be declared, negotiations entered into, or peace accords signed by its representatives after a military outcome, such a "war" can never be won, and therefore carries the very-real prospect of perpetual war.[16] In the words of James Madison,

> Of all the enemies to public liberty war is, perhaps, the most to be dreaded, because it comprises and develops the germs of every other...In war too, the discretionary power of the executive is extended...and all the means of seducing the minds, are added to those of subduing the force, of the people. No nation could preserve its freedom in the midst of continual war.[17]

LAWLESS CONDUCT

The Bush administration violated law governing the legitimate basis for and conduct of war,[18] maintaining that GWOT could not be restrained by international law, portraying the Geneva Conventions as irrelevant and international organizations as appeasers of evil.[19] It also violated the Nuremberg Principles.[20] These violations did not go unnoticed or unchallenged. Of the many voices of protest, one mainstream example was American writer and storyteller Garrison Keillor, who accused Bush of war crimes.[21]

The Bush administration held that "unlawful enemy combatants" are not entitled to the protections of international humanitarian law because they allegedly pose an unconventional threat in an ongoing war—a contention firmly rejected by the UN, EU, jurists, and legal scholars.[22] The 1949 Geneva Conventions provide for comprehensive categorization and treatment of all actors, even saboteurs. As then-UN secretary general Kofi Annan told the BBC in 2006, by U.S. logic prisoners at Guantánamo could be held in perpetuity without charge. The same "logic" applies to "the battlefield," which in GWOT may be anywhere in the world. The May 31, 2010, *New York Times* editorial, "Backwards at Bagram," addresses the evisceration of the right of habeas corpus as courts have deferred to excessive claims of executive power in GWOT. The *Times* notes that the creation of law-free zones "was dreamed up by Mr. Bush and subsequently embraced by

President Obama." A federal appeals court ruling on the U.S. military prison at Bagram Air Base in Afghanistan overturned a district judge's ruling that a detainee captured outside of Afghanistan, far from any battlefield, and then shipped to Bagram to be held indefinitely, has a right of habeas corpus. The appeals court reasoned that this would "hamper the war effort."

America's leadership has been undermined due to the discrepancy between its words and deeds. America, the moving force for the Nuremberg Trials, assisted emerging democracies to draft constitutions and establish institutions to uphold the rule of law. As noted by human rights attorney-scholar Scott Horton, the consistent application of the Nuremberg rules "seems to have been completely forgotten, and the rule seems to be: Scapegoat a few enlisted men, but no senior official or senior officer will be held to account for anything. It's the total abnegation of the Nuremberg rule."[23]

Impunity for criminal abuses of GWOT prisoners continues under the Obama administration, abetted by the decision not to investigate the history of criminal abuse under his predecessor, and the ongoing use of GWOT policy such as the state secrets defense to lawsuits alleging abuse.[24] Obama's Department of Justice announced on November 9, 2010, following a prolonged investigation into the destruction of videotapes of brutal interrogations of terror suspects, that it will not prosecute any of the CIA officers or top lawyers who were involved in obstructing justice by destroying evidence of torture and other criminality. The agency withheld the existence of the tapes from the federal courts and the September 11 Commission, which had asked the agency for records of the interrogations, because officials feared the devastating impact of their disclosure.

Following 9/11, some U.S. officials cast law as a weapon of the enemy.[25] The United States turned the rule of law on its head—linking judicial processes with terrorism, and ignoring its history shaping the norms and institutions it now denigrated.[26] The notion espoused by former attorney general Alberto Gonzalez that the United States may disregard law precedent is inimical to its jurisprudence. According to the *New York Times*, "Because Bush does not recognize that American law or international treaties apply to his decisions as commander in chief [hearings afforded Guantánamo detainees] mock any notion of democratic justice."[27] The Nuremberg Principles compel accountability for abuses, whoever bears responsibility. The lack of accountability of U.S. officials for detainee abuses at Abu Ghraib, Bagram, and elsewhere is stark.[28]

"TRUST US"

The GWOT enabled government secrecy and muzzling of dissent. Casting 9/11 as an act of war created a bunker mentality[29]—marked by a series of radical executive orders, and steamrolling legislation through a pliant Congress. The GWOT also entailed police harassment and unlawful detention of scores of citizens based merely on their name, national origin, and appearance.[30] In the media there was what has been aptly described as a "paralysis of skepticism" on issues such as Iraq's alleged weapons of mass destruction (WMD) and ties to al-Qaeda.[31] The major media outlets misled their viewers by presenting Pentagon propagandists as independent expert analysts.[32] Those who dissented were demonized. In the GWOT, Bush said, "you are either with us or you are with the terrorists." Thus, if you question GWOT tactics you are suspect.

Dissent is a core value guaranteed by the First Amendment. National security and free speech are often in tension, especially during times of armed conflict. National security has afforded policymakers with a long-standing rationale for bending the rules. Long before 9/11 officials deviated from norms of fairness and decency in fighting enemies: The Alien and Sedition Acts of 1798 criminalized speech critical of the government; Abraham Lincoln suspended habeas corpus; Red scares followed both world wars; more than 100,000 Japanese Americans were imprisoned without charge during World War II; in the 1950s anticommunist crusaders discarded the presumption of innocence. Tactics placing expediency over principle were also employed against witches and anarchists. In this regard, GWOT is not at all a different kind of war, but a continuation of long-standing antidemocratic practices.

GWOT tactics have deep roots, which transcend party lines and administrations. Bush-Cheney's bravado in going to "the dark side" was stylistically deviant, but the policy of kidnapping suspected terrorists was enabled by executive orders from the Clinton presidency. Today, Obama's crackdown on whistleblowers and condemnation of *Wikileaks* furthers executive secrecy, and secrecy abets the lawless use of force. As noted in the October 9, 2010, *New York Times* editorial, "Lethal Force Under Law," "The Obama administration has sharply expanded the shadow war against [alleged] terrorists, using both the military and the C.I.A. to track down and kill hundreds of them, in a dozen countries, on and off the battlefield."

Former U.S. Supreme Court justices Goldberg ("Power not ruled by law is a menace") and Brandeis ("Sunlight is the best disinfectant") sought to prevent abuse of power. Indeed, democracy rests upon mistrust by the people of the government at least as much as trust—that is why we have the Bill of Rights, and law mandating open government, access to information, and public disclosures.

DARK TIMES

Following the 9/11 attacks, Vice president Cheney said of the United States: "We have to work the dark side, if you will. Spend time in the shadows of the intelligence world."[33] In November 2005, the *Washington Post* broke the story of CIA-run secret prisons in Europe.[34] The "black sites" (the term used in classified U.S. documents) revelations led to an outcry in Europe with governments accused of consenting to American political prisons on their soil. The Council of Europe, which oversees compliance with the European Convention on Human Rights, found violations of international and European law "concerning the transfer and temporary detention of individuals, without any judicial involvement...individuals had been abducted and transferred to other countries without respect for any legal standards."[35]

Kidnappings of individuals suspected of having committed acts of terrorism were carried out by the CIA's counterterrorist center rendition group—whose agents wore black masks while abducting suspects—rather than by law enforcement officials making arrests and bringing indictments.[36] So-called extraordinary rendition bears no resemblance to extradition, the transfer of criminal suspects through proper legal channels. The rendered suspect is denied legal protections that accompany physical presence in a territory that respects the rule of law. With no criminal charges pending, suspects are abducted, hidden, and, according to Amnesty International and others, brutalized. Extrajudicial action, widely used by Bush and continuing under Obama,[37] is neither founded upon nor connected with any court of law.

The *New York Times* commented upon the case of Maher Arar, a Canadian citizen rendered to Syria:

> There, he was held for 10 months in an underground rat-infested dungeon and brutally tortured because officials suspected that he was a member of al-Qaeda. All this was part of a morally and legally unsupportable United States practice known as "extraordinary rendition," in which the federal government outsources interrogations to regimes known to use torture and lacking fundamental human rights protections.[38]

The Canadian government apologized to Mr. Arar and paid him financial compensation for its role in his abduction. The U.S. government has neither apologized nor acknowledged any wrongdoing—an all-too-familiar result for those who have suffered abuse in the war on terror. Another example is Khaled el-Masri, a German citizen who alleged he was kidnapped and tortured by U.S. officials, who had his claims verified by German state investigators but, as other such victims, was denied his day in court when the U.S. government said that to defend against the case would require the disclosure of state secrets.[39]

Abductees merely suspected of wrongdoing have been routinely locked up indefinitely and incommunicado and sent to countries known for human rights abuses, such as Jordan, Morocco, Syria, and Egypt.[40] With no judicial oversight, the same operatives who capture a suspect oversee their own actions. UN Commission on Human Rights Special Rapporteur Manfred Novak says extraordinary rendition is arbitrary detention and "a complete repudiation of the law."

The United States rendered terror suspects to Syria and Egypt while its own State Department Human Rights Report condemned these countries' use of torture. Former CIA director Porter Goss called waterboarding (pouring water over a prisoner's face until near drowning) a "professional interrogation technique," and when asked to define torture said it is "in the eye of the beholder." A UN report concluded that U.S. attempts to redefine torture in order to allow conduct "that would not be permitted under the internationally accepted definition of torture are of utmost concern."[41]

In December 2005 the House of Lords ruled that evidence obtained through torture is inadmissible in British courts regardless of who did the torturing. Britain's highest court noted the more than 500 years of English law and the moral weight of international treaties and obligations, adding, "The principles of the common law, standing alone...compel the exclusion of third party torture evidence as unreliable, unfair, offensive to ordinary standards of humanity and decency and incompatible with the principles which should animate a tribunal seeking to administer justice."[42]

The 1984 UN Convention against Torture, signed by the United States and 155 other states, establishes torture as unjustifiable and intolerable. The ticking-bomb scenario is oft-employed by those condoning torture via a cost-benefit approach. This scenario, whereby a terrorist in custody won't tell how to defuse the bomb, which will kill many innocents in a matter of minutes, is a fanciful tailor-made scenario used to justify torture. Nearly all experienced interrogators assert that torture does not produce useful information (since a person will say anything to stop the torture), but rather wastes precious law enforcement resources on a wild-goose chase.[43]

Torture soils the torturer, degrading the principles that were its greatest strength.[44] Torture leads to a no-win Catch-22. Having acted outside the bounds of law and decency, those who obtain information by torture find it inadmissible in a court of law, making the prosecutions of those tortured and many other criminals near impossible. And so, indefinite unlawful detention continues and places such as Guantánamo become their custodians' prisons too.[45] Obama's inability to fulfill his pledge to close Guantánamo is one more sign that U.S. officials have become prisoners of their unethical and unlawful practices.

An August 2010 report by *ProPublica* and *The National Law Journal* states that only 24 of the 779 men who have been held at Guantánamo have even been charged with a crime, and since the 2008 Supreme Court ruling that prisoners at Guantánamo can challenge their detention as enemy combatants under the constitutional right of habeas corpus the United States has lost 37 of the 53 such cases brought in federal court.[46] These cases largely turned on the inability to prove terrorist acts because the evidence was tainted by torture. Thus, torture is a bad act that brings bad results.

Secret Government

In his 1961 farewell address, President Eisenhower warned of the growing influence of the "military-industrial complex"—an alliance of military, economic, and political interests with "unwarranted influence" on American government.[47] The GWOT has enabled a military-security contractor complex. The rise of private contractors and their influence on public officials comprises a government within the government—one shrouded in secrecy, which is beginning to come to light.[48]

In July 2010 the *Washington Post* reported on the vastly expanded and transformed American national security operations post-9/11.[49] Top Secret America documents the existence of more than 1,250 government agencies and 1,930 private companies working on security-oriented programs at some 10,000 sites throughout the United States. An estimated 854,000 people have top-secret security clearance, 265,000 of whom are employees not of the government but of private, profit-making businesses. Defense Secretary Robert Gates told the *Post* he worries "whether the federal workforce includes too many people obligated to shareholders rather than the public interest—and whether the government is still in control of its most sensitive activities."[50]

Lawyer Glenn Greenwald writes, "Most of what the U.S. government does of any significance—literally—occurs behind a vast wall of secrecy, completely unknown to the citizenry."[51] Greenwald notes that close to 50 percent of all U.S. tax revenue now goes to military and intelligence spending.[52] According to the *Post*,

> The top-secret world the government created in response to the terrorist attacks of September 11, 2001, has become so large, so unwieldy and so secretive that no one knows how much money it costs, how many people it employs, how many programs exist within it or exactly how many agencies do the same work.[53]

The current U.S. intelligence budget is two and a half times its size on September 10, 2001.[54] A total of $75 billion was spent in 2009.[55] Intelligence and other security agencies were given "more money than they were capable of responsibly spending."[56] *The Post*'s two-year investigation found U.S. national security operations thoroughly lacking in oversight, with contractors playing an ever more important role.[57] "To have the country's most sensitive duties carried out only by people loyal above all to the nation's interest, federal rules say contractors may not perform what are called 'inherently governmental functions.' But they do, all the time in every intelligence and counterterrorism agency."[58] Defense Secretary Gates confessed, "I can't even get a number on how many contractors work for the Office of the Secretary of Defense."[59]

The Post reports, "Most [contractors] are thriving even as the rest of the United States struggles with bankruptcies, unemployment and foreclosures. The privatization of national security work has been made possible by a nine-year 'gusher' of money."[60] According to Professor Alison Stanger, this has helped the enemy by blurring the line between the legitimate and illegitimate use of force in war zones.[61] Contractors now comprise 69 percent of the Pentagon's workforce in Afghanistan, the highest ratio of contractors to military personnel in U.S. history.[62]

EVIDENCE OF FAILURE OF THE GWOT

Have kidnapping, torture, secrecy, and war brought about a better or safer world? Kishore Mahbubani argues that unethical and unlawful

GWOT practices such as torture and Guantánamo have brought America into disrepute—and serve as powerful recruiting tools for terrorists.[63] A comprehensive study by the Rand Corporation provides evidence supporting this claim.[64]

As for the avowed goal of the GWOT (to weaken militant jihadists), the military approach is in disarray. In September, 2010 became the deadliest year for NATO forces in the nine-year Afghan war.[65] Wars have failed to establish stable governance in Iraq or Afghanistan. After more than nine years of the GWOT, the *International Herald Tribune* reports that the trend is further deterioration: "Even as more U.S. troops flow into Afghanistan, the country is more dangerous than it has ever been during the war...The number of insurgent attacks has increased significantly."[66]

This fits with the findings of the key intelligence bodies of the U.S. government (the CIA and the NIE), which claims that the presence of U.S. armed forces in a foreign land is a magnet for insurgents, and the findings of leading scholars.[67] Former CIA antiterror expert Michael Scheuer writes, "U.S. forces and policies are completing the radicalization of the Islamic world...it is fair to conclude that the United States of America remains bin Laden's only indispensible ally."[68] Noam Chomsky argues that if we apply the law approach of relying on predictable outcomes as evidence of intent, we may conclude that the declared goals of GWOT are not the real ones.[69]

The 2006 National Intelligence Estimate (NIE), the cumulative assessment of all U.S. intelligence agencies, concluded that rather than improving its national security, the tactics used in the GWOT, especially in the war in Iraq, worsened the U.S. position by creating a recruitment vehicle for violent Islamic extremists and motivating a new generation of potential terrorists.[70] The Rand Corporation reached similar conclusions in 2008.[71] The past two years have seen the Iraqi government weakened and the Taliban strengthened. Al-Qaeda now has roots in Iraq, which it did not have before the GWOT.

On September 22, 2010, three key Obama administration officials testified to Congress that the threat of terrorism is spreading. Homeland security secretary Janet Napolitano said the United States was confronting "more diverse activity" as al-Qaeda had inspired a more diverse array of terror groups.[72] This follows the trend in U.S. government reports of an ever-increasing terrorist threat since 2001, especially since the 2003 invasion of Iraq.[73] A 2005 Chatham House study concluded "there is no doubt that the invasion of Iraq has given a boost to the al Qaeda network in propaganda, recruitment and fundraising, while providing an ideal training area for terrorists."[74]

The presence of U.S. forces in Afghanistan strengthens the Taliban and jihadists, just as the U.S. military presence in the Islamic holy lands of Saudi Arabia feeds militant jihadism throughout the Islamic world. As the Rand Corporation 2008 study concludes, "making a world of enemies is never a winning strategy."[75]

War is costly—in many ways. The secret war documents published in 2010 by *Wikileaks* provide first-hand accounts painting a grim portrait of the wars in Afghanistan and Iraq. These documents inject a dose of reality, countering the sanitized narrative used by officials and parroted by the media. They cut through euphemisms such as "collateral damage," revealing the carnage of these wars. The October 24, 2010, UK *Sunday Observer* editorial ("A Moral Catastrophe: The Final Reasons for Going to War are Being Swept Away") says the *Wikileaks* files

> reveal how allied forces turned a blind eye to torture and murder of prisoners held by the Iraqi army. Reports of appalling treatment of detainees were verified by the US army and deemed unworthy of further investigation...build[ing] a portrait of a military occupation deeply implicated in practices that were illegal under international law and unconscionable in the eyes of any reasonable observer.[76]

More than a million lives have been lost and more than a trillion dollars spent fighting wars in Iraq and Afghanistan since October 2001.[77] Great portions of the Middle East and Asia have been thrown into further chaos and suffering.[78] The wars have helped to sink the American economy into its worst recession since the 1930s. President Bush inherited a $281-billion federal budget surplus, the largest surplus in American history, when he took power in 2001. Today, the United States has record current account and trade deficits. Liberty has been eroded as privacy has given way to surveillance. And hope and prosperity have given way to fear and poverty.[79] In whose interest?

A BETTER APPROACH: PREVENT TERRORIST ATTACKS LEGALLY AND ETHICALLY

Clearly, the unethical, illegal, and antidemocratic tactics used in the GWOT have not made the world better or safer. The rule of law safeguards liberty, security, and justice. Policies rooted in abuse, illegality, and deception are doomed to fail because they degrade the very principles we strive toward. What can be done?

Take practical steps, don't overreact, and think through the consequences of policies. The sealing of the cockpits on airplanes was a sensible and effective remedy to the threat of terrorists hijacking planes to use as missiles. The war in Iraq was disastrous because ideology trumped commonsense. It was entirely foreseeable that occupying Iraq would incite terror attacks. Shifting Justice Department lawyers from white-collar crime to terror-funding prevention was likewise overzealous and senseless. It doesn't require much money to get a desperate enraged person to become a suicide bomber. Again, unforeseen consequences ensued, abetting financial recklessness, impunity, and our ongoing Great Recession.

The 2008 Rand study of terror groups since 1968 found they ended because they joined the political process or because local police and intelligence agencies arrested or killed key members. "Military force has rarely been the primary reason for the end of terrorist groups...[This] suggests fundamentally rethinking post-September 11 U.S. counterterrorism strategy."[80] The report criticizes the United States for making military force its primary policy instrument, arguing that police and intelligence work should be the backbone of U.S. efforts.[81]

Officials should better coordinate law enforcement and intelligence activities both domestically (local law enforcement, FBI, and CIA coordination is needed, not turf wars) and internationally. The Christmas Day 2009 failed bombing attempt by the troubled young Nigerian man who tried to ignite explosives in his underwear is a cautionary tale exposing the failings of the GWOT.[82] This was the very type of act the GWOT was supposed to prevent, all the warnings were there, and the would-be-bomber never should have been allowed to board the Northwest Airlines flight. The multiple systemic failings show that throwing money at the problem doesn't fix it. The bloated national security bureaucracy described in the *Washington Post*'s Top Secret America is a system that compiles so much information in such an uncoordinated manner that it cannot connect the dots even when they are laid out in a clear way, which is to say that the post-9/11 intelligence community can neither think nor see straight.

Use the criminal justice system to investigate and prosecute terror acts, not the Pentagon and CIA. Use proven methods of law enforcement, not extrajudicial means—the British police apparently foiled a plot to blow-up transatlantic airplanes by dogged police work using lawful surveillance and international cooperation. Europe's law enforcement approach has been relatively successful combating terrorism. That the vast majority of the prisoners held at Guantánamo have not yet had charges brought against them proves the failure of the lawless U.S. detention system. The May 28, 2010, the *New York*

Times reported there is no evidence against many of the detainees still being held at Guantánamo after more than seven years.[83]

Use the institutions and agencies established for collective defense and development, allowing them to do their jobs, rather than, for example, pressuring scientists and intelligence officials to distort their findings to fit some preconceived political agenda, or preventing the International Atomic Energy Agency (IAEA) from completing its inspections. Stop demonizing opponents; maintain channels of communication, even with perceived enemies, because "rogue states" are better than failed states—at least there is someone to negotiate with.[84] At home, keep secrecy and censorship to a bare minimum. Dissent and open debate are vital for democracy, as are transparency and accountability.[85] "Trust us" prevents us from knowing whether government claims of foiled terror attacks and new threats are legitimate. Impunity assures that war crimes and other immoral and unlawful acts will continue; lawbreakers must be punished.

Fund the UN Millennium Development Goals. Suicide bombers are born mainly out of desperation; fighting dire poverty will reduce terror. This implies that the U.S. government should no longer support corrupt oppressive regimes in Saudi Arabia and elsewhere, which use their countries' oil wealth primarily to further their own privileged position in society, but rather should use development aid to reduce poverty and inequity.[86] This further implies that spending for U.S. military and arms trafficking should be redirected toward economic and social development.[87]

Deterrence of terrorist attacks should be the goal of antiterrorism policy. Indeed, an ounce of prevention is worth a pound of cure. *The Economist* reports: "Does it matter to the United States that Somalia is becoming a hotbed of global jihad? The answer most often heard in Washington is impenetrable. 'Somalia is not important until it launches a terrorist attack which makes it important,' explains a Pentagon official."[88] This is like a doctor telling a healthy patient, "I'll give you an examination when you're in the ICU." The U.S. Constitution establishes civilian command of the military, yet policy often reflects the Pentagon's priorities. This must change if we are to de-escalate the GWOT and reduce terrorism.

LIVE AND LEARN

Philosopher George Santayana warned, "Those who do not remember the past are condemned to repeat it." A levelheaded analysis of the challenge of defeating terror makes clear what works and what doesn't.

At the Nuremberg Trials, U.S. chief counsel Robert Jackson stated:

> If certain acts of violations of treaties are crimes, they are crimes whether the United States does them or whether Germany does them, and we are not prepared to lay down a rule of criminal conduct against others which we would not be willing to have invoked against us... We must never forget the record on which we judge these defendants is the record on which history will judge us tomorrow. To pass these defendants a poisoned chalice is to put it to our own lips as well.[89]

Kant wrote, "a violation of rights in one part of the world is felt everywhere."[90] That is most true today—and the consequences of injustice include terrorism. The GWOT marks a low point in American history for the gravity, scope, and impact of its immoral practices. Making enemies is never a winning strategy. Hypocrisy is unethical and weak.

Treating the globe as a battlefield is certainly not the way to reduce terror or terrorism. FDR wisely said, "The only thing we have to fear is fear itself." Stopping the war-machine will not be easy—powerful industries and policymakers are profiting by spreading fear and war. It will require an actively engaged civil society to counter the fear mongering and carnage of the GWOT. Building peace requires greater strength than waging war. The U.S. government must be made to stop acting in ways that—predictably—enhance the threat of terrorism.[91]

NOTES

1. Civil disobedience is an act of individual conscience to deliberately violate a law seen as unethical based on the principle that one has a moral right to disobey an immoral law. See Henry David Thoreau's *Civil Disobedience* (1849) (available at http://thoreau.eserver.org /civil.html). See also, Rev. Martin Luther King, Jr., "Letter from a Birmingham Jail" (available at http://www.africa.upenn.edu/Articles _Gen/Letter_Birmingham.html), in which Dr. King writes that "one has a moral responsibility to disobey unjust laws" and "injustice anywhere is a threat to justice everywhere." Not all moral acts are lawful (e.g., King, Mohandas Gandhi, and Rosa Parks) and not all lawful acts are moral (e.g., tax havens, capital punishment). Rule of law principles help to align law with ethics. If the rule of law proves incapable of restoring ethical principles in the global response to terrorism then civil disobedience and other forms of unrest and rebellion are most relevant.

2. See John C. Yoo, "War, Responsibility, and the Age of Terrorism," *Stanford Law Review*, 57 (2004): 793; see also the legal opinions rendered by Bush administration lawyers Mr. Yoo, Jay Bybee, and Alberto Gonzalez (http://www.gwu.edu/~nsarchiv/NSAEBB/NSAEBB127/).

3. See David Cole, *What Bush Wants to Hear*, N.Y. Rev. Books, November 17, 2005; Ronald Dworkin, "Terror and the Attack on Civil Liberties," *New York Review of Books*, November 6, 2003 (http://www.nybooks.com /articles/archives/2003/nov/06/terror-the-attack-on-civil-liberties/); *Rights and Terror* (http://www.law.nyu.edu/clppt/program2003 /readings/dworkin.pdf); Laurence H. Tribe, *The Tanner Lectures on Human Values*, Oxford University, May 20 and 21, 2002 (http://www .tannerlectures.utah.edu/lectures/documents/volume24/tribe_2002 .pdf). See also the sources listed in note 22.

4. Aristotle, *Nicomachean Ethics*, Book V—On Justice and Fairness (350 BC).

5. There is a common misconception that the due process clause of the 5th and 14th Amendments of the Bill of Rights (protection against government action depriving an individual of life, liberty or property without due process of law) applies only to U.S. citizens. The framers of these amendments regarded life, liberty, and property as basic human or natural rights that do not depend upon citizenship, which is why these amendments refer not to citizens but to persons.

6. The International Bar Association issued a resolution in 2005: "The IBA, the global voice of the legal profession, deplores the increasing erosion around the world of the rule of law [which] is the foundation of a civilized society. It establishes a transparent process equal and accessible to all. It ensures adherence to principles that both liberate and protect." In 2009, the International Commission of Jurists concluding a three-year study of GWOT policies adopted by the United States, the United Kingdom, and others, stated: "We have been shocked by the damage done over the past seven years by excessive or abusive counter-terrorism measures in a wide range of countries around the world. Many governments, ignoring the lessons of history, have allowed themselves to be rushed into hasty responses to terrorism that have undermined cherished values and violated human rights" (http://www.harpers.org/archive/2009/02/hbc-90004415). See also icj.org, iba.org, William A. Cohn: "As Blackwater Rises, the Rule of Law Recedes," *The DePaul Rule of Law Journal* (Fall 2010); *Definitions of Convenience*, 8 The New Presence: Prague. *Journal of Central European Affairs* 28 (2006).

7. The United Nations Declaration of Human Rights and Covenant on Civil and Political Rights are rooted in Rule of Law principles.

8. Aristotle, *Politics* 51 (available at http://socserv2.mcmaster.ca/~econ /ugcm/3ll3/aristotle/Politics.pdf).

9. Immanuel Kant, *Perpetual Peace: A Philosophical Essay* (1795). Kant asserts that there exists international law founded on universal ethics.

He writes, "The peoples of the earth have thus entered in varying degrees into a universal community, and it has developed to the point where a violation of rights in one part of the world is felt everywhere." Dr. King's 1963 "Letter from a Birmingham Jail" echoes Kant. In *The Metaphysical Elements of Justice* (1797) Kant states that freedom exists only if universal laws govern, thus free will depends on universal laws.

10. See President Bush's address to a joint session of Congress on September 20, 2001 (http://www.americanrhetoric.com/speeches /gwbush911jointsessionspeech.htm). Although the Constitution (Article 1, Sec. 8) gives only Congress the authority to declare war, presidents have routinely engaged in warfare unlawfully, causing Congress to pass the War Powers Resolution of 1973, which requires the president to give Congress prompt notification when sending armed forces into military action. The wars in Iraq and Afghanistan (and the use of U.S. armed forces in Pakistan, Yemen, and elsewhere in the name of the GWOT) were never formally declared by Congress, raising questions about their legality under U.S. law, not to mention questions regarding illegality under international law. Important but largely ignored questions arise as to the appropriate steps to be taken when a leader circumvents a nation's constitutionally required process to declare and fight a war.

11. Angelo Gnaedinger, "Is IHL still relevant in a post-9/11 world?" (http://www.icrc.org/web/eng/siteeng0.nsf/html/ihl-article -300906). The 1907 Hague Convention and the 1949 Geneva Convention are the main sources of modern IHL.

12. The Center for Constitutional Rights conducted an April 1, 2010, an assessment of Obama's record on GWOT issues (http://ccrjustice.org /obamas-record) taking issue with ongoing: abuse of executive author- ity; ghost detentions; material support convictions; indefinite detention of suspects; habeas corpus denial; renditions; violation of civil liberties; lack of accountability for past crimes; abuse of the state secrets privilege; and human rights abuse by military contractors. See also the writings of Joanne Mariner at findlaw.com.

13. Quoted in Peter Baker, "Inside Obama's War on Terrorism," *New York Times*, January 5, 2010, which concludes, "much of the Bush security architecture is almost certain to remain part of the national fabric for some time to come, thanks to Obama."

14. See *In Pursuit of Justice: Prosecuting Terrorism Cases in the Federal Courts*, a white paper prepared by a team of experienced law enforce- ment lawyers headed by two former U.S. attorneys on behalf of Human Rights First in 2008. They conclude that "the existing criminal justice system is an established institution that has generally done a good job in handling international terrorism cases...it has proved to be adapt- able and has successfully handled a large number of important and chal- lenging terrorism prosecutions over the past 15 years without sacrificing national security interests or rigorous standards of fairness and due process" (page 129 of the report in http://www.humanrightsfirst.org

/pdf/080521-USLS-pursuit-justice.pdf). See also "The Memory Hole" and "Invisible Men" by Dahlia Latwick, at slate.com.

15. Hilary Benn, a senior aide to Tony Blair, said in 2007 that the phrase "war on terror" strengthens extremists: "In the U.K. we don't use the phrase 'war on terror' because we can't win by military means alone and because this isn't one organized enemy with a coherent set of objectives." The phrase "war on terror" has officially been replaced, in favor of the sanitized euphemism "overseas contingency operations," but GWOT's core—supplanting the criminal justice response to acts of terrorism with a military approach—endures.

16. See David Barash and Charles Webel, *Peace and Conflict Studies*, 2nd ed. (Los Angeles and London: Sage Pub., 2009), 62. The authors present a compelling argument that terrorism has always and will always exist, which makes the GWOT most threatening. As well, the GWOT professes to wage war against terror, a noun (thing), which is fallacious in itself. Although war has also been declared against poverty and drugs, this is using war in the broader meaning of battle or struggle. War in its traditional legal meaning of armed conflict may only be logically applied against an identifiable enemy.

17. Quoted in Fareed Zakaria, "What America Lost," *Newsweek,* September 13, 2010, 8. On "seducing the minds," see David Barstow's Pulitzer Prize report "Behind TV Analysts, Pentagon's Hidden Hand," *New York Times,* April 20, 2008. See, more recently, "Guantanamo Censors," *International Herald Tribune,* September 22, 2010, 6. On the implications of the endless war paradigm, see the writings of Andrew Bacevich, including *Washington Rules: America's Path to Permanent War* (New York: Macmillan, 2010).

18. The Bush Doctrine, used in Iraq, of "taking the battle to the enemy" is a direct repudiation to the UN Charter, which prohibits the use of international force unless in self-defense or via Security Council authorization. It would enable China to invade Taiwan and India to invade Kashmir. See Scott Horton, "Kriegsraison or Military Necessity? The Bush Administration's Wilhelmine Attitude towards the Conduct of War," 30 *Fordham Int'l L.J.* 576 (2006–2007): 576. Violations of law governing the conduct of war include failure to take steps to protect civilians, indefinite incommunicado detention, torture, kidnapping, and denial of Geneva and Hague Convention status review protocols. See, e.g., notes 19–23.

19. The U.S. attorney general's January 25, 2002, memo to the president refers to the Geneva Conventions as "quaint" and "obsolete." The ICRC found the United States guilty of systematic and serious violations of the Geneva Conventions of 1949 (e.g., Convention III governing the treatment of prisoners of war and Convention IV on protecting civilians in times of war). International law also prohibits incommunicado detention. The Geneva Conventions require that prisoners' whereabouts be documented and made available to family and governments, and that the

ICRC have access to all detainees and places of detention. Violations have occurred in Iraq, Guantánamo, Afghanistan, and the secret CIA prisons.

20. War crimes, "punishable as crimes under international law" under the Principles, encompass "Violations of the laws or customs of war which include...murder or ill-treatment of prisoners of war." The Center for Constitutional Rights filed charges seeking war crimes indictments against U.S. officials including former CIA chief George Tenet and former defense secretary Donald Rumsfeld. Together, the first four Nuremberg Principles establish personal responsibility and accountability for violations of law. In 2004, the International Committee of the Red Cross report found that some 90 percent of Iraqi detainees were mistakenly arrested and that inmates were routinely mistreated by being kept naked in totally dark, empty cells, subjected to brutality, humiliation, threats of imminent execution, and other abuses "tantamount to torture [and] used by the military intelligence in a systematic way to gain confessions." ICRC report: http://cryptome.org/icrc-report.htm. See also "Most Arrested by Mistake," *Los Angeles Times*, May 11, 2004, http://www.commondreams.org/headlines04/0511-04.htm. In 2005, Human Rights Watch reported that the United States has raised the use of torture to a "serious policy option" as abuse of detainees has become a "deliberate, central part of the Bush Administration's strategy for interrogating terrorist suspects." HRW report: http://www.hrw.org/. "When Human Rights Watch...focuses its annual review on America's use of torture and inhumane treatment...everyone who believed in the United States as the staunchest protector of human rights in history should be worried" ("Editorial: An Indictment of America," *The New York Times*, January 27, 2006).

21. Garrison Keillor, "When the Emperor Has No Clothes," *International Herald Tribune*, March 3, 2006.

22. See, e.g., David Cole, *What Bush Wants to Hear* (N.Y. Rev. Books, November 17, 2005); Ronald Dworkin, "The Threat To Patriotism," *New York Review of Books*, February 28, 2002; Justice Richard Goldstone, "U.S. Antagonism toward the International Rule of Law: The View of a Concerned 'Outsider,'" *Washington University Global Studies Law Review* 4.2 (2005): 205; Michael Ratner, "Moving Away from the Rule of Law: Military Tribunals, Executive Detentions and Torture," *Cardozo L. Rev.* 24 (2002–2003): 1513; and *Guantanamo: What the World Should Know* (Chelsea Green Pub. Co., 2004); Kenneth Roth, "Human Rights as a Response to Terrorism," *Oregon Review of International Law* (2004). See also icj.org, iba.org and aba.org.

23. Interview with Scott Horton in *Executive Intelligence Review*, January 28, 2005, http://www.larouchepub.com/other/interviews/2005/3204scott_horton.html.

24. The Obama administration has used the state secrets defense in cases on: Bush-era warrantless wiretapping; surveillance of an Islamic charity; its alleged planned assassination of a U.S. citizen (U.S. officials have

admitted that Anwar al-Awlaki is on an assassination list); and the torture and rendition of CIA prisoners. See the *New York Times* editorials: "Shady Secrets," Oct 1, and "Indefensible Defense," Oct 26, 2010. "Shady Secrets" notes that the public "still cannot distinguish between legitimate and self-serving uses of the national security claims. Worse, some of the [Obama] administration's claims clearly have fallen on the darker side of that line." Due to the failure of the United States to permit claims of abuse to be heard in its courts, other avenues have been sought in the search for justice. On September 21, 2010, lawyers with the Open Society Justice Initiative (OSJI) filed a petition to open an investigation into U.S. renditions to CIA-run secret prisons in Poland where they allege prisoners were tortured. Amrit Singh, OSJI's senior lawyer, said, "The quest for accountability for the CIA's illegal rendition program must continue in Europe, especially as U.S. courts appear to be closing their doors to victims of this program." Polish prosecutors have been investigating the country's alleged role in the U.S. worldwide system of secret prisons. "Poles urged to investigate claims on secret CIA jail," Associated Press, *International Herald Tribune,* September 22, 2010, 3.

25. Former U.S. homeland security secretary Michael Chertoff accused IGOs of using international law (IL) "as a rhetorical weapon against us." The Pentagon's 2005 National Defense Strategy also views IL as a threat to the United States: "Our strength as a nation will continue to be challenged by those who employ *a strategy of the weak using international fora, judicial processes and terrorism.*"

26. According to the annual report of Amnesty International: "Governments collectively and individually paralyzed international institutions and squandered public resources in pursuit of narrow security interests, sacrificed principles in the name of the 'war on terror' and turned a blind eye to massive human rights violations. As a result, the world has paid a heavy price, in terms of erosion of fundamental principles and in the enormous damage done to the lives and livelihoods of ordinary people. The war on terrorism is failing and will continue to fail until human rights and human security are given precedence over narrow national security interests." Hans Morgenthau wrote, the refusal to acknowledge the legitimate interests of others provokes "the distortion of judgment which, in the blindness of crusading frenzy, destroys nations and civilizations." See the statements of John Bolton, former U.S. ambassador to the UN, for the Bush administration's incendiary attitude toward international law and multilateral institutions.

27. "They Came for the Chicken Farmer," *New York Times,* March 8, 2006. The status review boards violate Geneva Convention protocols, and the military tribunals set up to conduct trials have been criticized as kangaroo courts (allowing hearsay evidence, denying attorney-client confidentiality and the right to see evidence and confront witnesses, and just about all the protections designed to ensure a fair hearing). Obama has continued the reliance on military tribunals. See "Editorial: Warped

Justice," *Times* November 8, 2010, on the case of Omar Khadr, which was to have been the first trial using the military commissions. The mockery of any notion of justice is exemplified by the treatment of U.S. citizen Jose Padilla, the alleged dirty bomber. Mr. Padilla was detained as a material witness in 2002, and then his classification changed from "enemy combatant" to crime suspect depending on the latest court ruling in the Bush administration's cat-and-mouse game to snub the courts. Padilla was held for more than three years in solitary isolation in a military brig.

28. We now know that every detail of the (mis)treatment of supposedly high-value detainees at CIA secret prisons, Guantánamo Bay, and prisons in Iraq and Afghanistan was monitored and sanctioned by high-level officials. We know that Bush, Cheney, Rumsfeld, Rice, Ashcroft, and Gonzales were present when torture was discussed and sanctioned. Yet no high-level military official, let alone the government lawyers who twisted the law to rationalize torture, or the cabinet members they sought to please, have been punished or otherwise put in peril. Such impunity is antithetical to the rule of law. See Sandra Coliver, "Bring Human Rights Abusers to Justice in U.S. Courts: Carrying Forward the Legacy of the Nuremberg Trials," *Cardozo L. Rev.* 27 (2005–2006): 1689; Mark Danner, "Torture and Truth," *New York Review of Books,* June 10, 2004; Kenneth Roth, *Getting Away with Torture? Command Responsibility for the U.S. Abuse of Detainees* (Human Rights Watch, 2005).

29. The noun bunker mentality is defined by the Merriam-Webster Dictionary as "a state of mind especially among members of a group that is characterized by chauvinistic defensiveness and self-righteous intolerance of criticism."

30. See the Human Rights Watch and ACLU report *Witness to Abuse: Human Rights Abuses under the Material Witness Law Since September 11, 2001* (http://www.aclu.org/national-security/us-scores-muslim-men-jailed-without-charge). On October 18, 2010, the U.S. Supreme Court agreed to hear former attorney-general John Ashcroft's appeal of a Ninth Circuit ruling that Abdullah al-Kidd may proceed with his lawsuit against Mr. Ashcroft alleging that he was a victim of the abusive use of the material witness law that Mr. Ashcroft used as a means of unlawful preventive detention. See "Editorial: Indefensible Defense," *New York Times,* October 26, 2010, discussing Ashcroft v. al-Kidd: "It turns on a sacrosanct principle: The government cannot arrest you without evidence that you committed a crime." Many observers of the Supreme Court believe the court agreed to hear the case so that it can overturn the Ninth Circuit ruling that the lawsuit against Mr. Ashcroft may proceed.

31. Ian Buruma, "Theater of War," *New York Times Sunday Book Review,* September 17, 2006, reviewing *The Greatest Story Ever Sold: The Decline and Fall of Truth from 9/11 to Katrina* by Frank Rich (Penguin Books, 2006).

32. See David Barstow's report mentioned in note 17.
33. Cheney made this statement on NBC's *Meet the Press* on September 16, 2001, adding, "A lot of what needs to be done will need to be done quietly, without any discussion..." (http://www.pbs.org/wgbh/pages /frontline/darkside/themes/darkside.html).
34. See the Pulitzer Prize-winning reporting of Dana Priest (http://www.washingtonpost.com/wp-dyn/content/article/2005/11/01 /AR2005110101644.html) and (http://www.washingtonpost.com/wp -dyn/content/linkset/2006/04/17/LI2006041700530.html).
35. Report at http://assembly.coe.int/CommitteeDocs/2006/20060606 _Ejdoc162006PartII-FINAL.pdf and further Council findings at http://www.coe.int/T/E/Com/Files/Events/2006-cia/.
36. Cohn, *Definitions of Convenience.*
37. http://www.nytimes.com/2009/08/25/us/politics/25rendition .html.
38. A Judicial Green Light for Torture," *New York Times*, February 26, 2006.
39. On September 7, 2010, a federal appeals court ruled that former prisoners of the CIA cannot bring lawsuits over their alleged torture in overseas prisons because such suits might expose secret government information. ACLU lawyer Ben Wizner commented, "To this date, not a single victim of the Bush administration's torture program has had his day in court. That makes this a sad day not only for the torture survivors who are seeking justice in this case, but for all Americans who care about the rule of law and our nation's reputation in the world. If this decision stands, the United States will have closed its courts to torture victims while providing complete immunity to their torturers." Charlie Savage, "Court Dismisses a Case Asserting Torture," *New York Times,* September 8, 2010. See also September 8 editorial, "Torture is a Crime, Not a Secret."
40. See Jane Mayer, "Outsourcing Torture," *New Yorker,* February 14, 2005. See also her *The Dark Side: The Inside Story on How the War on Terror Turned Into a War on American Ideals* (Doubleday, 2008).
41. See *UN Report,* February 16, 2006 (http://www.unhchr.ch/huricane/huricane.nsf/0/52E94FB9CBC7DA10C1257117003517B3?op endocument).
42. http://www.nytimes.com/2005/12/09/international/europe/09britain .html; http://www.guardian.co.uk/world/2005/dec/08/terrorism.uk.
43. http://www.independent.co.uk/opinion/commentators/fisk/robert -fisk-torture-does-not-work-as-history-shows-777213.html; http://www .vanityfair.com/magazine/2008/12/torture200812; http://www.nation aljournal.com/about/njweekly/stories/2005/1119njl.htm.
44. See Mark Danner, *Torture and Truth,* 2004, and "US Torture: Voices from the Black Sites," *New York Review of Books,* March 2009.
45. At his inauguration President Obama declared, "As for our common defense, we reject as false the choice between our safety and our ideals." Upon taking office his first act was to sign an executive order to close

Guantánamo prison. His subsequent GWOT policies and inability to close Guantánamo is testament to the U.S. government being trapped by its unlawful GWOT policies, which placed expediency over principle.

46. See http://www.nytimes.com/2010/08/27/opinion/27fril.html;http://www.law.com/jsp/nlj/PubArticleNLJ.jsp?id=1202466489442&Judges_reject_evidence_in_Gitmo_cases&slreturn=1&hbxlogin=1.

47. Eisenhower warned the American people, "We have been compelled to create a permanent armaments industry of vast proportions...The potential for the disastrous rise of misplaced power exists and will persist."

48. Jody Freeman and Martha Minow, eds., *Government by Contract: Outsourcing and American Democracy* (Harvard University Press, 2009); Scott Shane and Ron Nixon, "US Contractors Becoming a Fourth Branch of Government," *International Herald Tribune*, February 4, 2007 (http://www.nytimes.com/2007/02/04/world/americas/04iht-web.0204contract.4460796.html).

49. http://projects.washingtonpost.com/top-secret-america/.

50. Ibid.

51. http://www.salon.com/news/opinion/glenn_greenwald/2010/07/19/secrecy.

52. Ibid.

53. http://projects.washingtonpost.com/top-secret-america/. Retired army lieutenant. general John Vines says, "I'm not aware of any agency with the authority, responsibility or a process in place to coordinate all these interagency and commercial activities. Because it lacks a synchronizing process it inevitably results in message dissonance, reduced effectiveness and waste. We consequently can't assess whether it is making us more safe." Ibid.

54. Ibid.

55. The $75-billion figure does not include many military or domestic counterterrorism activities and programs. Ibid.

56. Ibid.

57. Ibid. See David Rose, "The People vs. The Profiteers," *Vanity Fair*, November 2007, (http://www.vanityfair.com/politics/features/2007/11/halliburton200711). See also "Billions Over Baghdad" (http://www.vanityfair.com/politics/features/2007/10/iraq_billions200710); Gary Shteyngart, *Absurdistan* 2006, for a sardonic fictionalized depiction of corrupt wasteful war culture; and William A. Cohn: "As Blackwater rises, the rule of law recedes," *DePaul University Rule of Law Journal* Fall 2010; "Democracy Devolved: Shrinking the Public Sphere" *New Presence (TNP)* 12.4 Fall 2009; "Government Inc.," *TNP* 11.1 Winter 2008. On the failure to punish contractors for their crimes, see James Risen, "U.S. Falters in Punishing Blackwater Personnel," *International Herald Tribune*, October 22, 2010, 5.

58. http://projects.washingtonpost.com/top-secret-america/.

59. Ibid.

60. Ibid.

61. Alison Stanger, *One Nation under Contract: The Outsourcing of American Power and the Future of Foreign Policy* (Yale University Press, 2009). The U.S. rationale for declaring enemy fighters in Afghanistan "unlawful enemy combatants" was that they did not wear uniforms, carry their arms openly, or follow a recognized chain of command. But of course the same is true for the contractors who comprise an ever-larger portion of the U.S. fighting force throughout the world.

62. http://www.alternet.org/story/144694/. As reported by the *New York Times* and the *Washington Post* in August 2009, the role of the contractor Blackwater has been expanding amid ongoing scandals. Blackwater spearheaded a secret CIA assassination program, partook in frequent CIA bombings in Afghanistan and Pakistan, and was privy to information deemed too sensitive for Congress. U.N. investigator Philip Alston said, "the Central Intelligence Agency is running a program that is killing significant numbers of people and there is absolutely no accountability in terms of the relevant international law." Quoted in "U.S. Use of Drones Queried by U.N.," *New York Times*, October 28, 2009, A17. See also Jeremy Scahill, including *Blackwater: The Rise of the World's Most Powerful Mercenary Army* (Nation Books, 2008).

63. Mahbubani, dean of the School of Public Policy at the National University of Singapore, writes of Asia's loss of respect for Western practices: "Few in the West understand how much shock Guantanamo has caused in non-Western minds. Hence, many are puzzled that Western intellectuals continue to assume that they can portray themselves and their countries as models to follow when they speak to the rest of the world on human rights." "End of Whose History?" *IHT*, November 12, 2009.

64. Seth Jones and Martin Libicki, *How Terrorists Groups End: Lessons for Countering al Qaida* (The Rand Corporation, 2008), drew its conclusion that the GWOT was failing by means of an examination of 648 terror groups that existed between 1968 and 2006. The authors note in conclusion that "making a world of enemies is never a winning strategy" (139).

65. "2010 Is Deadliest Year for NATO in Afghan War," *New York Times*, September 21, 2002.

66. "Afghanistan Growing More Dangerous," *IHT*, September 13, 2010, 1, continues: "In August 2009, insurgents carried out 630 attacks. This August, they initiated at least 1,353...'The humanitarian space is shrinking day by day' said Abdul Kebar, a CARE Afghanistan official...With one attack after another, the Taliban and their insurgent allies have degraded security in almost every part of the country...The most recent troop buildup comes in response to steady advances by the Taliban. Four years ago, the insurgents were active in only four provinces. Now they are active in 33 or 34."

67. University of Chicago political scientist Robert Pape has spent years conducting research on terror and suicide bombing. Pape finds that

al-Qaeda-style terror is "less a product of Islamic fundamentalism than of a simple strategic goal: to compel the U.S. and its Western allies to withdraw combat forces from the Arabian Peninsula and other Muslim countries." Pape and others note that Osama bin Laden turned against the United States in 1991 because he saw it as occupying the holiest Arab land in Saudi Arabia.

68. Cited in Noam Chomsky, "War on Terror," Amnesty International Annual Lecture, January 18, 2006, Trinity College, Dublin, Ireland (http://www.brianmay.com/experts/waronterror.pdf).

69. http://www.erich-fromm.de/biophil/joomla/images/stories/pdf -Dateien/Preis_2010_031.pdf.

70. See Rami Khouri, "A Bad Decade," *New York Times,* December 30, 2009, on the negative impacts of the past decade on the Middle East, and the rising clout of Iran; and his June 30, 2010, *NYT* op-ed.

71. Jones and Libicki, *How Terrorists Groups End.*

72. National Counterterrorism Center (NCC) director Michael Leiter, and FBI director Robert Mueller told the Senate Homeland Security and Governmental Affairs Committee that the threat of al-Qaeda using Americans and other Western nationals to attack the United States has grown, noting that at least 63 U.S. citizens have been charged or convicted of terrorist acts or related crimes since 2009. Homegrown plots have reached their highest level since 9/11 according to NCC (http://www.bbc.co.uk/news/world-us-canada-11392083).

73. According to U.S. officials quoted in the *New York Times,* in May 2005, the CIA reported that "Iraq has become a magnet for Islamic militants similar to Soviet-occupied Afghanistan two decades ago and Bosnia in the 1990s." The CIA concluded that "Iraq may prove to be an even more effective training ground for Islamic extremists than Afghanistan was in al Qaeda's early days."

74. Quotes cited in Chomsky, "War on Terror."

75. Jones and Libicki, *How Terrorists Groups End,* 139. See also "War & Consequences" (http://www.comw.org/pda/0609bm38.html).

76. *The War Logs* (http://warlogs.wikileaks.org/), and reporting on them in the *New York Times,* October 23–25, 2010. For information contained in *The War Logs,* which suggests that the sectarian bloodbath in Iraq has been part of an unofficial U.S. policy, see: http://www.guardian.co.uk /world/2010/oct/28/iraq-war-logs-iraq; and http://www.common dreams.org/headline/2010/11/01-6. On attacks against Wikileaks, see "Shooting the Messenger," *Prague Post,* November 3, 2010 (http:// praguepost.com/opinion/6263-shooting-the-messenger.html).

77. See Campbell, O'Hanlon, Shapiro and Unikewicz, "States of Conflict: An update," *New York Times,* October 6, 2009. See also "Defense Budget Shell Game" (http://www.inthesetimes.org/article/4452 /defense_budget_shell_game/); a June 2010 committee report, "Debts, Deficits and Defense: A Way Forward" (http://big.assets.huffington-post.com/bf.pdf; armscontrolcenter.org; and nationalpriorities.org).

78. For instance, Pakistan. Imtiaz Gul, author of *The Most Dangerous Place: Pakistan's Lawless Frontier*, writes that jihadist forces are strengthening in Pakistan in 2010. See http://www.foreignpolicy.com /articles/2010/06/10/pakistans_new_networks_of_terror.

79. One in seven Americans is now in poverty as the U.S. poverty rate has reached a 15-year high and appears to be getting worse, according to the September 17, 2010, *New York Times*; The U.S. working-age poor is at its highest levels since the 1960s according to the *International Herald Tribune*, September 17, 2010, 4, which also reports that U.S. Census released in September reports that 50.7 million Americans have no health insurance, an increase of almost 10 percent over the number of uninsured from the previous year (*IHT*, September 22, 2010, 4).

80. Jones and Libicki, *How Terrorists Groups End*, p. xiii.

81. "Our analysis suggests that there is no battlefield solution to terrorism. Military force usually has the opposite effect from what is intended: It is often overused, alienates the local population by its heavy-handed nature, and provides a window of opportunity for terrorist-group recruitment." See ibid., pp. xvii and 121–127.

82. http://www.telegraph.co.uk/news/worldnews/northamerica/usa /barackobama/6908709/Barack-Obama-admits-unacceptable-systemic -failure-in-Detroit-plane-attack.html; http://www.realclearpolitics.com /articles/2010/01/03/obamas_approach_to_terrorism_blows _up_99755.html. Red flag's included: The would-be bomber's father had warned U.S. authorities about his son's radicalism a month earlier; Britain had banned him from entry; and he had paid for his ticket in cash and had no luggage. Only a faulty detonator and quick action by the passenger sitting next to him saved the 278 passengers.

83. http://www.nytimes.com/2010/05/29/us/politics/29gitmo.html? _r=1. See also "Editorial: Civil Justice, Military Injustice," *New York Times*, October 5, 2010: "There are more than 170 inmates left in Guantanamo. Only 36 have been referred for prosecution...This is the choice: Justice in long-established federal courts that Americans can be proud of and the rest of the world can respect. Or illegal detentions and unending, legally dubious military tribunals. It is an easy one."

84. See Gilles Dorronsoro of the Carnegie Endowment for International Peace, "Face Reality: Talk to the Taliban," *International Herald Tribune*, September 15, 2010, 6. On the challenges of fostering dialogue, *Holder v. Humanitarian Law Project* was the first Supreme Court case of the post-9/11 era to pit free speech rights against national security. On June 21, 2010, the Court held that the government's compelling interest in preventing terrorism outweighed the plaintiff's free speech claims—reaching this conclusion without even asking the government to provide any evidence to support its claim that the goal of preventing terrorism would actually be served by the speech restrictions at issue. In a six-three ruling the court said that even advice on peaceful conflict resolution may be prosecuted under a law banning material support of

terrorists. Attorney David Cole of the Center for Constitutional Rights says, "When the Court allows unsupported speculation about 'terrorism' and disapproval of a speaker's viewpoint to justify making advocacy of human rights a crime, the First Amendment as we know it is in serious jeopardy." Human rights lawyer Scott Horton writes that after *Citizens United v. FEC*, the case in which the court struck down campaign finance restrictions as violating the free speech protections of corporations, "America stands alone as the only country in the world which grants human rights to corporations, just as it is curtailing human rights to humans. It's a curious sign of the times."

85. Former U.S. Supreme Court justice Potter Stewart noted, "Censorship reflects a society's lack of confidence in itself."

86. See the documentary *Black Money* at pbs.org/frontline. Changing course will be a challenge. *The Economist,* September 18, 2010, 7, reports that the Obama administration plans to sell Saudi Arabia some $90 billion dollars worth of arms in the coming decade in its biggest ever weapons sale. Thom Shankar and David Sanger, "US to propose a big sale of weapons to Saudi Arabia," *International Herald Tribune,* September 20, 2010, 6, report that scores of F-15 fighter planes, Apache attack and Black Hawk helicopters are part of the package, noting: "The purchase of these U.S. combat systems and related military support, including American trainers, would allow the U.S. armed forces to operate seamlessly in that part of the world, according to Pentagon officials." The U.S. Pentagon budget has increased each year of the first decade of the twenty-first century, an unprecedented run in the country's history, and under the government's current budget plans this steady rise will last for at least another decade. Is this a permanent war budget? Is the U.S. Department of Defense more aptly, as it was called until 1947, the Department of War? See Baker, "Inside Obama's War on Terrorism"; "The Pentagon Dodges the Bullet: Barack Obama is Spending More on Defence Than His Predecessors," *Economist,* February 6, 2010, 45; William A. Cohn, "De-based," *New Presence,* Winter 2010.

87. The United States, while preaching peace, has long held first place in the global arms race. It now spends as much as the next 14 countries combined, and maintains more than 700 military bases around the world. The Pentagon has been budgeted $704 billion for 2010, and according to its projections, which exclude supplementary war-fighhting spending, this will increase by 2.5 percent per year each year for the next ten years (a 25 percent increase over the next decade). In March 2010 the United States surpassed the $1 trillion mark in total for the Iraq and Afghanistan war-fighting thus far. According to the U.S. Office of Management and Budget, 55 percent of federal discretionary spending for 2010 will go to the military budget. UC professor emeritus Chalmers Johnson dates back to 1949 what he calls the U.S. "military Keynesianism—the determination to maintain a permanent war economy and to treat military output as an ordinary economic product

even though it makes no contribution to either production or consumption." See his trilogy *Blowback* (New York: Holt Paperbacks, 2004); *The Sorrows of Empire* (New York: Metropolitan Books, 2004); *Nemesis* (New York: Metropolitan Books, 2007).

88. "What's to be done?" *Economist*, September 18, 2010, 47.
89. Quoted in Whitney R. Harris, "Justice Jackson at Nuremberg," *The International Lawyer* 20 (1986): 867.
90. Immanuel Kant, *Perpetual Peace: A Philosophical Essay* (1795).
91. Albert Einstein defined insanity as "doing the same thing over and over again and expecting different results."

6

ACTS OF OMISSION IN THE "WAR ON TERRORISM"

Jørgen Johansen

"Terrorism"[1] is a contested term, and how to respond to it is also widely debated. A United Nations (UN) Ad Hoc Committee to Eliminate Terrorism was created by the General Assembly in 1996. They have remained in deadlock as they try to reach an agreement on a comprehensive draft convention to eliminate terrorism. In October 2010 they made another unsuccessful effort at drawing a distinction between "freedom fighters" and "state sponsored terrorism."[2]

In this essay, I will define this type of political violence in a way that is less influenced by the political rhetoric so frequently used by politicians and the mainstream media. I will also describe the complexity of these forms of violence. I am not arguing that "terrorism" does not exist; but that as defined by states it is a minor problem and that as a term it is so loaded that it is difficult to use. In the last part I will discuss the ethical dimensions of failure to act to reduce violence, "terrorism" included. A main point is that the task of reducing "terrorism" should not be left to state actors only. My conclusion: The morality of acts of omission in dealing with political violence should be judged similarly to acts of commission.

DEFINITION

"Terrorism" is, like many other elements in our society, a social, political, and ideological[3] construction. "Probably the most significant contribution of social thinking to our understanding of terrorism is the realisation that it is a social construction...terrorism is not a given in the real world but instead an interpretation of events and their presumed causes."[4]

Since the 9/11 attacks on the World Trade Centre and Pentagon,[5] the need for a clear understanding of what is meant by "terrorism" has escalated. The UN Security Council called on all member states to include antiterrorism laws in their criminal laws.[6] In addition, a number of state agencies and international bodies have expanded old, and created new, lists of "terrorist" organizations and individuals. Essential to any use of the term "terrorism" or "terrorist" in a legal document is an agreed upon, clear, and useable definition of the act of "terrorism." It is no secret that many struggled hard to come up with functional definitions and descriptions. When Schmid and Jongman published their first edition of *Political Terrorism* in 1984, they identified and discussed 109 different definitions of "terrorism."[7] Their new and expanded 2008 edition is crucial reading for anyone who wants to discuss "terrorism" as it clearly identifies the many difficulties in defining the term. The total number of definitions in use today is in the hundreds. Schmid and Jongman do not include them all, but their analyses and discussions of how definitions are constructed are still very relevant and useful.

Another useful definition was published in a special issue of the journal *Mobilization* in June 2007. In the article, Albert J. Bergesen presented a three-step model for how to identify and define "terrorist" violence, as opposed to other forms of violence. His main point is to separate the victim from the target. The *Perpetrator* harms or kills the *Victim*, but the *Victim* is not the ultimate *Target*.

Perpetrator (A)	$\Rightarrow$	Victim (B)	$\Rightarrow$	Target (C)

The perpetrator A attacks the victim B in order to influence the target C.

> In this model the victim is no longer the target whom the perpetrator is trying to influence or have an effect upon; in effect B is demoted from an ultimate end to an instrumental means for A to affect C. The essence of terrorism as a type of violence, then, is not that it is so labeled "terrorism," or that it is a strategy, or that it is clandestine, or nontraditional violence, but that it is violence where harm/damage is inflicted upon one set of actors for the sole purpose of affecting another set of actors.[8]

In addition to this separation of target from victim, at the core of "terrorism" as a political means we see not only the actual actions but also the threats of such actions as well. The threats of future acts of "terrorism" have a predictive function. The fear of new violent actions inspired by "terrorists" such as bin Laden will be around long after the perpetrators are dead. The main effect of "terrorism" is that it creates fear; and the fear is very often exaggerated far beyond any rational level.

Going by the definition given by Bergesen, 9/11 is obviously seen as an act of "terrorism." But none of the victims in the four hijacked planes, the Twin Towers, the Pentagon, or the flight crashing on the countryside in Pennsylvania, were the real targets. The victims were killed and harmed in order to influence the main target: power-holders in the U.S. empire.[9] Almost all letters and video-recordings from al-Qaeda argue that they wanted a change in the U.S. foreign policy, and hence the real target was the U.S. government.[10] This is similar to the case of Timothy McVeigh, who was convicted for the bombing of the Alfred P. Murrah building in Oklahoma City on April 19, 1995. His real target was the U.S. government, while the victims were the 168 people who were in the building at the time of the explosion.[11] Both of these cases are relatively undisputed cases of "terrorism." But the definition by Bergeson would just as well fit the allied bombing of Dresden and Hamburg during World War II as well as the U.S. atomic bombs on civilian targets in Hiroshima and Nagasaki in August 1945. In these cases, we can separate the victims from the real targets (the German and Japanese political leadership). The victims were not something that can be labeled "collateral damage." The allied forces knowingly attacked civilian targets, which is clearly a violation of international law. When the marshal of the Royal Air Force, Sir Arthur Travers Harris, also called "Bomber Harris," ordered and carried out bombing of civilians in Germany, he was very much aware of the expected consequences in terms of civilian deaths.[12] In the case of Hiroshima and Nagasaki, the cities were largely untouched during the nightly bombing raids and the Army Air Force agreed to leave them off the target list so accurate assessment of the atomic weapons could be made.[13] The numbers of civilians killed in such "terrorist" attacks by states vastly outnumber (by some estimates, of over 100/1) all of those killed in nonstate "terrorism" in the whole of history. Yet, to this day, such acts by the Allies are omitted from most discussions of "terrorism."

It is not only the use of heavy bombing and weapons of mass destruction against civilians that make such state actions "terrorist" acts: "Nicaragua took Mr. Reagan's America to the World Court for America's proxy and other attacks on it in the 1980s—those attacks fall pretty squarely under a lot of definitions of terrorism, including [their] own. The World Court found America guilty..."[14] There are many cases of state "terrorism," but in most legal documents and too many academic ones, states are excluded as actors in the definitions of "terrorism." The main reason these definitions do not specify what sort of actors are carrying out acts of "terrorism" is to avoid a definition with implications that might be seen as too political[15] by members of powerful states. However, it makes little sense to say that identical actions carried out by state and nonstate actors are completely different. But when lawmakers, political decision-makers, and their conventional advisers realized this discrepancy, they frequently claimed that acts of "terrorism" excluded state actors. These omissions are purposeful political decisions by state actors intended to protect them from being grouped together with the nonstate terrorists, and thus to avoid running the risk of prosecution for having committed crimes against humanity.

The U.S. National Counterterrorism Center in their annual reports omits state actors by defining "terrorism" to be "premeditated politically-motivated violence perpetrated against noncombatant targets by *sub-national groups or clandestine agents*, usually intended to influence an audience" (italics by the author).[16] We should separate how the actors publicly justify their use of violence from the actions themselves. States as well as all other actors using violent means have a strong tendency not to focus on their own *intentions* but on the *consequences* of actions by their opponents. This has serious ethical implications. The combination of excluding states as actors and at the same time concentrating only on the consequences of "acts by others" guarantees a biased picture of what "terrorism" is about. Core questions about responsibilities for such acts and for preventing them are not possible to answer when the dominant discourse is so biased by what has been omitted.

When the 9/11 attacks are described in Western media and by Western politicians, we see very clearly that the focus is on the consequences. They almost never try to understand the *intentions* and *motives* behind these actions. When the "war on terrorism" is described, they focus solely on what representatives of the main actors have said in public to defend and explain their actions in Iraq and Afghanistan, omitting other actors from the discussion. With the release of materials from *Wikileaks*, the evidence of atrocities committed by state actors is piling up. The *consequences* of acts committed by state actors are easily forgotten and often denied. The same tendency to focus on own intentions as contrasted with the consequences of the others is observable on websites and in clandestine documents: their own *intentions* are often mentioned; the human *consequences* have been omitted.[17] Brynjar Lia, in his book *Architect of Global Jihad*,[18] presents a nuanced and complex picture of al-Qaeda, including its internal conflicts, but the tendency of focusing on their own intentions and the consequence of what others are doing is clear.

Acts of, and threats of, "terrorism" should be understood and analyzed based on the action itself, not on *who* is committing the atrocities. To use a definition of "terrorism" that automatically excludes states as actors is neither wise nor helpful in legal or academic texts. Just as state actors frequently commit acts of war crimes, they also carry out acts of "terrorism," which, if the analysis is to be useful, must not be omitted from scrutiny.

Putting "Terrorism" in Perspective

In recent years, several world leaders have presented "terrorism" as the greatest threat to the world. Here follows a collection from *The Truth about the Real Threats to Our World*[19]:

Terrorism is the greatest twenty-first century threat.

—British prime minister Tony Blair,
May 2003

Terrorism is the greatest threat facing free democracies in the twenty-first century.

—German chancellor Angela Merkel,
May 2006

The greatest threat this world faces is the danger of extremists and terrorists armed with weapons of mass destruction.

—U.S. president George W. Bush,
September 2005

No challenge is greater than the threat of terrorism.

—Australian prime minister John Howard,
May 2006

Terrorism is the greatest threat to world peace.

—Russian president Vladimir Putin,
September 2000

None of these proclamations can be taken as anything but political rhetoric because they have no basis in actual facts. Statistical data on reasons for early deaths indicate that acts of "terrorism" are not a main cause of death.[20] The consequences of such statements by leading politicians are not only the creation of a misguided population, but also a disproportionate use of valuable resources. This rhetoric has direct ethical consequences. Since there are limits to the resources available in a society, every budget allocation will have ethical implications. Resources that are disproportionately allocated to a minor societal problem will reduce the amount of resources available for more serious and deadly problems. Within the health sector, transportation, and domestic violence there are more cost-efficient ways to save lives than what today is spent on counterterrorism activities.

The number of people dying as a direct consequence of "terrorism" is relatively limited. There are many causes of premature death other than by acts of "terrorists." For example, in the United States in 2001, food poisoning took more lives than the 9/11 attacks.[21] Death by firearms is a much more frequent cause of death in the United States than all the acts of "terrorism" together, including the 9/11 attacks.[22] Suicide took eleven times more lives and homicide almost six times more lives than "terrorism."[23] With some specific exceptions, politically motivated violence against innocent civilians is not on the top twenty list of leading causes of death in any country during any year. The exception is when states mobilize their armies to attack and occupy other states. In recent years we have seen huge numbers of civilians killed by politically motivated violence in Iraq and Afghanistan. In all other countries, more people are killed by a partner or a relative every year than by "terrorism." The most frequent reasons for early deaths are hunger and easily curable diseases. These causes result in around 100,000 deaths per day globally.[24] One conclusion that could be drawn from this data is that if any political actor wants to reduce the number of premature deaths, their resources would be much better spent on clean drinking water, nutrition, and medicine for poor people than on counterterrorist warfare.[25] However, it is unlikely that such a conclusion will be reached by a public that is misinformed by a political rhetoric that consistently omits the significance of social and health problems that are not related to "terrorism" by nonstate actors.

The relationship between the actual number of deaths attributed to acts of terrorism and the resources mistakenly devoted by states and other actors to reduce the problem of "terrorism" is problematic to understand and even more so to justify. The money spent on "antiterrorism" activities is skyrocketing,[26] while funding for the far more serious problems of fulfilling basic needs are declining.[27] There are a growing number of companies who make huge profits from the "terrorism-threat" and the security industry hits new peaks on the stock market after every spectacular bombing. The growth in tasks, equipment, and personnel for security companies after 9/11 has been exceptional. Combined with the outsourcing of military and police duties, the private security industry now captures a lucrative sector of the U.S. economy. A parallel is seen at universities and think tanks where there are growing numbers of academics doing research in this field. According to Shepherd, since 2001 a new book on terrorism is published every six hours in the English language.[28] Is this due to the seriousness of the problem, or are there other agendas behind these priorities? That researchers do their best to please their funding sources and write research proposals that fit the popular narrative is well known. It is not always what is most "important" that guides the search for financial support of research.

In the United States in the fiscal year 2002, federal spending for homeland security was $21 billion. By fiscal year 2006, federal homeland security spending had grown to $55 billion,[29] an increase of more than 161 percent. This total covers the homeland security funding and activities of all federal agencies, not just the programs funded through the Department of Homeland Security (DHS). The costs of some activities of agencies within the DHS are not included. The budget allocation going to support Coast Guard Search and Rescue activity, for example, is not included in the total funding for homeland security activities.[30] In contrast, the total sum for all development aid in the world is around 100 billion U.S. dollars a year.[31] This is money dedicated to cure diseases, deliver food, give people access to clean drinking water, and so on, in other words, to help poor people to fulfill their basic needs. Is it justified to spend more than half that sum on a threat that has a limited impact on our societies and that takes relatively few lives?

One preliminary conclusion is that the profit motives of armament and security companies could be a significant factor in encouraging more government spending on military solutions to "terrorism." More studies should be done on the impact of money and profit in the political handling of "terrorism" as a societal problem. As mentioned earlier, this development of allocating more and more resources to fighting "terrorism" has serious ethical implications because it will prevent resources from being spent on more needed and efficient life-saving activities.

There is no evidence that nonstate terrorism is a current threat to a state's existence. "We may require extraordinary patience in dealing with 'terrorism', but we can do so with some confidence that states will endure resiliently."[32] Professor Wilhelm Agrell argues that not even events such as the 9/11 attacks can be seen as threats against our societies.[33] That some Western governments, militaries, parts of the intelligence branches, and the security industry have described the possible threats as much more serious than what can be justified by actual data is due to factors other than the threats themselves.[34] Domestic political agendas, demands from the public to act, struggle for the next year's budgets, and catastrophic (in the dual meaning of the word) descriptions in the mass media are some possible explanations for the exaggerations.[35]

The threats from substate groups we have seen in the last decade should have been dealt with by police and criminal law, *not* with militaries and international law. The reason for this is clear when data on the threats of and casualties from "terrorism" are compared with the threats and casualties resulting from the "war on terrorism," however such comparisons have been omitted from discussions by news media and policymakers. Several authors have warned that the means used in combating "terrorism" constitute serious threats to Western societies and their values.[36] Benjamin Franklin was very clear when he stated in 1759: "Those who would sacrifice liberty for security deserves neither."[37] The argument here is that the counterterrorism actions carried out since 9/11 have seriously harmed the democracies involved and reduced respect worldwide for human and civil rights. Even among many former officers inside the secret services and think tanks close to governments, we hear voices that the remedy (the global war on terrorism) has done more harm than the illness it had hoped to cure. In addition, the number of people who engage in "terrorism" is growing due to some of the means used in the "war on terrorism."[38] Practices at Guantánamo and Abu Ghraib, the U.S. Patriot Act, long imprisonment without trials, torture, escalating surveillance, and the invasion and occupation of Iraq and Afghanistan have generated intense anti-American feelings thereby aiding the recruitment of new members to networks of nonstate "terrorists." Typical indications of the anti-American attitudes are seen the annual "Arab Public Opinion Poll 2010.[39] A sample of the results (all values in percentages):

- In a world where there is only one superpower, which of the following countries would you prefer to be that superpower? France, 55;

China, 16; Germany, 13; Britain, 9; Russia, 8; United States, 7; Pakistan, 6.

- Name *two* countries that you think pose the biggest threat to you. Israel, 88; United States, 77; Algeria, 10; Iran, 10; United Kingdom, 8; China, 3; Syria, 1.
- Which world leader (outside your own country) do you admire most? (partial list) Recep Erdogan (Turkey), 20; Hugo Chavez, 13; Mahmoud Ahmadinejad, 12; Hassan Nasrallah (Hezbollah/ Lebanon), 9; Osama bin Laden, 6; Saddam Hussein, 2. (Barack Obama not mentioned, 1)

In the months following 9/11, 80,000 predominately Arab and Muslim persons were required to register in the Special Registration Program. It resulted in not a single terrorist conviction. Of the 8,000 young men of Arab and Muslim descent sought out for FBI interviews, and more than 5,000 foreign nationals placed in preventive detention in the first two years after 9/11, virtually all Arab and Muslim, not one stands convicted of "terrorist" crime up till today.[40] It is easy to understand that some of these persons might feel justified in joining "terrorist" networks after such humiliating treatments. In fall 2010, we have seen the first cases of prisoners from Guantánamo facing trials in civilian courts. The courts have so far only accepted a few of the prosecutors' charges. Anti-Americanism has not only grown in the Muslim regions of the world, but also close allies distanced themselves from the United States during the Bush era.[41] Steven Kull presented a paper based on several surveys at the Center for the Study of Islam and Democracy's annual conference in 2010. He found that the anger against America has not diminished following President Obama's speech in Cairo in June 2009.[42]

NOT ONLY THE STATE

Traditionally "terrorist" acts were dealt with by the combination of police work, criminal laws, trials, and prison. In other words, they were handled as other forms of crimes. This had been a relatively successful strategy that reduced and removed the classical leftist terrorism in Europe in the 1970s.[43] Since 9/11 we have witnessed a growing use of military means in the fight against "terrorism." This changeover from police to militaries in the fight against "terrorism" had a tremendous impact on the whole concept of "counterterrorism" work. Not only do the military forces use a more deadly and advanced range of weaponry, but of even greater significance is that they are required to follow international law, not criminal law. However, international law, as it has developed since the Peace Treaties of Westphalia in 1648, has been designed to handle conflicts between states, not between a state and a network of nonstate actors. There are good reasons to have two separate sets of rules/laws for handling these two types of crimes, but the UNSC Resolution 1368[44] erased the important distinction between them. It is problematic to apply a set of rules to a conflict for which they were not constructed to handle, as in the case of Resolution 1368:

> *The Security Council,*
>   *Reaffirming* the principles and purposes of the Charter of the United Nations,
>   *Determined* to combat by all means threats to international peace and security caused by terrorist acts,
>   *Recognizing* the inherent right of individual or collective self-defence in accordance with the Charter."[45]

Just as criminal law is not designed to handle conflicts between states, international law is not constructed to handle conflicts between a state and a network that has no specific territorial base. It is only "state-terrorism" that to some degree can be treated with international law, because the conventions, treaties, and regulations for *jus in bello*[46] do define what sorts of weaponry, tactics, targets, and so on are legal.

The main problem in the contemporary way of handling non-state "terrorism" is not the lack of legal justifications for the means used. There are two principal weaknesses in the present strategy: the over-militarization of state responses to "terrorist" attacks and the lack of state engagement with actors other than state actors. Louise Richardson expressed a commonly held view among "terrorist" researchers in her book *What Terrorists Want*:

> We cannot defeat terrorism by smashing every terrorist movement. An effort to do so will only generate more terrorists, as has happened repeatedly in the past. A policy informed by the work of the terrorism studies community would never have declared a global war on terrorism, because we know that such a war can never be won...A policy informed by those of us who have studied this subject for years would never had as an objective the completely unattainable goal of obliterating terrorism and would have sought, instead, the more modest and attainable goal of containing terrorist recruitment and constraining resort to the tactic of terrorism.[47]

Richard English, an expert on terrorism and political conflicts in Northern Ireland, expresses it this way in his book *Terrorism, How to Respond*: "Despite the frequent assumption that military retaliation can deter future terrorists, the reality seems very different; 'defeating or diminishing the overall threat of terrorism is not something that either small- or large-scale retaliations have yet been able to achieve.' "[48] Others argue that the military war on terrorism has been counterproductive: "There is a widespread misconception that using terror to defeat terror will ultimately work. On the contrary, the evidence is that this policy is counterproductive."[49]

The war on terror can hardly claim many victories. Secret services and politicians frequently argue that they have been successful in preventing acts of "terrorism." However, while it is difficult to prove preventive actions, it seems that if these claims were valid there should have been more people convicted for planning and preparing "terrorist" activities. As described earlier, the backfire[50] mechanisms have been more visible than the intended effects.

EXPAND THE NUMBER OF ACTORS

Why have only state actors had the central role in the struggle to reduce nonstate "terrorism" while other actors have been omitted from discussion of potential solutions? The most important work for all who are engaged in handling conflicts is to identify the multiple actors who are influencing the outcome of the conflict. Conventional diplomacy has been extremely narrow in its engagement in conflicts between alleged "terrorists" and their adversaries. When diplomats engage in negotiations, it is rare that more than two actors will be invited into the process. This is far from enough. Through conflict analyses it is possible to identify many more than two. By "actor" I mean any group, individual, company, society, or community that have an influence on the outcome. They can be domestic, international, or transnational. They can be part of a state, an NGO, a business entity, a media company, religious community, or any other organization that in some way influences or can influence the conflict.

The geographical distance between the observer and the conflict has a big impact on the understanding of how many actors are involved in a conflict. For example, students in Ramallah, on the West Bank of Palestine, can easily list 40–50 different actors in the Israeli/Palestine conflicts, but seldom more than a handful from the civil wars in Colombia. And the students in Bogota can without difficulty list 40 actors in their country but very seidom more than

5 in Palestine/Israel. The mass media, which are usually the main source of information, are the main reason for these disparities. By failing to recognize all the main actors, the possibilities to act are limited. For conflicts where acts of "terrorism" have been used, it is possible to include many more actors than those normally regarded as actors. It is essential to expand the list of actors if we want to expand the possibilities for more engagement. To leave the struggle against "terrorism" to the police and military alone is a serious mistake that omits many potential sources of understanding and help.

FOUR PHASES IN THE STRUGGLE AGAINST "TERRORISM"

I have identified four different stages in dealing with "terrorism" (table 6.1). Phase one is to identify what can be done to prevent future acts of "terrorism." The next is to clarify what can be done in order to stop ongoing "terrorism." The third phase is to specify what can be done to reduce the effects of "terrorism." Finally, there is the phase of healing and reconciliation. By combining the categories of possible actors with these four stages of counterterrorism efforts, it is possible to discover many more activities by many more actors than what has been done to date.

The main objective in using this matrix is to expand the number of actors outside the state sphere. That state actors such as militaries,

Table 6.1 Expansion of Actors Within the Four Phases of Addressing Terrorism

	Prevent	Stop ongoing	Reduce effect	Heal and reconcile
Military forces				
Police				
Politicians				
Fire brigades				
Ex-"terrorists"				
Religious communities				
News media				
Victims				
Public figures				
Civil society				
Security industry				
Educational institutions				
Researchers				

police, and fire brigades have acted against "terrorism" is well known, but many more "new" actors and activities are possible for those who want to reduce "terrorism." There is currently a lack of constructive proposals about what can be done to prevent and counter "terrorist" acts. Future research should examine specific possible actions in all four phases for each category of actors.

Politicians have, until now, done more to expand the problem than to reduce it and put it in a useful perspective. In contrast, new approaches have come from some unexpected sources. For example, former "terrorist" Noman Benotman gave an interview about the inner workings of al-Qaeda's leadership to CBN on June 3, 2010.[51] His change of sides and decision to go public about it was not only brave but had the potential to discourage suicide bomber candidates from participating in attacks. In another case, when Shaykh-ul-Islam Dr. Muhammad Tahir-ul-Qadri, the founding leader and patron-in-chief of Minhaj-ul-Quran International, issued his more than 600-page fatwa against "terrorism," he might have done more to prevent future acts of "terrorism" than any ongoing police surveillance.[52] Within the next years we will know the real impact of such actions by nonstate actors such as ex-terrorists, religious leaders, and others.

The mainstream mass media, with very few exceptions, have generated fear with their reporting after acts of nonstate "terrorism." They have used war-related terms in overly dramatic headlines to report both actual attacks and speculations about possible future actions. If a primary goal of nonstate "terrorists" is to create fear, then the news media must be seen as (unconscious?) supporters of the "terrorist" agenda. In contrast, for state-"terrorism" mainstream media have in general functioned as a justifier, not as a critic or reporter. Typical cases are found throughout the coverage of the wars and occupations of Iraq and Afghanistan.

Victims of "terrorism" can play important roles in all of the four phases of counterterrorism efforts mentioned earlier. The U.S. organization *September Eleventh Families for Peaceful Tomorrows* was created by surviving victims and relatives of those who died in the 9/11 attacks.[53] Their outspoken goal was to oppose the use of their suffering to justify U.S. wars of occupation and more civilian causalities as a consequence of these wars. Their courageous, ethical stand went unreported in most U.S. news media, but should be seen as a model for more to follow. Another example of a group of people opposing the war on terrorism is "Courage to Resist." It is a group of concerned community members, veterans, and military families who support war resisters. While there are those who would like to dismiss war resisters as cowards, the reality is that it takes exceptional courage for soldiers to resist unjust, illegal, or immoral orders. For many resisters, it was their first-hand experiences as occupation troops that compelled them to take a stand. For others, "doing the right thing" and acting out of conscience began to outweigh their military training in unquestioned obedience.

Public figures are often role models for young people. Their views on what is right and wrong are taken as truths by their fans. Obvious cases such as Nelson Mandela and John Lennon are well known, and many more could play important roles in preventing acts of "terrorism" as well as in healing and reconciling. When famous persons encourage people to take a stand against violence, to oppose extremism, to respect human rights, and not engage in "fundamentalist networks" they will influence many young minds. This can be done via political speeches, written texts, music, or the movies. The main point is to support tolerance and peaceful means when confronted with injustices.

Civil society, in all its variety, has not played a prominent role in the issue of "terrorism." With the exception of protests against parts of state-"terrorism," the traditional peace, women's, solidarity, trade union and other movements have been silent. These acts of omission run counter to values these movements have kept high, such as nonviolent processes for conflict prevention and resolution. To open channels of communication between different parts of the society could help to build friendships. Maybe more important is intra- rather than interreligious communication. Dialogs between open-minded and tolerant representatives of different religions seems less important than the tolerant from each religion engaging in dialogs with fundamentalists and extremists of their own religion. And for secular, political, and cultural networks, the same is true: There is a lack of communication between different camps. As Mark Perry argues in his book *Talking to Terrorists* (2010): it is essential to talk to your enemies, and this should take place on several levels, not only on a governmental level.[54] In their failure to seek constructive dialogue with enemies, civil societies have committed serious acts of omissions that will effectively prevent satisfactory resolution of conflicts.

The security industry is one of the main winners in the war on "terrorism." From locksmiths to security guards, from producers of screening equipment to fence factories, we have seen an exceptional growth in the size of these companies as well as in their profits. Much of their activities contribute more to the illusions of control and security than to effective prevention strategies. Airport security personnel will not let you take your nail clippers and mouth wash on board but they won't stop you from bringing a bottle of vodka from the tax-free shop on-board! How much of the expansion of the security industry is a psychological game to pretend to have control and how much is in fact helpful? There are several ongoing research projects on these topics, but few substantial contributions have delivered to date. Berndtsson (2009) in his *The Privatisation of Security and State Control of Force: Changes, Challenges and the Case of Iraq* has published some of the best analyses so far.[55] He is currently working on a new research project to be published in 2012.

There are also important ethical questions regarding the role of universities, both as educational institutions and as research facilities. The field of "terrorism" and security studies has expanded enormously in recent years, often with major funding from national defense agencies. The majority of courses and publications are biased and limit discussion of the problem to a state point of view, with dissenting views omitted. The network of Critical Studies of Terrorism was established following an article in *European Political Science*.[56] The authors of the article, Jackson, Gunning, and Smyth, claim that the Western state-centrism of "terrorism" studies and the surrounding discourse has led to a "moral certitude" and reluctance to consider the motivations of terrorists. The orthodox discourse, which casts all "terrorists" as evil (rather than their acts), eliminates opportunities for consideration of motivation because of the risk of appearing to justify or condone their actions. Within this framework, attempts to examine the motivations of "terrorists" can be labeled apologetics and dismissed or researchers themselves can be demonized. In addition, there is a serious lack of solution-oriented approaches in "terrorism" studies. Most of the academic studies focus on explaining how and why nonstate terrorism occurs. Only a few present ideas for how to cope with the problems. This is very different from medical research and training where positive results are at least as important as describing the problem.

CONCLUSIONS

The concept of "terrorism" is often used with a political bias. In order to act effectively on "terrorism" there is a need for a clear and operational definition that does not omit potentially significant concepts or actors. Without an objective (scientific) understanding of the complexity of these conflict processes, there is little hope for effective and wise actions.

The simplifications and naïveté in typical news media reports provide a distorted picture of what is going on as well as what is needed.

There are many more actors than states who could act to reduce the problem of "terrorism." Outside the state sphere (with its biased emphasis on military interventions), few actors are involved in the important task of reducing "terrorism." This general lack of engagement is a serious ethical issue because without a multitude of new actors and methods the important task to reduce "terrorism" is left to those who so far have partly failed and partly expanded the problem. And if the goal is to reduce the number of premature deaths there are many more efficient ways to do that. The failure to engage or not to act enough seems to be typical for most nonstate actors in the struggle against "terrorism." There is no reason why the problem of "terrorism" should be left to state actors only. Like all other human evils, the civil society, in its widest definition, should engage and act to reduce the problem. This is not to say that states should not act. The main critique of states in the "war on terror" is that most of their means have so far been counterproductive. The limitations of military means in fighting political motivated violence are obvious and there is a lack of engagement with other tools for building peace.

Not acting is just as difficult to justify ethically as to act with a negative impact. I have indicated a number of possible activities and am sure there are many more to be found and tested. But this in not only an ethical problem; the purposeful, reckless, or negligent absence of an action is considered a voluntary action and therefore fulfils the voluntary requirement of *actus reus*.[57] Not to intervene when serious crimes are committed can also be a crime according to criminal laws. And on the global arena there are similar principles in international law; acts of omission can be violations of the law and conventions.[58]

Media have so far focused too much on the consequences of acts of terror against states and the good intentions of the state actors in the "war on terror." There is a need to add the consequences of what states are doing as well as the intentions of those fighting against foreign troops in Iraq, Afghanistan, Yemen, and other places. In addition most of the media have omitted proposals for peaceful solutions in this "global civil war."[59]

Without more engagement, by far more actors than present, the acts of omissions will face a tough scrutiny by history. It is the responsibility for each potential actor to do their best to reduce "terrorism" of all sorts in the world.

NOTES

1. I frame "terrorism" and "terrorist(s)" in quotation marks because I believe these are too loaded to be proper terms in a scientific text—they are too vague and elastic.
2. December 1, 2010, http://english.aljazeera.net/indepth/features/2010/11/20101124114621887983.html.
3. See chapter one of this volume.
4. A. Turk, "Sociology of Terrorism," *Annual Review of Sociology* 30 (2004): 271.
5. These events are in the following referred to as "9/11."
6. UNSC Resolution 1368.
7. Alex Peter Schmid and A. J. Jongman, *Political Terrorism: A New Guide to Actors, Authors, Concepts, Data Bases, Theories, & Literature*. rev. ed. (New Brunswick, NJ: Transaction Publishers, 2008).
8. A. J. Bergesen, "Three-Step Model of Terrorist Violence," *Mobilization, The International Quarterly of Research in Social Movements, Protest, and Contentious Politics* 12.2 (2007): 115.
9. I use "empire" in the same sense as Johan Galtung and make a distinction between the U.S. empire and the U.S. republic. See Galtung, "The Fall of the US Empire—And Then What? Successors, Regionalization or Globalization? US Fascism or US Blossoming?"
10. O. bin Laden and B. B. Lawrence, *Messages to the World: The Statements of Osama Bin Laden* (London, New York: Verso, 2005).
11. D. Hoffman, *The Oklahoma City Bombing and the Politics of Terror* (Venice, CA: Feral House, 1998).
12. Norman Longmate, *The Bombers: The RAF Offensive against Germany 1939–1945* (London: Hutchinson, 1983).
13. See documents from the Target Committee, Los Alamos, May 10–11, 1945: http://www.dannen.com/decision/targets.html.
14. T. Honderich, *After the Terror* (Edinburgh: Edinburgh University Press, 2002).
15. See C. Webel, *Terror, Terrorism, and the Human Condition* (New York: Palgrave Macmillan, 2004).
16. National Counterterrorism Center, *2007 Report on Terrorism,* April 30, 2008: http://www.fbi.gov/stats-services/publications/terror_07.pdf/view?searchterm=definition%20of%20terrorism.
17. These Internet sites are moving around on the web all the time. This is done partly because they are regularly closed down and partly to avoid the detection of those running them.
18. B. Lia, *Architect of Global Jihad: The Life of Al-Qaida Strategist Abu Mus'Ab Al-Suri* (New York: Columbia University Press, 2008).
19. C. Abbott, P. Rogers, et al., *Beyond Terror: The Truth about the Real Threats to Our World* (London: Rider, 2007).
20. See statistics from WHO and national databases.

21. T. Heldmark, A. Ryman, et al., *Hotbilder och Hjärnspöken: Forskare om Terrorism* (Stockholm: Vetenskapsrådet, 2008), 160.

22. http://www.cdc.gov/mmWR/preview/mmwrhtml/ss5002a1.htm.

23. Jiaquan Xu and Betzaida Tejada-Vera B.A. "Deaths: Preliminary Data for 2007," *National Vital Statistics Reports*, U.S. Dept. of Health and Human Services, 2009, 5.

24. See Johan Galtung, *A Theory of Development—Overcoming Structural Violence* (Kolofon Press, 2010), 11.

25. World Health Organization has several databases presenting reliable statistics for mortality and risk factors: http://www.who.int/research/en/.

26. Budget of the U.S. government 1996–2011: http://www.gpoaccess.gov/usbudget/browse.html.

27. The UN has estimated the cost of ending world hunger at $195 billion annually.

28. J. Shepherd, "The Rise and Rise of Terrorism Studies," *Guardian*, July 3, 2007.

29. Organisation for Economical Co-operation and Development (OECD), *Aid Targets Slipping Out of Reach?* 2008, 1.

30. See the report from the U.S. Office of Management and Budget (2006), *Analytical Perspectives, Budget of the United States Government, Fiscal Year 2006* (Washington, DC: Government Printing Office, 2001), 37–52.

31. OECD, 2008, 1.

32. R. English, *Terrorism: How to Respond* (Oxford: Oxford University Press, 2009), 123.

33. Heldmark, Ryman, et al., *Hotbilder och Hjärnspöken*, 160.

34. L. Zedner, *Security* (New York: Routledge, 2009), 89–115.

35. N. M. Ahmed, *Behind the War on Terror: Western Secret Strategy and the Struggle for Iraq* (East Sussex: Clairview, 2003); R. Jackson, *Writing the War on Terrorism: Language, Politics, and Counter-terrorism* (Manchester: Manchester University Press, 2005).

36. D. Cole, *Terrorism and the Constitution: Sacrificing Civil Liberties in the Name of National Security* (New York: New Press, 2002); L. K. Donohue, *The Cost of Counterterrorism: Power, Politics, and Liberty* (Cambridge: Cambridge University Press, 2008).

37. N. M. Ahmed, *The War on Freedom: How and Why America Was Attacked, September 11th, 2001* (Joshua Tree, Calif.: Media Messenger Books, 2002), 9.

38. See *Newsweek* (http://www.newsweek.com/2009/09/29/homecoming.html) and the *Washington Post* (http://www.washingtonpost.com/wp-dyn/articles/A28876-2005Feb16.html) among many.

39. http://www.brookings.edu/~/media/Files/rc/reports/2010/08_arab_opinion_poll_telhami/08_arab_opinion_poll_telhami.pdf.

40. D. Cole and J. Lobel, *Less Safe, Less Free: Why America is Losing the War on Terror* (New York: New Press, Norton, 2007).

41. J. R. Nassar, *Globalization and Terrorism: The Migration of Dreams and Nightmares* (Lanham, MD: Rowman & Littlefield, 2005).
42. http://www.worldpublicopinion.org/pipa/articles/brmiddleeastn africara/663.php.
43. J. Johansen, "Militären Jagar Terrorismens Skugga," in *Laglöst Land*, ed. J. Flyghed and M. Hörnqvist (Stockholm: Ordfront, 2003), 59; English, *Terrorism*, chapter 4.
44. The first U.N. Security Resolution dealing with 9/11: "Threats to International Peace and Security Caused by Terrorist Acts" (http://daccess-ods.un.org/TMP/7979316.71142578.html).
45. United Nations Security Council, "Resolution 1368," United Nations Security Council Resolutions, 2001.
46. *Jus in bello* is a set of rules regulating the limits to acceptable wartime conduct.
47. L. Richardson, What Terrorists Want: Understanding the Enemy, Containing the Threat (New York: Random House, 2006), 10–11.
48. English, *Terrorism*, 128.
49. P. Wilkinson, *Terrorism versus Democracy: The Liberal State Response* (London Portland, OR, Frank Cass, 2001), 69.
50. See Brian Martin, *Justice Ignited: The Dynamics of Backfire* (Lanham, Md.: Rowman & Littlefield, 2007).
51. http://www.cbn.com/cbnnews/world/2010/March/Ex-Terrorist-Gives-CBN-Glimpse-Inside-Al-Qaeda/.
52. http://www.minhaj.org/english/tid/9959/Historical-Launching-of-Fatwa-Against-Terrorism-leading-Islamic-authority-launches-fat wa-against-terrorism-and-denounces-suicide-bombers-as-disbeliever s-Anti-terror-Fatwa-launched.htm.
53. See http://www.peacefultomorrows.org/.
54. Mark Perry, *Talking to Terrorists: Why America Must Engage with Its Enemies* (New York: Basic Books, 2010).
55. Joakim Berndtsson, *The Privatisation of Security and State Control of Force: Changes, Challenges and the Case of Iraq* (Göteborg: Peace and Development Research, School of Global Studies, University of Gothenburg, 2009).
56. http://www.allacademic.com/meta/p_mla_apa_research_citation /2/0/8/8/5/p208859_index.htm.
57. The objective element of a crime.
58. See William Shabas. *Genocide in International Law: The Crimes of Crimes* (Cambridge: Cambridge University Press, 2000).
59. A term used by Stein Tønneson in a lecture at the University of Tromsø on April 24, 2002. The ongoing conflicts between states and networks have many similarities to civil wars, but the conflicts are not confined to a specific territory. The networks can hit almost anywhere in the world and the actions by states are similarly global.

BIBLIOGRAPHY

Chomsky, N. "The Evil Scourge of Terrorism: Reality, Construction, Remedy," chapter one in this volume.

Galtung, J. *Peace by Peaceful Means: Peace and Conflict, Development and Civilization.* London: Sage Publications, 1996.

———. "The Fall of the US Empire—And Then What? Successors, Regionalization or Globalization? US Fascism or US Blossoming?" Transcend University Press, 2009.

Lederach, J. P. *Building Peace: Sustainable Reconciliation in Divided Societies.* Washington, D.C.: United States Institute of Peace Press, 1997.

Part III

Winning the Public Relations War: Journalism as a Weapon

OVERVIEW

Charles P. Webel and John A. Arnaldi

This part examines the powerful rhetorical frames used to communicate about the "global war on terrorism" (GWOT). As in all wars, adversaries in the GWOT must fight on two primary battlefronts: the physical war waged with lethal weapons and the information war waged using communication media as weapons. Controversies that arise in every war are: how to determine the ethical obligations of journalists as they investigate and report on the war, how to recognize and manage the pressures from interested parties who seek to influence the messages communicated, and how to assess the fulfillment of these obligations.

Stephen D. Reese and Seth C. Lewis provide a critical analysis of the narrative framing of the GWOT and discuss findings from their original research on the frequency that "war on terrorism" was mentioned in a U.S. national newspaper from 2001 to 2006. They examine how powerful rhetorical frames acting at a symbolic level were used by the Bush administration to promote its national security policy and how those frames influenced media reports. They find that "news and editorial reports went beyond 'transmitting' the label as shorthand for administration policy, to 'reify' the policy as uncontested, and 'naturalize' it as a taken-for-granted common-sense notion." They conclude that by internalizing the administration's framing of policy, journalists and the media abrogated their responsibility to provide the "space for deliberative scrutiny" that is necessary in healthy democracies.

John Arnaldi examines the ethical challenges facing journalists during the GWOT. Ideally, in a democratic society, journalists try to live up to the ethic of service to the public by providing the accurate information citizens need in order to make informed judgments about their government. However, in times of war and terrorism, journalistic ethics of devotion to the truth and service to the public may be sacrificed to their more immediate needs for safety, employment, funding, and social approval. The media companies that employ journalists are driven by a combination of consumer fears/desires, economic interests, and political forces. Together, such factors favor news reports that avoid challenging administration policies and mainstream views related to the GWOT. Additionally, the coalition of states fighting the GWOT and the nonstate terrorist organizations attempt to control the media's messages. As the GWOT has progressed, investigative journalists have uncovered deceptive and possibly illegal attempts by the U.S. government to influence the press, as in the Pentagon's military analyst program. The chapter concludes with discussion of *Wikileaks*, a highly controversial alternative news media organization, which has released stolen secret government and corporate documents because it claims mainstream news organizations have failed to report the information needed by citizens to hold governments accountable for war crimes and other illegal acts that harm the public.

Molly Bingham, a photojournalist and filmmaker, discusses lessons she learned while filming *Meeting Resistance*[1] with codirector Steve Connors and in question and answer sessions that followed screenings. She finds that the "story of the human effort for self-determination by violent means cannot be told in America." From her perspective as a journalist who has lived within war zones, she explores the government misuse of language in support of the GWOT. She argues that the mischaracterization of resistance to the occupation as an "insurgency" has contributed to the coalition's "dramatically flawed" strategy to combat it—counterinsurgency. Bingham maintains that "the highest form of patriotism...is expecting our country to live up to the promises it makes and the values it purports to hold." She concludes that the news media are "undeniably failing today" in assisting the public to ensure that those values and human rights are reflected in reality.

These essays explore how language has been used to frame the GWOT so it communicates specific, culturally powerful understandings to decision-makers and the public. These frames have influenced the understanding of the nature of terrorism, the choice of strategies intended to deal with it, and judgment of their outcomes. The press's internalization of administration framing of the GWOT, together with the largely unaddressed vulnerabilities of the press and news media to the powerful influences of conflicting interests, have weakened the public's ability and motivation to hold coalition governments accountable for effective antiterrorism strategies.

Note

1. *Meeting Resistance* focuses on interviews with members of the Iraqi resistance to the U.S.-led occupation. See http://www.meetingresistance.com/index.html.

7

FRAMING THE WAR ON TERROR: THE INTERNALIZATION OF POLICY IN THE U.S. PRESS

Stephen D. Reese and Seth C. Lewis

The challenge of political violence has grown with new means of global coordination and access to weapons of mass destruction. The Bush administration's response to this threat, following the now iconic policy reference point of 11 September 2001, has had far-ranging implications for national security strategy, relations with the world community, and civil liberties. Labeled the "war on terror,"[1] the policy was framed within a phrase now part of the popular lexicon, becoming a natural and instinctive shorthand. More than phrases though, frames are "organizing principles that are socially shared and persistent over time, that work symbolically to meaningfully structure the social world."[2] As would any policy advocate, administrations seek compelling frames to define the issues and help win the discursive struggle, as opponents, in turn, seek to resist those definitions and find more favorable ones.[3] As a particularly powerful organizing principle, the "War on Terror" created a supportive political climate for what has been called the biggest U.S. foreign policy blunder in modern times: the invasion of Iraq. Thus, in the scope and consequences of its policy-shaping impact, the War on Terror may be the most important frame in recent memory.[4]

STUDY PURPOSE

In this essay, we consider how the War on Terror became a socially shared organizing principle through its transmission via the U.S.

press. Captivated by a powerful master narrative after 9/11 and in the run-up to the Iraq War, American journalists found it difficult to resist being drawn into the national anxiety and general pro-Bush patriotic fervor. Since Iraq, of course, the criticism of administration policy has been widespread, including a host of books.[5] But that critical scrutiny was most needed *before* major decisions were made and the public enlisted. While the explicit cultural components of the frame have been carefully assembled by its sponsors in policy documents and presidential speeches, we are concerned here with precisely how the War on Terror has been absorbed into media (and therefore public) discourse and grown beyond its original policy usage to take on a life of its own. Arguing that the news media have been active participants in propagating the framing, we examine reporting of the War on Terror from its launching after 9/11, as represented by a prototypical national newspaper (*USA Today*), and we confirm our inferences from news discourse by interviewing some of the journalists who wrote the stories. In our model of the interpretive framing process, we differ from the view of frames as a lower-level construct with more specific, clearly competing recommendations for short-run political action. Instead, we regard the War on Terror as a macrolevel cultural structure that functions in its scope as an ideological expression: in Thompson's expression, "meaning in the service of power."[6] We describe the key components of the frame, and examine how that structure was assimilated by the press, a process that can be seen in news texts and journalists' own reflections on them. More specifically, we examine the extent to which professional routines and cultural assumptions led the media to internalize the frame: indications that ranged from simple transmission, to reification, and to naturalization.

THE BUSH POLICY FRAME

In the now well-known evolution of the administration's policy, influential neoconservatives within the administration had advocated regime change in Iraq for some time, but the events of 9/11 gave them a compelling way to fast-track their ideas and justify a new policy of preemptive war, first in Afghanistan and then in Iraq. The *National Strategy for Combating Terrorism*[7] defined the attacks of 9/11 as "acts of war against the United States of America and its allies, and against the very idea of civilized society." It identified the enemy as terrorism, an "evil" threatening our "freedoms and our way of life."[8] The related *National Security Strategy of the United States of America*[9] clearly divides "us" from "them," linking terrorism to rogue states that "hate the United States and everything for which it stands."[10] Presenting himself as God's agent, Bush's Manichean struggle pitted the United States and its leader against the evildoers.[11]

Arguably, the most significant outcome of the War on Terror construction was in giving a rhetorical (if not empirical) rationale for the invasion of Iraq. Gershkoff and Kushner showed how Bush clearly framed the Iraq strategy within the War on Terror by juxtaposing Iraq and 9/11.[12] He underscored that link the following year in proclaiming a military success: "The battle of Iraq is one victory in a war on terror that began on Sept. 11, 2001, and still goes on."[13] Indeed, public support for the war hinged crucially on whether or not one believed the link between 9/11 and Saddam Hussein, which a majority of Americans did.[14] This link continued to provide retroactive justification for the invasion. Vice President Cheney, for example, claimed falsely on September 14, 2003, that success in Iraq would strike a major blow at the *"geographic base* of the terrorists who had us under assault now for many years, but most especially on 9/11."[15] In a 2004 news conference responding to continued resistance in Iraq, President Bush declared that "the terrorists have lost...an ally in Baghdad..."[16] Bush argued that 9/11 taught the lesson that threats must be anticipated before they materialize, and that he had seen such a threat in Iraq.[17] This nonfalsifiable "lesson" expanded the scope of the frame even further.[18] Although the terminology showed signs of strain, Bush could not easily abandon the slogan after using it as justification for Iraq.[19]

Conservatives have largely embraced the underlying principle, but others more skeptically bracketed the policy in ironic reference: "war on terrorism" or Bush's so-called war on terrorism, signaling that the framing itself is flawed—an argument made even by critics in the national security community.[20] Critics on the left regard it as a front for an imperialistic project and reject the uncritical celebration of American life. In spite of such resistance, the War on Terror received wide acceptance across the political spectrum. In terms of Entman's model of White House influence, the administration achieved "frame dominance" among official elites with no evidence of a viable competing narrative.[21] The success of this dominance needs to be better understood.

A MODEL FOR INTERPRETIVE FRAMING

As Smith argues, war is not just something that elites decide to do with the help of public relations techniques.[22] They make use of preexisting cultural resources, codes, and genres of interpretation to mobilize support and legitimize military action. As an expression of power, wars happen when policy actors successfully align their goals with favorable cultural codes. This supports our view of framing as an ideological process within a larger political context, with the task for analysis one of showing more precisely how these meanings are connected and support certain interests.[23] The sweep of the War on Terror calls for this more interpretive approach—which we contrast with other research comparing issues presented more narrowly within one frame or another—as suggesting a specific problem definition and policy response. Entman, for example, ostensibly considers the War on Terror,[24] but identifies a problem solution within it as war-with-Iraq, as opposed to the "counterframing" war-with-Saudi Arabia suggested by influential journalists Seymour Hersch and Thomas Friedman. But this discourse still occupies boundaries set by the larger macro-frame, which is given no viable competitor. Bennett and colleagues criticize the press for failing to challenge official framing during that time, but again they operate at a more specific level—whether, for example, Iraq's Abu Ghraib prison torture scandal was referred to as "torture" or "abuse."[25]

Like Hertog and McLeod we emphasize a broader cultural approach to frames, which they regard as "structures of meaning made up of a number of concepts and the relations among those concepts."[26] Underlying master narratives structure those concepts and guide the processing of new content. This approach emphasizes the dynamic aspect of frames, which are used to assimilate and make sense of new information. Regarding the present case, the familiar metaphor of war has been applied before to more abstract social problems including poverty and drugs.[27] Although asymmetric warfare has no "front," identifiable armies, or fixed duration, the president insisted on declaring Iraq the "front line," a claim made easier within the controlling metaphor, which in turn enables connections to other conflicts deeply rooted in American psychology. Concerning terrorism itself, official definitions such as the FBI's reinforce the role of government as the protagonist: "*unlawful* use of force or violence" excludes state-sponsored, presumably "lawful" terrorism. These definitions allow even repressive states to classify challenges to state power as "terrorism." Framing terrorism as the global equivalent of a hijacking brackets off criticism of state actors as they reassert their authority in dealing with threats to security.

JOURNALISTS AND THE WAR ON TERROR

The War on Terror describes a vague enemy, opposes a "tactic," has no clear measure of success, privileges the state and the status quo—who "we" are versus who "they" are—and thus lifts the problem out of political, economic, and historical contexts. But these concerns have received little attention from the U.S. press.[28] In fact, journalists have easily adapted to this perspective, with all of its discussion of allies, fronts, borders, and national threats. (The Tyndall Report, which monitors the news broadcasts of the major networks, called the "War on Terror" the top story of 2002.) But to what extent do U.S. journalists remain committed to a frame even after its validity has been so seriously challenged? Journalists often follow official namings, but this must be done carefully, lest reports no longer describe the administration's "war on terrorism" but how things are going in "America's war on terror."[29] In reporting, for example, the combat death of a former National Football League athlete, a *Los Angeles Times* story described how Pat Tillman "was mourned as a fallen fighter in the war on terrorism...and hailed as a hero."[30]

Numerous other examples suggest that the frame became uncritically accepted as a way of viewing the world. The ultimate closing of the loop came when journalists, after having helped brand the policy, labeled the frame as public opinion: "the struggle that most Americans call the war on terrorism."[31] Other clues include the writings and statements of high-profile journalists who express the common wisdom. NBC's *Meet the Press* host Tim Russert spoke out, sounding very similar to the president himself: "We are at war, and all of us must come together as never before...Simply put: there are those who want to destroy us, our people—men, women and children—our institutions, our way of life, our freedom."[32]

Self-reflection among professionals, at think tanks and elsewhere, provides other clues. In their resulting book from a Brookings and Harvard-sponsored forum on the media and the War on Terrorism shortly after 9/11, Hess and Kalb acknowledged that the War on Terror served as a framing device for the media, but then quickly emphasized *how* it had been covered. They declare 9/11 as *"day one* of the war on terror"[33] and that "the war on terror *erupted* on 9/11."[34] This dehistoricizes the problem and conceals any U.S. responsibility for what the editors described as the circumstances "the US *had been thrust into*."[35]

PROBLEM STATEMENT

The administration constructed its framing of national security policy and gave it a name, but *how* was this framing communicated by the press, and to what extent was it taken for granted? To answer these questions, we assume that any reference in news discourse to the War on Terror signals an engagement, critical or (most often) not, with the administration's policy framing. We focus our attention on these engagements as a way to identify the relevant news texts. Although we focus on journalists' own word choices, we want to identify overall features of the discourse; so, whether attributed statements or the reporter's own words, we assume that any reference to the War on Terror communicates a framing choice on the part of the journalist.[36] Beyond frequency and emphasis, the particular power of a frame lies in it being an organizing principle, guiding (even if mentioned in passing) policy discussions through its resonance with supportive cultural elements. We examine the extent to which the frame was reinforced and internalized, as suggested by features within journalistic texts and from responses by journalists themselves about their work. Here we are not concerned with whether media did the leading or simply indexed elite opinion, but with how the news media *participated* in this framing. We take then the administration's framing of the War on Terror as a starting point and examine how it was, in turn, communicated.

With its emphasis on the dramatic, easily summarized conflict, television news, and Fox news channel in particular, have embraced the War on Terror from the start as an onscreen organizing device. Print media, however, provide a more nuanced view of how journalists respond to administration framing. Specifically, we focus on the Washington-based *USA Today*, with the largest daily newspaper national circulation and a publication that seeks to speak with a national voice.

SUMMARY AND DISCUSSION

Although the War on Terror no longer dominates news discourse as it did after 9/11, the trends suggest that it still lives on. Our findings from the textual analysis and interviews suggest that the frame was internalized by the U.S. news media—in ways beyond Entman's "cascading" process of frame influence from White House to press.[37] In addition to simply repeating the preferred terminology of the President, journalists reified the policy—treating it as an uncontested "thing"—and naturalized it, suggesting they accepted its use as a way of describing a prevailing condition of modern life. It's tempting to regard these as sequential stages, but elements of each were found throughout the period. Follow-up interviews with journalists from our sample suggested that, to the extent that it has become more deconstructed and politically controversial, they have used the War on Terror with greater care. From their comments, we conclude that the frame was quickly accepted post-9/11 and was vulnerable to challenge only after the "execution" of one key component failed—after the administration lost credibility with Iraq.[38]

So, as we have argued, the War on Terror was more than a policy label; it was a powerful organizing principle and, to the extent that journalists shared that way of structuring the world as indicated in their reports and analysis, created a favorable news discourse climate for military action in Iraq. This status quo frame—pitting "us" versus "them," obscuring concerns for state-sponsored violence, and casting a broad net of undifferentiated "terror"—made it easier to regard Iraq as a legitimate response to 9/11. Mutual participation in that framing allowed both the administration and the media to disavow making such a link—the president because he never made it explicitly and journalists who could say they were only passing it along.

The post-9/11 consensus has been eroded, with Democrats now openly questioning its assumptions.[39] The War on Terror, however, has resilience and its deep cultural structure was given renewed currency in the 2008 presidential campaign. Republican candidate Rudy Giuliani, for example, made 9/11 the centerpiece of his campaign, arguing that the War on Terror and Iraq were both examples of the country having gone "on offense" to defeat terrorism.[40] A well-funded advocacy group, Freedom's Watch, announced plans to support the war in Iraq as the solution to the "9/11 problem." Former Bush press secretary and group leader Ari Fleischer acknowledged that Iraq was not responsible for 9/11, "but 9/11 should be a vivid reminder to everyone about how vulnerable our country is, and that's why we need to win in Iraq."[41] Such illogical claims are hard to refute when packaged within the all-encompassing War on Terror.

Something fundamental about this principle lives on in news reports, especially on television. In a 2006 CBS News broadcast, Katie Couric introduced a story: "Tonight, it was the first front in the war on terror, and in Afghanistan now the Taliban are back with a vengeance." Reporter Lara Logan went on to say, "For many Americans today, it was back to work and back to school, but in the war on terror, you have to wonder, is it back to the drawing board?" Couric, in the same newscast, confirmed the received wisdom of the 9/11-as-genesis: "The war on terror began, of course, with the September 11th attacks on the United

States."[42] Similarly, NBC News anchor Brian Williams declared that we are a "nation at war because of what happened in New York."[43]

We posed our questions primarily at the professional level: How did journalists in the U.S. press participate in reinforcing and internalizing a key administration frame? Making inferences about the internal psychology of journalists is always tricky, and not to be made solely on the basis of their outputs, which are institutional and cultural, as well as personal creations. In this case, their reflections coupled with their reporting helped reveal the process, which should provide an object lesson for the U.S. news media and journalistic community. Even when the opposition party does little to mount an alternative counterframe, competing instead on who can be toughest in execution, the news media cannot abrogate their responsibility to critically examine policy assumptions embedded in frames. The internalization of policy short-circuits democratic debate by allowing little space for deliberative scrutiny from citizens and meaningful action by elected officials. We need to understand better how dominant frames become so with the active participation of the news media.

NOTES

Reproduced by permission of SAGE Publications Ltd., London, Los Angeles, New Delhi, Singapore, and Washington DC, from Stephen D. Reese and Seth C. Lewis. "Framing the War on Terror: The Internalization of Policy in the US Press," *Journalism*, 10.6 (2009): 777–797, Copyright (© The authors, 2009).

1. Various phrases have been used in this context, including the "war on terrorism," the "war against terror," and the "war on terror." Henceforth, the capitalized "War on Terror" will be used when referring to the frame itself and otherwise a lowercase "war on terror(ism)" when quoted or paraphrased in its use by others.
2. S. D. Reese, "Framing Public Life: A Bridging Model for Media Research," in *Framing Public Life*, ed. S. D. Reese, O. H. J. Gandy, and A. E. Grant (Mahwah, NJ: Lawrence Erlbaum, 2001), 7–31.
3. Z. Pan and G. M. Kosicki, "Framing as a Strategic Action in Public Deliberation," in *Framing Public Life*, ed. S. D. Reese, O. H. J. Gandy, and A. E. Grant (Mahwah, NJ: Lawrence Erlbaum, 2001), 35–65.
4. S. D. Reese, "The Framing Project: A Bridging Model for Media Research Revisited," *Journal of Communication* 57.1 (2007): 148–154.
5. M. Isikoff and D. Corn, *Hubris: The Inside Story of Spin, Scandal, and the Selling of the Iraq War* (New York: Crown Publishers, 2006).
6. J. Thompson, *Ideology and Modern Culture: Critical Social Theory in the Era of Mass Communication* (Stanford, CA: Stanford University Press, 1990), 7.

7. White House, *National Strategy for Combating Terrorism*, Washington, D.C., 2003.

8. Ibid., 1.

9. White House, *National Security Strategy of the United States of America*, Washington, D.C., 2006.

10. Ibid., 14.

11. D. Domke, *God Willing? Political Fundamentalism in the White House, the "War on Terror," and the Echoing Press* (London: ML Pluto Press, 2004).

12. A. Gershkoff and S. Kushner, "Shaping Public Opinion: The 9/11-Iraq Connection in the Bush Administration's Rhetoric," *Perspectives on Politics* 3.3 (2005): 525–537.

13. L. McQuillan and R. Benedetto, "Bush Hails Win, Looks Ahead," *USA Today*, May 2, 2003, p. A1.

14. Concerning casualties in Iraq a month after the beginning of the conflict, one New Yorker compared the 88 American dead to the 3,000 who died on September 11, 2001: 'Those, to me, are casualties of this same war, which is a war against terrorism," said Daphne Scholz, co-owner of a gourmet food store in the Park Slope section of Brooklyn. "We took the first casualties, and the balance of dead is still on our side"' (Wilgoren and Nagourney, 2003).

15. *Meet the Press,* "Transcript for Sept. 14," 2003: http://www. msnbc .msn.com/id/3080244/ (last accessed July 2009).

16. G. W. Bush, "President Bush's Opening Statement on Iraq," *New York Times*, April 14, 2004, p. A11.

17. G. W. Bush, President Discusses Homeland Security with WI First Responders (Washington, D.C.: White House, 2004).

18. Overall Republican political strategy further amplified the link between Iraq and 9/11. Pollster Frank Luntz recommended always placing the war in Iraq within the greater war on terror, arguing that it is better to fight it on the streets of Baghdad than New York, and adding, "Don't forget the Sept. 11, 2001, attacks. '9/11 changed everything' is the context by which everything follows" (Harris and Faler, 2004).

19. In the summer of 2005 reporters noticed a transition in the "catchphrase," although the alternative "global struggle against violent extremism" was still cast by Defense Secretary Donald Rumsfeld as an apocalyptic conflict "against the enemies of freedom, the enemies of civilization" (Schmitt and Shanker, 2005). For the military, in any case, the global war on terrorism (including Afghanistan and Iraq) remains an official theater of operation and category of service medals.

20. Z. Brzezinski, *The Choice: Global Domination or Global Leadership* (New York: Basic Books, 2004); J. Record, *Bounding the Global War on Terrorism* (Monograph) (Carlisle, PA: Strategic Studies Institute, U. Army War College, 2003).

21. R. M. Entman, "Cascading Activation: Contesting the White House's Frame after 9/11," *Political Communication* 20.4 (2003): 415–432.

22. P. Smith, *Why War? The Cultural Logic of Iraq, the Gulf War, and Suez* (Chicago, IL: University of Chicago Press, 2005).

23. K. M. Carragee and W. Roefs, "The Neglect of Power in Recent Framing Research," *Journal of Communication* 54.2 (2004): 214–233.

24. Entman, "Cascading Activation."

25. W. L. Bennett, R. Lawrence, and S. Livingston, "None Dare Call it Torture: Indexing and the Limits of Press Independence in the Abu Ghraib Scandal," *Journal of Communication* 56.3 (2006): 467–485.

26. J. K. Hertog and D. M. McLeod, "A Multiperspectival Approach to Framing Analysis: A Field Guide," in *Framing Public Life*, ed. S. D. Reese, O. H. J. Gandy, and A. E. Grant (Mahwah, NJ: Lawrence Erlbaum, 2001), 140.

27. J. Lule, Daily News, Eternal Stories: The Mythological Role of Journalism (New York: Guilford Press, 2001).

28. Among the rare criticisms within the professional community, Levenson (2004) reinforced the view of our journalists by arguing that the press malfunctioned when continuing to use without questioning the label beyond its original rationale for Afghanistan.

29. Reese, "The Framing Project."

30. S. Farmer, T. Bonk, and J. Honduran, "Player Who Swapped NFL for Army Killed in Action," *The (Austin) American-Statesman*, April 24, 2004, p. A1.

31. J. Hoagland, "War's Global Casualties," *Washington Post*, October 17, 2002, p. A21.

32. P. Johnson, "Tim Russert: War Changes the Rules," *USA Today*, November 1, 2001, p. D4.

33. S. Hess and M. L. Kalb, eds, *The Media and the War on Terrorism* (Washington, D.C.: Brookings Institution Press, 2003), 183.

34. Ibid., 223.

35. Ibid., 2.

36. B. Van Gorp, "The Constructionist Approach to Framing: Bringing Culture Back in," *Journal of Communication* 57.1 (2007): 60–78.

37. Entman, "Cascading Activation."

38. See also S. C. Lewis and S. D. Reese, "What is the War on Terror? Framing Through the Eyes of Journalists," *Journalism & Mass Communication Quarterly* 86.1 (2009): 85–102.

39. M. Bai, "America's Mayor Goes to America," *New York Times (Magazine)*, September 9, 2007, p. 46.

40. Ibid.

41. P. Baker, "9/11 Linked to Iraq, in Politics if Not in Fact," *Washington Post*, September, 12, 2007, p. A1.

42. CBS News, Transcript of *CBS Evening News with Katie Couric*, September 5, 2006.

43. F. Rich, "Too Soon? It's too Late for 'United 93,'" *International Herald Tribune*, May 8, 2006, p. 7.

BIBLIOGRAPHY

Benedetto, R. (2002) "Poll: High Approval for Bush Due Partly to His Character," *USA Today*, May 3, 2002, p. A4.

Benedetto, R. and J. Keen. "Bush Alters Political Strategy after Democrats' Hammering," *USA Today*, February 6, 2004, p. A2.

Bush, G. W. "Bush: 'Enemies of Freedom Are Not Idle, and Neither Are We,'" *USA Today*, May 2, 2003, p. A2.

Di Rita, L. "Don't Tie Our Hands: Congress Shouldn't Set Limits on Interrogating Captured Terrorists," *USA Today*, August 5, 2005, p. A12.

Dorell, O. "Bush Visit Puts Focus on Concerns over Russia's Path," *USA Today*, May 5, 2005, p. A5.

Dorell, O., J. Drinkard, K. Kiely, S. Kirchhoff, and S. Ko. "The Key Points and Their Context: The State of the Union," *USA Today*, February 1, 2006, p. A7.

Editorial. "Defense Plan Doesn't Adapt to New Face of War," *USA Today*, November 5, 2001, p. A14.

———. "An Election of Many Hues, and Not Just Red and Blue," *USA Today*, November 5, 2004a, p. A14.

———. "...and Why Third-Party Votes Matter," *USA Today*, November 2, 2004b, p. A16.

———. "Bin Laden's Message," *USA Today*, November 1, 2004c, p. A20.

———. "Crowds and Calm at the Polls," *USA Today*, November 3, 2004d, p. A24.

Gannon, J. P. "How Bush Can Right the Ship," *USA Today*, November 3, 2005, p. A15.

Glueck, M. A. "Thanks, Arizona and New York, for a Great World Series," *USA Today*, November 7, 2001, p. A14.

Grossman, C. L. "President Draws on the Bible to Comfort a Grieving Nation," *USA Today*, February 3, 2003, p. A5.

Hall, M. "Questions about Terror Threat Answered," *USA Today*, August 5, 2004, p. A10.

Hampson, R. "Fear as a Weapon: Terrorist Tactics Rarely Triumph," *USA Today*, November 1, 2001, p. A1.

Harris, J. F., and B. Faler. "Talking Iraq: Some Things Are Better Left Unsaid," *Washington Post*, June 20, 2004, p. A4.

Kasindorf, M. "We Cannot Win this Election," *USA Today*, November 4, 2004, p. A4.

Keen, J. "President's All-out Campaigning for GOP a Gamble," *USA Today*, November 4, 2002, p. A10.

———. "Talk on Terrorism Draws Cheers; Tough Stance Revs Up Crowds," *USA Today*, August 2, 2004, p. A5.

Keen, J., and J. Diamond. "Bush to Act on Some of 9/11 Report Today," *USA Today*, August 2, 2004, p. A2.

Kelly, M. "Rove Lauds Ill. GOP for Voter Registration," *Associated Press*, May 15, 2004.

Kerry, J. "Why You Should Vote for Me Today," *USA Today*, November 2, 2004, p. A17.

Levenson, J. "The War on What, Exactly? Why the Press Must Be Precise," *Columbia Journalism Review* 43.4 (2004): 9–11.

Locy, T. "New Tribunal for Detainees Faces Challenge: Lawyers Question System," *USA Today*, November 1, 2004, p. A19.

Luce, E. "How Republicans and Democrats Alike Are out-Bushing Bush," *Financial Times*, March 11, 2006, p. 11.

News Analysis. "GOP Challenge: Small Wins or Enduring Dominance," *USA Today*, November 4, 2004, p. A26.

Page, S. "Corporate Credentials Weigh down Bush's Team," *USA Today*, August 7, 2002a, p. B1.

———. "The New New Economy," *USA Today*, May 3, 2002b, p. A4.

———. "Swing States Lean to Kerry; Democrat Ties Bush Nationally," *USA Today*, November 1, 2004, p. A1.

Sanger, D. E. "Bush Compares Responses to Hurricane and Terrorism," *New York Times*, September 22, 2005, p. A24.

Schaeffer, F. "For War Families, it's Not Political," *USA Today*, May 6, 2004, p. A13.

Schmitt, E., and T. Shanker. "New Name for "War on Terror" Reflects Wider U.S. Campaign," *New York Times*, July 25, 2005, p. A7.

Seiler, A. "The Wizards of Cinema," *USA Today*, November 2, 2001. p. E1.

Shapiro, W. "Democrats May Have Edge, but it Won't Be a Sharp One," *USA Today*, November 1, 2002, p. A14.

———. "Graham's Next Job is Playing Catch-up," *USA Today*, May 7, 2003, p. A8.

Spielvogel, C. "'You Know Where I Stand': Moral Framing of the War on Terrorism and the Iraq War in the 2004 Presidential Campaign," *Rhetoric & Public Affairs* 8.4 (2005): 549–569.

Suskind, R. *The One Percent Doctrine: Deep inside America's Pursuit of its Enemies since 9/11*. New York: Simon & Schuster, 2006.

Wickham, D. "Democratic Herd Needs Culling," *USA Today*, May 6, 2003, p. A15.

Wilgoren, J., and A. Nagourney. "While Mourning Dead, Many Americans Say Level of Casualties is Acceptable," *New York Times*, April 8, 2003, p. B1.

Wolf, R., and D. Jackson. "Cutting Medicare Will Be Tough Sell in Election Year," *USA Today*, February 7, 2006, p. A5.

8

IN WHOSE INTEREST? ETHICS IN JOURNALISM AND THE WAR ON TERRORISM

John A. Arnaldi

> Until lions have their historians, tales of the hunt shall always glorify the hunter.
>
> —African proverb

SHARED MORAL DUTIES OF PROFESSIONS

Journalism[1] shares a common ethical context with professions that serve the public interest, such as medicine and law. Professions are expected to develop standards for ethical conduct, usually presented in a code of ethics. Ideally, both society and profession benefit when ethical standards are met: society receives the maximum benefit with the lowest possible risk of harm when professionals perform ethically, and the profession benefits by earning the public's respect as trustworthy sources of valuable services. Additionally, professionals are often expected to contribute to the betterment of society.

Professions ideally share at least two fundamental ethical principles. First, members are duty-bound to act in the best interests of those persons they serve: they are expected to put their clients' interests above all other interests that could influence the performance of their work. They should base their judgments on the relevant facts of each case and standard practices, not upon personal, financial, or other conflicting interests that could influence their judgment. Acting in the best interests of their client contributes to the welfare and safety of the public. Second, ethical standards should be universal: they should apply equally without discrimination, as in Kant's categorical imperative, where the same moral standard required of one group is required of all.

ETHICAL RESPONSIBILITIES OF THE PRESS

For journalists, the client is the public and the public's best interest is access to relevant, accurate information. According to the *Code of Ethics* for the Society of Professional Journalists: "Journalists should be free of obligation to any interest other than the public's right to know."[2] Public access to relevant, accurate information usually promotes public welfare and safety. The principle of universality asserts that the same ethical standards should apply to the press in all nations.

The ethical responsibilities in journalism relate to the value and integrity of information. Communication of meaningful information is highly valued as key to the advancement of knowledge and social progress. Freedom to communicate information increasingly has been recognized as a basic human liberty essential for democratic governance. In the United States, freedom of the press is rooted in the Declaration of Independence and the Constitution, which lay out the basis for natural rights of individuals, including the rights to "life, liberty, and the pursuit of happiness." The founders recognized that one of the most serious threats to liberty and democratic government is the possibility that certain interests might gain unfair advantage over the best interests of the public. The First Amendment protection of the press affirms the value of the press as a check on attempts by any party, including the government, to overpower the interests of the citizenry.

The press also holds significant power to legitimize any narrative, which increases its vulnerability to exploitation by government and others seeking legitimization of their cause. When a narrative dominates the news, the increased coverage adds legitimacy to it and confers power on the group promoting it. Increased coverage makes it worthy of more coverage, which yields more legitimacy and power. As the cycle repeats, power accrues to the most powerful. This dynamic subverts the main purposes of the Constitution—to establish a democratic government that prevents the abuse of power and guarantees that leaders serve only by consent of the governed. Failure of the press to address this dynamic virtually guarantees that power will be concentrated in the most powerful hands (government, political groups, and corporations), while the rights and interests of the public are weakened. When prowar narratives are allowed to dominate the news unchallenged, the risk grows that policy and military/security actions will be implemented without the consent of the public and therefore unlikely to serve their interests.

Because war is among the greatest threats to human life (and liberty and happiness), if decisions involving military actions, national security, and counterterrorism are to be ethical, human lives must be valued above narrowly defined self- and national interests. It is those who argue *for* war who must provide the burden of proof for deviating from society's moral prohibition of killing.[3] Similarly, those who abandon human rights and the rule of law must provide the burden of proof. Those who dissent the call to war speak for society's prohibition of killing and therefore should have equal opportunity to participate when war is debated.

Such government and military decisions remain subject to (1) moral, ethical, legal, and religious constraints based upon the moral presumption that human life is sacred, and (2) the consent of the citizens. The authority for these decisions does not automatically reside with the government or military—rightful authority is derived from the *continuing* consent of the citizens. Valid consent requires voluntary agreement (free of coercion) based upon full understanding of the potential consequences (costs, risks, and benefits). To give valid consent, citizens must have access to relevant, understandable information. When government controls the available information, public understanding may automatically reflect the government views, which cannot be the basis for valid consent.

Propaganda is manipulation of information for the purpose of influencing others and constitutes a form of coercion. Recognizing propaganda as a threat to liberty and democratic government, Congress has repeatedly prohibited the government from directing propaganda at the U.S. public.[4] Citizens who have been subjected to state propaganda or censorship are unable to give valid consent (1) because they cannot access accurate information, and (2) because propaganda is coercive and hence consent cannot be voluntary. Likewise, when the press favors nationalistic or government-military-industrial interests, unbiased information is unavailable to the public. Only a press independent of government influence can provide the information needed by citizens to validate the legitimacy of their government. Lacking the valid consent of the governed, the government cannot claim legitimate authority to plan or wage war.

Nationalism and Ethics

On the evening of September 11, 2001, former president George W. Bush called for unity, asserting that "those who want peace and security in the world" will "stand together to win the war against terrorism."[5] Within the first weeks following the attacks, most of the world did stand in unity with the United States. For example, many Arabic and Muslim leaders offered condolences and condemned the attacks; and on September 13, the headline of *Le Monde* proclaimed, "Nous sommes tous Américains"[6] (We are all Americans). Many U.S. journalists also felt called to support the commander-in-chief. For example, six days after the attacks, one news anchor asserted, "George Bush is the President, he makes the decisions, and, you know, as just one American, wherever he wants me to line up, just tell me where."[7]

It is understandable that immediately following the attacks U.S. journalists would have strong personal feelings about defending the nation. However, as the initial shock lessened, journalists should have recognized that their personal feelings, interests, and biases could conflict with their professional responsibilities. In times of threat and war, it is inevitable that journalists will be challenged to sort out their loyalties: whether, in the interest of public safety (defense) and welfare, they should support the administration's narrative, or, in the interest of informing the pubic, they should challenge and scrutinize all sides of the issue. They must determine how to keep true to their professional mission of serving the people's best interests. They also must decide how to respect universality (if foreign journalists are expected to report facts, even when harmful to their government's interests, what should be required of U.S. journalists?).

Evidence from 9/11 forward suggests that in most cases the mainstream press and media were influenced more often by nationalism (and other interests) than by professionalism: they have provided virtually unlimited coverage of administration views, while alternative views have been rarely featured. This observation is supported by several studies. One study examined on-camera news interviews on four networks in early 2003 (just prior to the attack on Iraq) and found that 75 percent of the sources were current or former U.S. government officials. Of 393 sources, only 68 (17 percent) were skeptical about or critical of attacking Iraq and only 3 sources "(less than 1%) were identified with organized protests or anti-war groups"[8]—a striking imbalance in coverage. A later study focused on the *PBS NewsHour* from October 2005 through March 2006, and found that "current and former government and military officials totaled 50 percent of all sources."[9] Sources advocating continued occupation of Iraq "outnumbered pro-withdrawal sources more than 5-to-1. In the entire six months studied, not a single peace activist was heard on the *NewsHour*."[10]

Some journalists have echoed these findings,[11] charging that mainstream news consistently and uncritically favors the administration's views. "The burden of proof, implicitly or explicitly, was put on these dissenting views and persons" and not "on an administration that was demonstrably moving towards a large-scale military action."[12] The absence of other views cannot be attributed to a scarcity of experts because respected peace activists as well as experts in counterterrorism, intelligence, foreign policy, political and military sciences, peace and conflict studies, ethics, and theology who favored alternatives to the wars are plentiful and easily accessible for interviews. How such a consistently nationalistic bias could have become the unchallenged standard dominating mainstream media for a decade demands close scrutiny.

Journalistic procedures also can introduce bias. One analysis found that the traditional "inverted pyramid style of reporting" gives priority placement within a report to the highest administration officials.[13] The researcher found that the press emphasizes the administration's designated issues, narrative frames, and policy priorities, leaving little time or space for alternatives. Additionally, when multiple media draw from press pools to lower overseas costs, reports tend to be homogeneous.

THREE INTERESTED PARTIES

Information is valuable and during war control of information is highly coveted. As a major information provider, the press is vulnerable to and targeted for control by interested parties seeking advantages that cannot be won on the battlefield alone. Three powerful parties seek to influence the news: officially designated terrorist and insurgent groups, news media owners, and governments. Understanding how interested parties may influence the press requires critical analysis of their interests—discovering what motivates and rewards them.

Terrorist Groups' Influences on Reporting

Long before the 9/11 attacks, terrorists discovered they could gain visibility by attacking civilians and symbolic targets. Spectacular, terrifying attacks proved to be a dependable strategy for relatively weak antigovernmental groups to leverage more power than they could acquire by directly combating powerful governments—hence the term, "asymmetric warfare." Questions about ethical judgments arise: when the press reflexively follow the principle that "when it bleeds, it leads," are they informing the public or inadvertently providing the visibility sought by perpetrators? Shouldn't the "people's right to know" be applied universally, to cover nonstate terrorists, insurgents and freedom fighters,[14] peaceful dissenters, experts who challenge government views, and state-supported terrorists who perpetrate wars and other human-rights violations?

Corporate Influences on Journalists and Media

Media owners are influenced by legitimate business realities, such as the potential to earn high profits from advertising during periods of high interest, such as elections, wars, and disasters, and the potential to lose profits by reporting news that alienates viewers and advertisers. These economic incentives pressure owners to be competitive and risk-averse—they cannot expend finite resources on stories that don't attract viewers or that cannot compete with stories featured by other companies. Additionally, owners may have conflicts of interest, which they may handle ethically or unethically. For example, news shows on NBC and MSNBC, which are owned by General Electric (GE), ethically should disclose GE's financial interests as a major military/government contractor, but they don't.

Media owners control the work of journalists and "have enforced their political views and other preferences by installing senior editors whose careers depend on delivering a news product that fits with the owner's prejudices."[15] Stories and images that don't fit their needs may not be published and journalists who don't meet their needs may be reassigned or dismissed. Independent journalists often face similar pressures because they must find media willing to publish their stories. Print journalists and editors have been fired, *Politically Incorrect* was cancelled (allegedly because ads were withdrawn),[16] and the Donahue show was cancelled for "low ratings" when its ratings were highest.[17] A leaked report claimed Donahue presented a "difficult public face for NBC in a time of war…He seems to delight in presenting guests who are anti-war, anti-Bush and skeptical of the administration's motives" and his show may become "a home for the liberal antiwar agenda at the same time that our competitors are waving the flag at every opportunity."[18]

Critics in media watchdog and reform groups, such as *Fairness and Accuracy in Reporting* and *Free Press*, argue that many media problems, including risk-avoidance and homogeneity of content, result from deregulation, which enabled the consolidation of news media into a handful of corporate owners.[19] For some owners, such as CBS owner Viacom, ABC owner Disney, and NBC and MSNBC owner GE, the news business is a relatively small part of the business they conduct, which may lead them to favor broad corporate business interests over journalistic ethics.

Government Influences on Journalists and Media

The standard claim of government is that national security supersedes all other considerations, including freedom of the press, because government's highest obligation is to protect its citizens' lives. Failure to control information gives the advantage to the enemy. Information warfare experts claim, "today's military commanders stand to gain more than ever before from controlling the media and shaping their output"—the press must be used "as an instrument of war."[20] These experts, understanding that news can influence the outcome of individual battles as well as entire wars, have regarded the press as an ally, an adversary, and even a "combatant" (not covered under Geneva Conventions' protections for journalists).[21] One defense department document argued, "Arab hate-media are themselves equivalent to weapons of mass destruction"[22] (which means they can be attacked).

U.S. government control of information during war is neither new nor uncommon. From the early days of the republic, the government has restricted the press during war. For example, in the Civil War, President Lincoln suspended constitutional rights, including the *writ of habeas corpus,* so those who were "disloyal" could be indefinitely detained without trial; and First Amendment freedoms, so telegraph lines could be seized, newspapers closed, reporters barred from battle, and editors arrested.[23]

A prime example of information warfare was CIA funding of the Iraqi National Congress (INC) and the Rendon Group (experts in selling wars) to provide false intelligence verifying Hussein's weapons of mass destruction. In 2001, INC leader Ahmad Chalabi arranged for reporter Judith Miller to go to Thailand to interview Adnan al-Haideri, an Iraqi defector who claimed to have direct knowledge of Hussein's weapons programs. She described Iraq's hidden weapons program in a front-page story. Even though the CIA had discredited al-Haideri's stories, George W. Bush, Colin Powell, and other top administration officials publicly argued their case for attacking Iraq based in part on al-Haideri's fabrications. In 2004, al-Haideri accompanied the CIA to each location he had claimed was a weapons site, but he failed to locate any evidence.[24]

An example of how state security interests may conflict with the public's right to know occurred in 2004 when CBS News yielded to government pressure by delaying their exclusive *60 Minutes* report of the murder and torture of prisoners by U.S. personnel at Abu Ghraib prison in Iraq.[25] The request was based upon concerns that public knowledge of the abhorrent conduct could endanger U.S. troops and their mission. However, after graphic photographs were anonymously circulated worldwide the military relented, allowing CBS to broadcast their report. To this day, the government has refused to release additional photographs and all of the videos taken in Abu Ghraib.

However, military influence was not the only factor that delayed news about Abu Ghraib. Another factor may have been media self-censorship: some journalists had heard about the torture for at least a year before *60 Minutes*, but most did not investigate. On November 1, 2003, journalist Charles Hanley working for "the Associated Press was among the first to raise alarms about abuse at Abu Ghraib—but few of the AP's clients showcased the story, if they ran it at all."[26] Also, journalists repeatedly received credible information about prisoner torture in Afghanistan and Guantánamo from respected human rights organizations beginning two years before the *60 Minutes* report.[27] If the earlier crimes had been reported, could the Abu Ghraib crimes have been prevented? Why did the media showcase claims about Iraq's alleged weapons that the CIA had discredited, and give negligible coverage to continuing allegations of torture made by respected human rights organizations?

Additional methods of information warfare employed by the U.S. government include:

- Planting propaganda stories overseas, knowing they would make their way back into U.S. news reports, as happened in the INC-Rendon-al-Haideri case.
- Running covert campaigns to discredit persons who challenged administration views, as when the Bush administration illegally leaked classified information identifying Valerie Plame as a CIA agent in order to discredit her husband, former U.S. ambassador Joseph Wilson, who had investigated and then publicly disputed Bush's claim that Hussein tried to buy enriched yellowcake uranium from Niger.[28]

- Making false statements, as in a study by the Center for Public Integrity, which found that "President George W. Bush and seven of his administration's top officials...made at least 935 false statements in the two years following September 11, 2001, about the national security threat posed by Saddam Hussein's Iraq."[29] These falsehoods contributed to the "campaign that...led the nation to war under decidedly false pretenses."
- Prohibiting press access to specific areas, such as prisons, secret rendition sites, battlefields, and cities under siege (as during the Second Battle of Fallujah).[30]
- Embedding press in military units[31] to build rapport with the troops and to limit coverage to approved areas.
- Holding press conferences and news briefings to keep control of a story.[32]
- Recruiting, briefing, and then feeding talking points to news consultants, as in the Pentagon's covert military analysts' program, which after years of use was exposed in David Barstow's Pulitzer Prize–winning investigation.[33] Barstow stated, "Most of the analysts have ties to military contractors vested in the very war policies they are asked to assess on air."[34] Other than Barstow's employer, neither his investigation nor the reasons he won the Pulitzer received much coverage and television news continues to use the analysts without disclosing their conflicting interests.[35]
- Applying sanctions against or closing unsympathetic Middle East media.[36]
- Possibly targeting of press and media for attacks.[37]
- Speeding the kill: complete military missions rapidly—before media can respond—as illustrated in the two battles of Fallujah. "The hostile global media, led by al-Jazeera, won the First Battle of Fallujah" because the Marines used "deliberate urban operations [to avoid high civilian casualties], which gave the media time to muster world opinion against us and break the nerve of key leaders." "We won the Second Battle of Fallujah because we used overwhelming force, we didn't shirk from doing what was necessary [obliterating the city]—and we did it fast."[38] Journalists were prohibited during the second battle.

Are All Casualties Equal?

Not everyone who bleeds receives the same coverage. Public understanding of a war is affected by which casualties make the news and which do not. Decisions about who gets covered may depend upon factors such as geography, national interests, race, culture, religion, and economics. Violence receives major coverage in some locations, but not in others (such as least developed countries). For example, in the U.S. wars in Afghanistan, Iraq, and Pakistan, civilian casualties and refugees number in the millions, but receive significantly less coverage than the few thousands of U.S. casualties.

In contrast to the nearly constant coverage of victims of nonstate terrorists, victims of state-sponsored attacks receive scant coverage. For example, the "Shock and Awe" attack on Iraq in 2003, which had the stated objective "to frighten, scare, intimidate, and disarm,"[39] was enthusiastically and uncritically promoted in the U.S. press for months. During one news report, a Pentagon official bragged, "there will not be a safe place in Baghdad," while Harlan Ullman, an author of the plan, noted, "You also take the city down. By that I mean you get rid of their power, water."[40]

Given the U.S. government's intent to inflict terror on the residents of a densely populated city of over 5 million people and to destroy their power and water systems, "Shock and Awe" could serve as a textbook example of state-sponsored terrorism. Instead, U.S. television coverage repeatedly portrayed the massive bomb and missile attacks as a spectacular fireworks display accompanied by enthusiastic, nationalistic commentary and unsubstantiated reassurances that precision weapons would kill the Iraqi leaders while sparing civilians, claims seldom questioned in their coverage. Mainstream news did not say much about the more than 6,600 civilians killed in the first days of "Shock and Awe."[41] And in their flood of interviews with military experts speculating on how the war would proceed, they omitted International Law experts who might have challenged "Shock and Awe" as war crimes under the Geneva Conventions, which prohibit destruction of power, water, food, farms, livestock, irrigation, and all infrastructure that are "indispensable to the survival of the civilian population."[42]

The limited coverage of U.S.-caused civilian deaths in Afghanistan, Iraq, Somalia, Yemen, and Pakistan shields from scrutiny the administration's myth of American exceptionalism, which characterizes Americans as exceptional people who don't kill in cold blood or commit war crimes. In contrast, this myth is challenged by foreign and independent U.S. media, which have reported extensively on civilian victims of U.S. troops and air war. For example, 50 combat veterans described widespread misconduct and crimes, directives to cover-up killings, and "rules of engagement" that hampered discrimination of civilians from combatants.[43] When Arab media show civilian victims,

U.S. leaders claim only combatants were killed and criticize the reports as anti-American propaganda. For example, after one incident, Secretary of Defense Donald Rumsfeld insisted, "I can definitely say that what Al Jazeera is doing is vicious, inaccurate and inexcusable." Our troops "don't go around killing hundreds of civilians. That's just outrageous nonsense."[44] Administration officials did not comment on the report by civilian hospital officials that of 600 Iraqis killed in that battle, "more than half of the dead are women and children."[45]

Destroying and rebuilding countries also has been costly in dollars. However, the press has given little attention to how the high costs of the war on terrorism have damaged the U.S. economy while war-related businesses continue to make record-breaking profits. Recent news coverage of the proposed 2011 budget has focused on deficit reduction that targets entitlements such as social services, Social Security, and Medicare, while mostly ignoring military spending, which has doubled in the last ten years and now accounts for half of the discretionary budget.[46]

WIKILEAKS AND THE PRICE OF SECRECY

The world is in the middle of dramatic changes in the way news is gathered, reported, and published. Catalysts include the growth in communications technology and the loss of trust in traditional news media. A 2010 Gallup Poll reported that only 25 percent of those polled expressed confidence in either newspapers or television news.[47] Recent democratic uprisings in the Middle East exemplify how the public is using electronic communication to distribute news. One surprising result is that the Obama administration seems to be rethinking Al-Jazeera's contributions to democracy in the Middle East: Secretary of State Hillary Clinton told a Congressional Committee that the United States was losing the information war:

> Viewership of al Jazeera is going up in the United States because it's real news. You may not agree with it, but you feel like you're getting real news around the clock instead of a million commercials and, you know, arguments between talking heads and the kind of stuff that we do on our news which, you know, is not particularly informative to us, let alone foreigners.[48]

A recent development in the news revolution is *Wikileaks,* which claims to be a "new model for journalism" that functions like an online newswire service from which journalists can access information leaked anonymously. *Wikileaks* was founded in 2007 in response to the "media becoming less independent and far less willing to ask the hard questions of government, corporations and other institutions."[49] Its mission is to "publish material of ethical, political and historical significance...thus providing a universal way for the revealing of suppressed and censored injustices."

Information posted on *Wikileaks* includes hundreds of thousands of secret government materials and private corporate communications. One video shows U.S. troops killing twelve unarmed Iraqi civilians, including children and journalists.[50] Responses to *Wikileaks* have included death threats, sabotage, the loss of banking and Internet services, and the arrest of one of its founders, Julian Assange. The alleged source of secret military and government information, Private Bradley Manning, has been in solitary confinement for many months, facing multiple charges, including aiding the enemy (a death penalty offense).[51] It should be noted that war crimes are also punishable by death.

An important ethical consideration in sorting through these issues is the contrast between exaggerated threats and factual historical data. For example, one of the most serious criticisms of *Wikileaks* is that release of secret information might endanger the safety of troops, diplomats, and informants. While this is a possibility, hard evidence has not been presented—claims of potential endangerment usually rely more on the rhetoric of fear than tangible evidence. The Vietnam War is replete with examples of military and government leaders, including the president, claiming dire threats and promoting noble missions while repeatedly lying to the public and Congress, as was revealed when secret documents were made public in *The Pentagon Papers*. The human costs for the rhetoric and secrecy the government used to falsely justify waging that war included the deaths of 58,000 Americans[52] and at least part of the estimated 1.3 million Vietnamese people killed.[53]. Those human lives lost are not fear-based rhetoric—they are tragic facts.

The secret information released by *Wikileaks* and *The Pentagon Papers* reveal that presidents, their administrations, and military leaders lie to justify wars. Facts are hidden and not relinquished willingly even when legitimate requests for information are made. For example, on October 12, 2001, "in a memo that slipped beneath the political radar, U.S. Attorney General John Ashcroft vigorously urged federal agencies to resist most Freedom of Information Act requests made by American citizens."[54]

During the Vietnam War, the administration argued that in the interest of national security a court injunction prohibiting the *New*

York Times from publishing the stolen classified documents known as *The Pentagon Papers* should be allowed to stand. In speaking for the court's majority and rejecting the administration's claims, Supreme Court justices Black and Douglas stated:

> In the First Amendment the Founding Fathers gave the free press the protection it must have to fulfill its essential role in our democracy. The press was to serve the governed, not the governors. The Government's power to censor the press was abolished so that the press would remain forever free to censure the Government. The press was protected so that it could bare the secrets of government and inform the people. Only a free and unrestrained press can effectively expose deception in government. And paramount among the responsibilities of a free press is the duty to prevent any part of the government from deceiving the people and sending them off to distant lands to die of foreign fevers and foreign shot and shell. In my view, far from deserving condemnation for their courageous reporting, the New York Times, the Washington Post, and other newspapers should be commended for serving the purpose that the Founding Fathers saw so clearly. In revealing the workings of government that led to the Vietnam war, the newspapers nobly did precisely that which the Founders hoped and trusted they would do.[55]

The government's claim that the rights of the press could be restricted in the interests of national security also were rejected:

> The word "security" is a broad, vague generality whose contours should not be invoked to abrogate the fundamental law embodied in the First Amendment. The guarding of military and diplomatic secrets at the expense of informed representative government provides no real security for our Republic. The Framers of the First Amendment, fully aware of both the need to defend a new nation and the abuses of the English and Colonial governments, sought to give this new society strength and security by providing that freedom of speech, press, religion, and assembly should not be abridged.[56]

CONCLUSION

The opinion of Justices Black and Douglas in *The Pentagon Papers Case* reaffirms the importance of the press to the health of the nation and lays out the moral and Constitutional Law basis for a press kept free from government influence. Likewise, the profession of journalism asserts that the core ethical obligation for journalists is to be guided by a fierce loyalty to the people's right to information. Justices

Black and Douglas clearly believed that receiving and publishing stolen secret government documents in hopes of stopping a dishonest war was a perfect example of how the founders intended the press to function.

I have presented examples where conflicting interests have influenced the mainstream press and media. News programming that has a pro-government bias and is "not particularly informative"[57] cannot serve the best interests of any nation. As the traditional press continues to flounder in its misplaced loyalties, one source of hope is that new strategies and organizations will arise and fulfill the nation's need for "real news." If traditional journalism is to survive, it must recover its mission and assert its integrity in the face of conflicting interests. However, the best hopes for democratic government and a more peaceful world may emerge from new forms of journalism, such as *Wikileaks*.

> Paramount among the responsibilities of a free press is the duty to prevent any part of the government from deceiving the people and sending them off to distant lands to die.[58]

NOTES

1. "Journalism" and "press" are used as synonymous and inclusive of all forms of U.S. news and journalistic work, i.e., print, broadcast, Internet, and documentary reporters, photographers, videographers, and related production staff. However, owners of news media organizations ("media") are not included, as some of their interests and priorities may differ significantly from those of the press. Criticisms of press and media in this chapter point to general trends. Many notable exceptions in mainstream reporting meet high ethical standards, as in the reports on Abu Ghraib by Charles Hanley in the *Associated Press* and *60 Minutes* and in David Barstow's *New York Times* report on the Pentagon's covert military analysts.
2. Society of Professional Journalists. *Code of Ethics.* 2010 (http://www.spj.org/ethicscode.asp).
3. William J. Hawk, "Pacifism: Reclaiming the Moral Presumption," In *Ethics in Practice,* ed. Hugh LaFollette 3rd ed. (Hoboken, NJ: Wiley-Blackwell, 2006), 735.
4. Sheldon Rampton, "Pentagon Pundit Scandal Broke the Law," *PR Watch,* April 28, 2008 (http://www.prwatch.org/node/7261).
5. George W. Bush, "Statement by the President in his Address to the Nation," The White House. September 11, 2001.
6. J. Colombani, "Nous Sommes Tous Américains," *Le Monde,* September 13, 2001.
7. Dan Rather, *The Late Show with David Letterman,* September 17, 2001.

8. "In Iraq Crisis, Networks are Megaphones for Official Views," Fairness and Accuracy in Reporting, March 18, 2003 (http://www.fair.org).

9. "Study Finds Lack of Balance, Diversity, Public at PBS NewsHour," Fairness and Accuracy in Reporting, October 4, 2006 (http://www.fair.org).

10. Ibid.

11. For example, Norman Solomon, Chris Hedges, Robert W. McChesney, Bill Moyers, Amy Goodman, Danny Schechter, and Glenn Greenwald.

12. Dan Rather, "Dan Rather Slams Corporate News at National Conference for Media Reform," *Free Press.* June 8, 2008 (http://www.freepress.net/node/41471).

13. Susan D. Moeller, *Media Coverage of Weapons of Mass Destruction.* Center for International and Security Studies at Maryland. March 9, 2004. 12–14.

14. See, e.g., the award-winning documentary film by Molly Bingham and Steve Conors in which they interview insurgents in Iraq: *Meeting Resistance* (2007) (http://www.meetingresistance.com/trailer.html).

15. Robert Parry, "The Price of the 'Liberal Media' Myth," *ConsortiumNews.com,* January 1, 2003 (http://www.consortiumnews.com/2002/123102a.html).

16. Peter Hart and Seth Ackerman, "Patriotism and Censorship," *Fairness and Accuracy in Reporting,* November/December 2001 (http://www.fair.org/index.php?page=1089).

17. Rick Ellis, "The Surrender of MSNBC," *Allyourtv.com,* February 25, 2003 (http://www.allyourtv.com/index.php?option=com_content&view=article&id=259:surrendermsnbc&catid=78:featurescoveringmedia).

18. Ibid.

19. *FreePress.Net* (http://www.freepress.net/media_issues/consolidation).

20. Kenneth Payne, "The Media as an Instrument of War," *Parameters,* (Spring 2005): 81–93.

21. Ibid.

22. U.S. Department of Defense, "White Paper: 'Rapid Reaction Media Team' Concept," *The National Security Archive,* January 16, 2003 (http://www.gwu.edu/~nsarchiv/NSAEBB/NSAEBB219/index.htm).

23. Ronald K. L. Collins, "Civil War Tested Lincoln's Tolerance for Free Speech, Press," *First Amendment Center,* February 11, 2009 (http://www.firstamendmentcenter.org/analysis.aspx?id=21225).

24. James Bamford, "The Man Who Sold the War: Meet John Rendon, Bush's General in the Propaganda War," *Rolling Stone,* November 17, 2005.

25. Rebecca Leung, "Abuse At Abu Ghraib: Dan Rather has Details of One Man Who Died in the Custody of Americans," *60 Minutes,* May 5, 2004 (http://www.cbsnews.com/stories/2004/05/05/60II/main615781.shtml).

26. Sherry Ricchiardi, "Missed Signals," *American Journalism Review,* August/September 2004 9http://www.ajr.org/article.asp?id=3716).

27. Ibid.
28. Barton Gellman and Dafna Linzer, "A'Concerted Effort' to Discredit Bush Critic," *Washington Post,* April 9, 2006 (http://www.washingtonpost.com/wp-dyn/content/article/2006/04/08/AR2006040800916_pf.html).
29. Charles Lewis and Mark Reading-Smith, "Overview: False Pretenses," *The War Card: Orchestrated Deception on the Path to War,* January 23, 2008 (http://projects.publicintegrity.org/WarCard/?gclid=CI3y-bHuyacCFQli2godyz5jDg).
30. Payne, "The Media as an Instrument of War," 86.
31. Ibid., 86–87.
32. Ibid., 87–88; Josh Rushing and Sean Elder, *Mission Al Jazeera* (New York: Palgrave Macmillan, 2007).
33. Sheldon Rampton, "Pentagon Pundit Scandal Broke the Law," *PR Watch,* April 28, 2008 (http://www.prwatch.org/node/7261).
34. David Barstow, "Behind TV Analysts, Pentagon's Hidden Hand," *New York Times,* April 20, 2008 (http://www.nytimes.com/2008/04/20/us/20generals.html?_r=1&ex=1366689600&en=eefc8e0bdd6ffc91&ei=5124&partner=permalink&exprod=permalink).
35. Glenn Greenwald, "The Pulitzer-Winning Investigation that Dare Not Be Uttered on TV," *Salon.com,* April 21, 2009 (http://www.salon.com/news/opinion/glenn_greenwald/2009/04/21/pulitzer).
36. Jacqueline E. Sharkey, "Al Jazeera Under the Gun," *American Journalism Review,* October/November 2004 (http://www.ajr.org/article.asp?id=3760).
37. Payne, "The Media as an Instrument of War," 89–92.
38. Ralph Peters, "A Grave New World: 10 Lessons from the War in Iraq," *San Diego Union-Tribune,* April 17, 2005 (http://www.signonsandiego.com/uniontrib/20050417/news_mz1e17peters.html).
39. Harlan Ullman et al., *Shock and Awe: Achieving Rapid Dominance,* Defense Group Inc., 1996, 34 (http://www.dodccrp.org/files/Ullman_Shock.pdf).
40. "Iraq Faces Massive U.S. Missile Barrage," *CBS News,* January 24, 2003 (http://www.cbsnews.com/stories/2003/01/24/eveningnews/main537928.shtml).
41. *A Dossier of Civilian Casualties 2003–2005.* Iraqbodycount.org(http://www.iraqbodycount.org/analysis/reference/pdf/a_dossier_of_civilian_casualties_2003-2005.pdf).
42. Protocol Additional to the Geneva Conventions of August 12, 1949, and relating to the Protection of Victims of International Armed Conflicts (Protocol I), June 8. 1977, Part IV: Civilian population, Section I—General protection against effects of hostilities, Chapter III—Civilian objects, Article 54—Protection of objects indispensable to the survival of the civilian population (http://www.icrc.org/eng/war-and-law/treaties-customary-law/geneva-conventions/index.jsp).

43. Chris Hedges and Laila Al-Arian, *Collateral Damage: America's War against Iraqi Civilians* (New York: Nation Books, 2008).

44. "Al Iraqiya Offers Alternative View," *Washington Times,* April 27, 2004 (http://www.washingtontimes.com/news/2004/apr/27/20040427 -105458-3420r/).

45. "Fallujah," Global Security (http://www.globalsecurity.org/military /world/iraq/fallujah.htm).

46. Friends Committee on National Legislation (FCNL), "Ten Reasons Why Congress Should Cut the Pentagon Budget," September 21, 2010(http:// www.fcnl.org/issues/item.php?item_id=4010&issue_id=18).

47. Lymari Morales, "In U.S. Confidence in Newspapers, TV News Remains a Rarity," *Gallup's Confidence in Institutions,* August 13, 2010 (http://www.gallup.com/poll/142133/Confidence-Newspapers -News-Remains-Rarity.aspx).

48. Hillary Clinton, "Clinton: Al Jazeera is Real News," *ABC News,* March 2, 2011 (http://abcnews.go.com/Politics/video/hillary-clinton -al-jazeera-real-news-13042310).

49. "What is *Wikileaks?*" *Wikileaks* (http://www.wikileaks.ch/About .html).

50. "Leaked U.S. Video Shows Deaths of Reuters' Iraqi Staffers," *Reuters,* April 5, 2010 (http://www.reuters.com/article/2010/04/06/us-iraq -usa-journalists-idUSTRE6344FW20100406).

51. "Bradley Manning Faces Death under New Charge of 'Aiding Enemy,'" *Bradley Manning Support Network,* March 2, 2011(http://www .bradleymanning.org/16235/bradley-manning-facing-possible-death -penalty-under-new-charges/#ixzz1FsDshJed).

52. "American War and Military Operations Casualties, Table 7," Navy Department Library, 2005 (http://www.history.navy.mil/library/online /american war casualty.htm).

53. Matthew White, *Necrometrics,* 2011 (http://necrometrics.com/).

54. Ruth Rosen, "The Day Ashcroft Censored Freedom of Information," *San Francisco Chronicle,* January 7, 2002 (http://www.commondreams .org/views02/0108-04.htm).

55. Justice Black and Justice Douglas, "New York Times Co. v. United States (The Pentagon Papers Case)," 403 U.S. 713 (1971).

56. Ibid.

57. Clinton, "Clinton: Al Jazeera is Real News."

58. Justices Black and Douglas.

9

HOME FROM IRAQ: JOURNALIST URGES AMERICANS TO SEARCH FOR TRUTH AND FREEDOM

Molly Bingham

Fellow journalist Steve Connors and I spent ten months in Iraq from August 2003 through June 2004 working on a story. We sought to understand who the people attacking U.S. and other foreign troops are—who is fighting, why do they fight, what are their fundamental beliefs, what kinds of backgrounds are they from, what education and jobs have they had, and so on? Are they former military? Are they Iraqi or foreign? Are they part of al-Qaeda? What we came up with is a story in itself, and one that *Vanity Fair* ran in July 2004 with my text and photographs. Steve Connors shot video of our reporting, turning it into a documentary film that is still waiting to find a home. But the basic point for this discussion is that we both thought it was really journalistically important to understand who it was who was resisting the presence of the foreign troops in Iraq. If you didn't understand that, how could you report what was clearly becoming an "ongoing conflict"? And if you were reading the news in America, or Europe, how could you understand the full context of what was unfolding if what motivates the "other side" of the conflict is not understood, or even discussed?

The process of working on that story has revealed many things to me about my own country. I'd like to share some of them with you.

LESSON ONE

Many journalists in Iraq could not, or would not, check their nationality or their own perspective at the door.

One of the hardest things about working on this story for me personally, and as a journalist, was to set my "American self" and perspective aside. It was an ongoing challenge to listen open-mindedly to a group of people whose foundation of belief is significantly different from mine, and one I found I often strongly disagreed with.

But going to report with a pile of prejudices is no way to do a story justice, or to do it fairly, and that constant necessity to bite my tongue, wipe the smirk off my face, or continue to listen through a racial or religious diatribe was a skill I had to develop. In America, we would never walk in to cover a union problem or political event without seeking to understand the perspectives from both or the many sides of the story. Why should we as journalists not do the same in Iraq?

LESSON TWO

As a society, we seemed to have learned little from our history—even recent history. Just as it was during the lead up to the war in Iraq, questioning our government's decisions and claims and what it seeks to achieve today is criticized as unpatriotic.

Along these lines, the other thing I found difficult was the realization that, while I was out doing what I believe is solid journalism, there were many (journalists and normal folks alike) who would question my patriotism, or wonder how I could even think that hearing and relating the perspective "from the other side" was important.

Certainly, over the last three years I've had to acquire the discipline of overriding my emotional attachment to my country, and remember my sense of human values that transcend frontiers and ethnicity. And with a sense of duty to history, I needed to just get on with reporting the story. My value of human life and rights don't fluctuate depending on which country I'm in. I don't see one individual as more deserving of fair treatment than another.

Now, I realize I'm in Kentucky, a state with many military connections, and there are many of you here who may have served, or have family members who serve, and let me take this moment to say that I have the utmost respect and sympathy for the American soldiers overseas right now, particularly in Iraq. They have been sent on a most difficult mission, to quell a population that will not be quelled, in a land awash with weapons. The American military is being used to find a solution to what is essentially a political problem, an assignment that rarely ends up well. As if that were not enough, our soldiers have been sent with insufficient resources to protect themselves. In my mind, that is all inexcusable.

LESSON THREE

To seek to understand and represent the reasons behind the Iraqi opposition is considered by many Americans as being practically treasonous.

Every one of the people involved in the resistance with whom we spoke held us individually responsible for their security. If something happened to them—never mind that they were legitimate targets for the U.S. military—they would blame us. And they would try to kill us. We soon learned that they had the U.S. bases so well watched that we had to abandon our idea of working on the U.S. side of the story—that is, discovering what the soldiers really thought about who might be attacking them. There were so many journalists working with the American soldiers that we believed that story would be well told. More practically, if we were seen by the Iraqis going in and out of the American bases, we would be tagged immediately as spies, informants, and most likely be killed.

As terrifying as that was to manage and work through, there was another fear that was just as bad. What if the American military or intelligence found out what we were working on? Would they tail us and round up the people we met? Would they kick down our door late one night, rifle through all our stuff, and arrest us for collaborating with the enemy? Bear in mind that there are no real laws in Iraq. At the time that we were working, the American military was the law, and it seemed to me that they were pretty much making it up as they went along. I was pretty sure that if they wanted to "disappear" us, rough us up, or even send us for an all-expenses-paid vacation in Guantánamo for suspected "al-Qaeda connections," they could do so with very little, or even no, recourse on our part.

I could go into a long litany of the ways in which the American military has treated journalists in Iraq. Recent actions indicate that the U.S. military will detain any journalist who happens to be caught covering the Iraqi side of the militant resistance, and indeed any journalist killed while covering the "other side" would be considered by the U.S. military to be the enemy not to just be covering the enemy. This behavior at the moment seems to be limited to journalists who also happen to be Arabs, or Arab-looking, but that is only a tangential story to what I'm telling you about here.

The intimidation to not tell the story of the resistance was evident. Any journalist in Baghdad who revealed to a U.S. military officer that they were planning or had interviewed a member of the "resistance" would have been given a cold shoulder, at best. As Steve and I were leaving Baghdad a writer for a major newspaper told us that he'd become friendly with a U.S. commander, meeting up frequently, and talking beyond the issues and work at hand. Asked during one meeting by the commander to meet again the writer declined saying that he had lined up an interview with a "bad guy" and hence couldn't come. In the writer's retelling, the commander's face changed, turning stony cold upon hearing that and he made a brief comment to the effect that the military "has a position on that." The relationship was not as friendly going forward even though the writer had cancelled the appointment with the "bad guy."

Being treated in a less friendly manner by a commander wasn't so bad. At worst, journalists reporting on the "resistance" could have been denied access to U.S. military briefings, bases, and embeds, something particularly problematic for any journalist requiring access to the biggest institution in town. If you were Arab or Iraqi, you could end up arrested with or without charge and languish in a U.S. or Iraqi prison. The U.S. military actively sought to discourage journalists from telling the story of the resistance by tenor, language, and implication. The impact seemed to be that many journalists just didn't "go there"—or at least didn't try until it was too late and nigh impossible or way too dangerous. They covered U.S. military briefings, did embeds, and covered breaking news stories on the streets.

I'm not telling you this as criticism of the military; they have a war to win, and dominating the "message" or the news is an integral part of that war. The military has a name for it, "information operations," and the aim is to achieve information superiority in the same way they would seek to achieve air superiority. If you look closely, you will notice there is very little, maybe even no direct reporting on the resistance in Iraq. We do, however, as journalists report what the Americans say about the resistance. Is this really anything more than stenography?

And many American journalists often refer to those attacking Americans or Iraqi troops and policemen as "terrorists." Some are indeed using terrorist tactics, but calling them "terrorists" simply shuts down any sense of need or interest to look beyond that word, to understand why human beings might be willing to die in a violent struggle to achieve their goal. Pushing them off as simply "insane, wild Arabs" or "extremist Muslims" does them no service, but even more, it does the United States no service. If we as Americans fail to understand who attacks us and why, we will simply continue on this same path, and continue watching from afar as a war we don't understand boils over.

LESSON FOUR

The gatekeepers—by which I mean the editors, publishers, and business sides of the media—don't want their paper or their outlet to reveal the compelling narrative of why anyone would oppose the presence of American troops on their soil. Why would anyone refuse democracy? Why would anyone not want the helping hand of America in overthrowing their terrible dictator? It's amazing to me how expeditiously we turn away from our own history. Think of our revolution. Think of our founding fathers. Think of what they stood for and hoped for. Think of how, over time, we have learned to improve on our own Constitution and governance. But think, mostly, about the words I just used: It was *our* decision and *our* determination that brought us where we are now.

Recall Patrick Henry's famous speech, encouraging the Second Virginia Convention gathered on March 20, 1775, to fight the British, "Give me liberty or give me death!" Why is it that we, as Americans, presume that any Iraqi would feel any differently? If the roles were reversed, do you think for a moment that our men wouldn't be stockpiling arms and attacking any foreign invader with the temerity to set foot on our soil, occupy our buildings of government, and write us a new constitution?

Wouldn't we as women be joining with them in any way we could? Wouldn't the divisions between us—how we feel about President Bush, whether we're Republican or Democrat—be put aside as we resisted a common enemy?

Then why is it that this story of human effort for self-determination by violent means cannot be told in America? Are we so small, so confused by our own values that we cannot recognize when someone emulates our own struggle? Even if it is the United States that they are struggling against? I want to be careful to explain that I am not saying that the Iraqis fighting against us are necessarily fighting for *democracy*, but they are fighting for the right to decide for themselves what their nation looks like politically.

LESSON FIVE

What it's like to be afraid of your own country.

Once the story for *Vanity Fair* was finished and set to come out on the street, I was rushing back to the United States—mostly because we could no longer work once the story was published—and I found I was scared returning to my own country. And that was an amazingly strange and awful feeling to have. Again, you could call me paranoid, but the questions about what might happen to me once in America—where at least I would have more rights—kept racing through my brain. I'm still here, so you could say that my frantic mental gymnastics about what could happen to me in my own country were paranoid anxieties.

But I would turn that question around.

How many other American journalists, perhaps not as secure in their position as I, have thought to do a story and decided that it's too close to the bone, too questioning of the American government or its actions? How many times was the risk that our own government might come in and rifle through our apartment, our homes, or take us away for questioning in front of our children a factor in our decision not to do a story? How many times did we as journalists decide *not* to do a story because we thought it might get us into trouble? Or, as likely, how often did the editor above us kill the story for the same reasons? Lots of column inches have been spent in the discussion of how our rights as Americans are being surreptitiously confiscated, but what about our complicity, as journalists, in that? It seems to me that the assault on free speech, while fear and intimidation are in the air, comes as much from us—as individuals and networks of journalists who censor ourselves—as it does from any other source.

We need to wake up as individuals and as a community of journalists and start asking the hard and scary questions. Questions we may not really want to know the answers to about ourselves, about our government, about what is being done in our name, and hold the responsible individuals accountable through due process in our legal or electoral system.

We need to begin to be able to look again at our government, our leadership, and ourselves critically. That is what the Fourth Estate is all about. That's what American journalism can do at its zenith. I also happen to believe that, in fact, that is the highest form of patriotism—expecting our country to live up to the promises it makes and the values it purports to hold. The role of the media in assisting the public to ensure those values are reflected in reality is undeniably failing today.

Go ahead, take a hard look in the mirror, ask the questions—if there is something in our nation that needs repair or change, that is how it will get done, by asking those questions, getting answers, and reporting them.

We still have the freedom in this country as individuals and as journalists to defend the rights enshrined in the Constitution, to defend the values that we as individuals still hold dear—so why aren't we doing it? Are we scared? If we're scared, then who will be there to defend those rights and values when it is proposed that they be taken away?

I still believe in that country that I love so dearly, the place I think of when the words "freedom," "opportunity," "liberty," "justice," and "equality" are spoken on lips, but I want it to be a country I see, hear, and feel every day, not one that lives in my imagination.

It's time we looked in the mirror and began to take responsibility for what our country looks like, what our country is and how it behaves, rather than acting like victims before we actually are.

Or do I need to start facing the reality that all I love and believe in is simply self-delusion?

ADDENDUM: AUGUST 2010

Five years have passed since I delivered this speech at Western Kentucky University and it was published in the *Courier-Journal*. Since then, Steve Connors and I have completed the documentary *Meeting Resistance,* which reveals what we found during our reporting in Iraq. The film has won awards at festivals around the world, played to veterans from the Iraq and Afghan wars, for peace activist organizations in the United States, general audiences in theaters, community centers as well as universities, and, most interestingly for us, to active duty military and diplomatic audiences in the United States and in Baghdad. Steve and I spent almost eighteen months traveling with the film, doing hour-long Q&As after almost every screening.

Here is what we've learned since I delivered the speech in 2005.

One of the most important things I've learned, as simple as it sounds, is the critical importance of language. Components within the U.S. government, The White House, State Department, and Defense Department most notably, participated in a deft and understandable rush to "name" the aspects of the conflict in Iraq. By early on defining the terminology used to describe the conflict the U.S. government ensured that their language dominated the conversation. Mainstream media carried, and repeated many times over, the language used by government officials on and off the record to describe events and people in Iraq. As a result, the American public perceived the conflict in the terms and language that had been defined and utilized by the U.S. government—rather than in accurate language that would describe the conflict as revealed by on-the-ground reporting.

Hence, the word "resistance" only rarely appeared in any mainstream media to describe the violence in Iraq. The resistance to occupation and the civil war—fundamentally two separate conflicts—have been lumped into one inaccurate term, which was used early on by government officials and adopted by everyone: that term is "insurgency."

An "insurgency" is widely defined as an uprising, usually internal, against a constituted government. Iraq didn't have an elected government until 2005 and many would argue that an election conducted under foreign occupation is illegitimate. Hence, the use of the term in 2003 and 2004 is simply inaccurate, even if the Iraqi government is accepted as legitimate in 2005. But more importantly for our conversations—it was inaccurate because no one was trying to overthrow any government. I will explain this in depth later, but fundamentally there was a resistance to the occupation of the country and there was (from 2004 on) a civil war. Yet the use of the word "insurgency" has reigned supreme in descriptions of all kinds of violence, lumping it into an inscrutable (for the U.S. media-consuming public) mess. And seemingly, by intent.

This is clearly not an entirely new phenomenon. Tag words such as "D-Day," "Vietnamization," and others were created to have the same effect. The differences lie in the fact that so *much* of the terminology was driven by specific language chosen and used by U.S. officials and that the war itself was so brazenly initiated on trumped up, or even false, information. The third difference—perhaps not so different from World War II, but important—is the extent to which the mainstream media played along with the game, rarely challenging any of the core implications of those word choices. Repeating them. And by repeating them, building a narrative of the conflict that was fundamentally built in a U.S. government public relations office rather than by events reported and explored on the ground.

Since so much of our critique of the realities in Iraq raise the issue of the role played by the mainstream media, Steve and I almost always end up pointing out that we have spent our careers in that same mainstream media. Steve worked for twenty years for outlets such as *Newsweek*, *Stern*, and British newspapers including the *Guardian* and *Observer*. I have, in my turn, worked for many U.S. and U.K. dailies, the *New York Times*, the *Houston Chronicle*, the *Guardian*, or *Telegraph*, newsweeklies, *Newsweek*, and *U.S. News*, as well as *Sports Illustrated* and *People Magazine*. We are not people who have spent our careers at "alternative" news outlets. And we are talking about our peers, people we have worked with and often like, but whose reporting decisions we fail to understand when it comes to Iraq.

Following are the main issues Steve and I have consistently addressed in our Q&As as we traveled with the film.

We often spend time at the beginning of a Q&A unraveling what the audience "thinks" it knows about the Iraq conflict—learned from consuming mainstream media—a deconstruction that is critical to having an accurate discussion of the conflict. Redefining the term "insurgency" and explaining events in the context of a civil war and resistance to occupation is the most important step. Once accurate language can be used to describe events a completely different conversation of the conflict is possible.

We introduce the concept that there is not one war in Iraq; there are at least two wars. The first is a resistance to occupation, and the second is a civil war. The civil war is a fight between two competing visions of Iraq's political future. One vision is fundamentally "nationalist," embracing the concept of Iraq as one nation, with a strong, unified central government and, most important, the collective public ownership of Iraq's natural resources. The competing vision for Iraq's future seeks a "federalized" or "partitioned" Iraq, with strong regional governments, a weak or nonexistent central government, areas of the country divided along sectarian and ethnic lines, and privatized natural resources. This "partitionist" vision has also been the vision most favored by the U.S. government.

There are Sunni and Shia on both sides of that fight, so describing a "sectarian civil war," a phrase that has been used by government officials and repeated regularly in the media, is inaccurate. Without a doubt, Sunni on Shia violence occurs, as does Shia on Sunni. But when there is also Shia on Shia violence and Sunni on Sunni violence as aspects of the society split depending on where they see Iraq's future—as partitioned or as one nation—then explaining a civil war as "sectarian" becomes wholly inaccurate and misleading. Describing the civil war as "sectarian" has the added benefit—for the U.S. government trying to maintain U.S. public support for the conflict—of building a narrative in which the U.S. military is in Iraq on an honorable mission, standing between two warring and irreconcilable forces, and that the very survival of the Iraqi population depends upon our presence. Built on language and terminology that are not accurate, that narrative is inaccurate as well.

The resistance to occupation is a grassroots, indigenous, classic resistance to occupation. For our discussion here the key is to understand that the resistance as a whole represents, and has the support of, the broad Iraqi public. Polling data of Iraqis since 2003 has shown that by overwhelming numbers Iraqis living outside Kurdistan want foreign troops to leave their soil, even if they have concerns about what will happen afterward.[1] Polling also shows that Iraqis want one, unified nation—not a divided or partitioned state.[2] The broadest segments of the society support Iraqis fighting to evict foreign troops from Iraqi soil in order to create a political space in which Iraqis can determine their political future. We call this the "first war" because it also contains the majority of the violence in Iraq, though not the majority of its deaths. U.S. military quarterly reports to Congress have between 2003 and 2008 revealed that 73 percent of significant attacks (those are attacks that require planning and resources) in Iraq target U.S.-led coalition forces—the occupation. The same reports show that 13 percent of attacks target Iraqi army and police forces, which some resistance groups (and Iraqis) see as collaborators and hence legitimate targets of the resistance. And 14 percent of attacks target civilians.[3]

We have drawn the following conclusions from those statistics. First, it cannot be denied that the overwhelming amount of violent energy—86 percent—targets the foreign troops in Iraq and their perceived (rightly or wrongly) collaborators. Second, the violence that targets Iraqi civilians is actually only a fraction of the total number of violent attacks, though understandably more individuals die in them since civilians—unlike U.S. military and Iraqi police—are physically unprotected. However, U.S. government talking points and the mainstream media's representation of the conflict would imply that the number of attacks is the exact inversion—that the majority of violent energy goes toward killing civilians while the minority are those who seek to dislodge the American troops from Iraqi soil.

In the history of warfare, no resistance to occupation has ever survived by attacking its own support base. Iraqi resistance groups have publicly and broadly condemned unequivocally any attacks against civilians—a fact that is little covered in the U.S. media. A clandestine resistance, such as the one in Iraq, absolutely requires the complicity and support of the community around it. Otherwise it can neither function, survive, nor even hope to succeed.

The reasonable question then is this: Who is attacking the civilians? The answer is that those engaged in the civil war, the second war, are attacking and killing civilians by targeted assassination, by bombs placed in markets, and other devices devised to separate and divide a society whose natural inclination is toward nationhood—whose identity is "Iraqi."

At this point, we were inevitably asked, "but hasn't the surge been successful? Violence is down." The "surge" and reworking of the counterinsurgency or "COIN" manual were the beneficiaries of fabulous public relations. If Iraq is in a political civil war, and as the occupying army you face a resistance to your presence—why would you apply a counterinsurgency strategy to that problem? Unless you had already defined the problem for the American public as an "insurgency" and hence were pinned into solving the problem you had publicly named inaccurately. Using COIN for resistance and civil war is like rushing to repair a leaky dam by whacking it with a sledgehammer.

When you recognize that the people attacking U.S. troops are neither fringe elements of society, nor unpopular, the entire premise becomes a bit strange, even Orwellian. "Clear, hold and build"— the main premise of the U.S. counterinsurgency policy—is dramatically flawed when viewed within the information presented here. "Clearing" may indeed be clearing an area of people who are attacking the U.S. military—but they are the people who live there, they are part of the community, and they will only come back. Or, since some of the resistance fighters we met do attacks in neighborhoods and villages *other* than the ones they live in, by "clearing the area" the U.S. military is collectively punishing the population for something they didn't do. All you have done by "clearing" the area is upset the population further, giving them further justification for violence and maybe temporarily disrupting their cell and communications structures.

The COIN manual itself defines insurgency, and resistance, but I have yet to hear anyone in the U.S. military address the issue that their policy is in direct contradiction to the reality revealed by statistics from Iraq. COIN practices, largely designed to divide and conquer, inappropriately applied as they have been here to a resistance, have done more to divide Iraq and inflame the civil war than calm or stabilize the country.

At the seven-year point in this war, the terminology of the conflict has been defined by the U.S. government. The public has consumed and accepted it. The mainstream media has failed to successfully challenge or redefine it and hence the conflict fundamentally continues on the terms the government proposes with little effective objection from the U.S. public.

Violence has indeed dropped since its height—and blessedly for most Iraqis. But the violence was also at its height at the *height* of the surge, meaning, when there were the most U.S. troops on the ground in Iraq conducting operations in May and June of 2007.[4] The drop in violence wasn't due to the success of the surge alone but more likely due to the general withdrawal of U.S. troops from the streets of Iraq and several other factors that coincided with the drawdown,[5] including the Sunni Awakening movement and Moqtadr Sadr's forces' observation of a voluntary peace. It is interesting to note that between 2003 and 2008, whether violence in Iraq was up or down, the percentages of attacks targeting occupation forces or civilians remained largely the same.

The Obama administration has carried on the use of the same terminology and yet by pulling U.S. forces back from the streets and out of the country is seeing a continued decrease in the violence. The terminology of "withdrawal" as applied by the Obama administration seeks to relegate the problems of having misnamed the conflict in the first place to the dustbin of history. The August 31, 2010, U.S. "withdrawal of combat forces" deadline is a consistent twist of language regarding Iraq. Those troops who are staying will be prepared to engage in combat as necessary and as called on. In addition, the vast size of the U.S. embassy compound in Baghdad will require significant troop presence (some have estimated at least 30,000 U.S. troops) long into the future just to keep it secure. Iraqis will still see the U.S. troop presence in Iraq as significant. No matter what the U.S. government calls it.

The last topic we usually touch on in our Q&As is the issue of "information warfare" or the "information battlespace"—places where this war is being fought as aggressively as it is on the ground by the U.S. military. If we return to the issue of language and the use of it in the conflict, some of the earliest words coming out of the U.S. government to describe those who were attacking U.S. soldiers were "dead-enders," "Ba'athi diehards," "common criminals," "al-Qaeda," "foreign fighters," and "religious extremists." All of these terms had the effect of indicating to the U.S. public that it was not "normal" Iraqis who opposed our presence or were committing violence, but it was "fringe elements" of Iraqi society that most Iraqis wouldn't interact with. While those descriptions may not be entirely wrong—there are certainly some criminal elements, some people who have extreme religious views in our perspective, and others who may have been Ba'ath party members—but the overarching implication of the language is misleading and inaccurate.

From the beginning, by manipulating the language to describe events in Iraq, the U.S. government took ownership of how the war would be perceived by the U.S. public. The mainstream media did little to question or present counterarguments regarding the narrative the government was constructing. The words used to describe those attacking U.S. forces had another misleading implication: If it is simply "fringe elements" of Iraqi society that oppose our presence in Iraq then (i) the majority of Iraqis want us there, (ii) those fringe elements can be successfully isolated from the wider community, and (iii) the fringe elements can be "eliminated" or killed, taking care of the problem and delivering a peaceful society to the Iraqis. America can be the hero. Most Americans share the aspiration of delivering a peaceful society to the Iraqis. So, building that narrative further encourages the American public to "stay onboard" and support the war.

At the end of our Q&A sessions many people ask us why the information we discuss isn't more broadly available or represented in the press and where they can glean such knowledge and insight. Our website has a list of the blogs that Steve reads regularly to keep abreast of events in Iraq. Yet we also believe that there is rarely a replacement for having spent fourteen months on the ground in Iraq and that our time there informs our reading of everything we come across. Steve likes to add that if we as westerners were less dismissive of local media in the Middle East, we could easily find these topics being covered and discussed from significantly different angles.

Finally, I would like to add that many people who have heard or read the speech I gave in 2005 ask me whether Steve and I think we were right to be so "paranoid" about our safety. Yes, we were right to be paranoid. This has been demonstrated in the intervening years as more information comes out about the U.S. use of extraordinary rendition; detention without trial and treatment of journalists in Iraq; and the 2008 revelation that the NSA was eavesdropping on personal calls by journalists, aid workers, and others who were in Iraq in 2003 and 2004. Some of our fears were justified, and I am simultaneously very happy that none of them have been realized. Perhaps that gives me some hope that while challenging the dominant narrative may not make you popular in the United States, for an American journalist it is not yet apparently fatal. Indeed, there is still a demand in America for real journalism that can tell us uncomfortable truths, something only fearless reporting can ultimately provide.

NOTES

Originally published May 9, 2005, by the *Courier-Journal* of Louisville, KY. This article is adapted from a plenary speech given by photojournalist Molly Bingham at Western Kentucky University's "First Amendment First" Celebration in Bowling Greens, Kentucky on April 21, 2005.

1. Amit R. Payley, *Washington Post*, "Most Iraqis Favor Immediate U.S. Pullout, Polls Show: Leaders' Views Out of Step With Public." September 27, 2006 (http://www.washingtonpost.com/wp-dyn/content/article/2006/09/26/AR2006092601721_pf.html) and "Iraq Poll September 2007: In Graphics," *BBC News,* May 10, 2007 (http://www.washingtonpost.com/wp-dyn/content/article/2006/09/26/AR2006092601721_pf.html). Note specifically the overwhelming response of Iraqis to two questions: "How long do you think U.S. and other Coalition forces should remain in Iraq?" and answers in the "Is Violence Justified?" section.

2. See "Where Things Stand" polling report by ABCnews/BBC/NHK, released September 10, 2007; and *ABCnews* analysis, "Iraqi's Own Surge Assessment: Few See Security Gains," by Gary Langer September 10, 2007. Of particular attention for our discussion, download the PDF of the polling data by clicking "Click here for full report with charts and questionnaire" on this page: http://abcnews.go.com/US/story?id=3571504&page=1; look at the polling responses on p. 9, "Presence of Coalition Forces in Iraq." On p. 30 you can see the responses to "Do you think the separation of people on sectarian lines is a good thing or a bad thing for Iraq?" Across the board, 98 percent of Iraqi Arabs responded that it is a "bad thing," while 95 percent of Kurds agreed.

3. Note the estimation of attacks broken down in this way stops in 2008 because the U.S. Department of Defense changed the way it reported numbers. Continuing to break it out in this way was no longer possible. For a look at the statistics, visit a copy of the last chart showing the previous five years and comments by Steve at: http://www.meetingresistance.com/DoDgraph.html.

4. See the Department of Defense violence chart on the *Meeting Resistance* site: http://www.meetingresistance.com/DoDgraph.html.

5. Yochi J. Dreazen, "Officer Questions Petraeus's Strategy," *The Wall Street Journal,* April 7, 2008. See par. 13 and Col. Steve Boylan's (General Petraeus's spokesman) comments there: "The surge was definitely a factor. It wasn't the only factor, but it was a key component" (http://online.wsj.com/article/NA_WSJ_PUB:SB120753402909694027.html).

PART IV

EXAMINING THE DARK SIDE OF THE GLOBAL WAR ON TERRORISM

OVERVIEW

Charles P. Webel and John A. Arnaldi

We also have to work, though, sort of the dark side, if you will. We've got to spend time in the shadows in the intelligence world. A lot of what needs to be done here will have to be done quietly, without any discussion, using sources and methods that are available to our intelligence agencies, if we're going to be successful. That's the world these folks operate in, and so it's going to be vital for us to use any means at our disposal, basically, to achieve our objective.

—Former U.S. vice president Dick Cheney,
September 16, 2001

Part four questions whether specific initiatives in the U.S.-led GWOT have remained true to the moral high ground that democratic nations aspire to or have slipped over to the dark side that is beyond the reach of domestic and international law and natural human rights. Specific areas of concern, all related to radical departures from established rule of law, include expanded government secrecy and surveillance, enhanced interrogation and torture, extralegal detention, extraordinary rendition, and lowered standards for domestic prosecution of terrorism cases (including the use of preemptive prosecution and unreliable informants). Although all of these important issues have made headline news at times, most of the details and implications have not been given extensive news coverage.

Michael German lived as a terrorist and counterterrorist while working as an undercover FBI special agent investigating violent American white supremacist groups. Effective counterterrorism strategies require an accurate understanding of terrorism, which German says has not been true in the GWOT. He argues that U.S. intelligence and security services were ineffective in preventing 9/11 because of "bureaucratic inefficiency and managerial incompetence,...not a lack of intelligence and certainly not an over-reliance on criminal law enforcement." Terrorists need to trigger severe government overreactions in order to stir popular resentment against the government and to validate terrorists' propaganda that "they" (the government) are persecuting "us" (the aggrieved citizenry). Rather than improving security and weakening terrorist organizations, the government's unchecked secrecy and departures from the rule of law have "handed a victory to the terrorists." Fair public trials of accused terrorists in courts subject to judicial review would strengthen U.S. credibility globally. In the "battle for legitimacy" between a democracy under the rule of law and the jihadist movement, an effective counterterrorist strategy, according to German, would uphold honesty and accountability, and not "square the error" of doubling, rather than reevaluating, a failed strategy.

Lisa Hajjar discusses another of the coalition's secret departures from the rule of law: the use of torture in the GWOT, either directly or by proxy (as in extraordinary rendition to another country that tortures). The prohibition of torture is "absolutely non-derogable because the law recognizes no exceptions, including in times of war or national emergency. There is no right to torture." The prohibition is universal—it applies everywhere and to all persons. Contrary to claims by former president George W. Bush and some officials in his administration, there is no evidence that torture is effective in obtaining actionable intelligence, yet their unsubstantiated framing retains some credibility in shaping public understanding that torture is necessary and it works.

Cris Toffolo examines ethical controversies raised by recent U.S. efforts to fight terrorism in Pakistan. Since its formation in 1947, Pakistan has been engaged in a precarious struggle to sustain and develop democratic governance. The United States has pressured Pakistan to pursue policies that are not always seen by Pakistan's citizens or government to be in their national interest. Further, U.S. policy has resulted in the death and disappearance of hundreds, perhaps thousands, of innocent civilians. Two U.S. policies, in particular, raise critical ethical concerns for Toffolo. The first includes use by the United States of drone attacks and other military actions inside Pakistani territory without the permission of the Pakistani government. According to Toffolo, these actions violate international law and frequently result in the killing of innocent civilians. The second questionable policy is extraordinary rendition, the extralegal disappearance of people for interrogation purposes, which in many cases amounts to torture and sometimes results in death. Toffolo asks whether such policies advance democracy or instead incite the growth of terrorist insurgencies and strengthen repressive regimes.

Mark Arax investigates the sensational terrorism trial of a young American man accused of being a member of an al-Qaeda sleeper cell in California's wine country. Like so many of the U.S. terrorism trials, after years of investigation at a cost of millions in tax dollars, the federal prosecutors built a weak, preemptive case on the *possibilities* that this defendant *could be thinking* like a terrorist rather than on any solid evidence of wrongdoing. Central to the government's case against him, Hamid Hayat carried a common Muslim prayer in his wallet, had visited his grandfather's village in Pakistan, was taped talking with a government informer who tried to incite Hayat to "do something," and finally "confessed" to ridiculous and contradictory statements fed to him by inexperienced FBI interrogators. A key expert witness (an award-winning FBI agent who had recently retired after 35 years of service) called by the defense to challenge the interrogation and confession was not allowed to testify. Trials such as this one represent a significant post-9/11 shift away from the fundamental principles of Western jurisprudence and rely on public hysteria for successful convictions.

These contributors have argued that important elements in the GWOT have operated on the dark side that is out of reach of necessary oversight and accountability. Intentional legal maneuvering and secret directives working outside normal government processes have enabled and protected serious breaches of law and human rights. The violations of law and human rights that might be the expected norm within violent extremist organizations and tyrannical states are inexcusable in a democracy.

10

SQUARING THE ERROR

Michael German

I have taken as the title to my essay a phrase that British counter-insurgency expert Sir Robert Thompson used to critique American military strategy in Vietnam during the 1960s.[1] When the military force applied in Vietnam failed to achieve the desired results, rather than reevaluate the strategy, we simply doubled the effort, and in doing so, squared the error. If the terrorist attacks of September 11, 2001 (9/11), taught us anything, it is that doing nothing in response to terrorism is unacceptable, and there is no doubt but that we are now making great efforts. But we also have to recognize that terrorism is a complex problem, and an incorrect response may compound our problems rather than resolve them, regardless of the amount of effort we apply to the task.

In the *Art of War*, Sun-Tzu counsels that we must know both our enemy and ourselves to ensure victory.[2] Knowing ourselves is the easy part. We are a constitutional democracy; a nation of laws, a free and open society in which individual rights are inalienable, and government power is limited. Global terrorism threatens us by exploiting the very freedoms and openness that define us as a democratic society. Government's primary obligation in a hostile world is to protect its citizens.

But the efforts now underway to protect us from terrorism are changing America and changing the world in ways that actually assist the terrorists, because amid all this change, very little effort has been made to truly understand terrorists. This is where I think my experience might be helpful since I have been on both sides, living simultaneously as a terrorist and as a counterterrorist.

In the early 1990s, working as a Federal Bureau of Investigation (FBI) undercover agent, I spent over a year with white supremacist extremist groups engaged in a racial holy war. A few years later, after the Oklahoma City bombing, I spent another six months under-cover with militia groups in the Pacific Northwest. I later served as a counterterrorism instructor at the FBI National Academy, but it is my experience working within terrorist groups and seeing the world from their perspective that has most influenced my understanding of the nature of the threat we are facing. My repeated success using constitutionally sound, proactive law enforcement techniques to infil-trate terrorist groups and prevent acts of terrorism convinces me that a criminal law approach to counterterrorism can be effective.

In my experience, terrorism, quite simply, is what "they" do to "us." Terrorist groups almost never refer to themselves as terrorists, but rather as soldiers, revolutionaries, holy warriors. And govern-ments, no matter how oppressive, conduct only counterterrorism operations. You'll never see a Department of Terrorism on a govern-ment's organizational chart. As bodies pile up on both sides, each sees himself as the victim. In addition, terrorist acts are often so heinous they are seen not only as unjustified, but as unjustifiable. Anyone suggesting a rationality supporting the terrorist's behavior is branded a sympathizer, which chills intelligent discourse about the root causes of terrorism and the behavior of terrorists.

This again is where my experience helps. I am clearly not a terrorist sympathizer. The terrorists I befriended all went to prison because I betrayed them. Now some could argue that my experience with domes-tic terrorists, particularly right-wing extremists, is irrelevant to a dis-cussion focusing on Islamic terrorism because right-wing extremists are just lightweights and amateurs compared to the al-Qaeda. I would simply remind them that while the al-Qaeda failed in their first attempt to bring a building down in the United States, right-wing extremists succeeded in Oklahoma City, and while no weapons of mass destruc-tion (WMD) were found in Iraq, a cyanide bomb capable of killing every person in a 30,000 square-foot building was discovered in a stor-age locker in Noonday, Texas.[3] We ignore domestic terrorists at our peril. "Amateurs" is probably a fair description of them, though, in the sense that they never had state sponsorship like the al-Qaeda enjoyed with the Taliban. But that they are able to continue operating without financing and without a safe haven arguably makes them a more formi-dable threat, not less of one. I often hear terrorism experts remark that the al-Qaeda's evolution into decentralized cells after the invasion of Afghanistan is a sign of organizational genius,[4] but they are really just imitating the leaderless resistance and lone wolf strategies right-wing extremists pioneered decades ago.[5] Nobody ever called them geniuses.

More to the point though, as a criminal investigator, I did not focus on the ideology of the group I was investigating, mainly because the First Amendment to the U.S. Constitution guarantees their right to their beliefs, but also because their beliefs were not going to hurt anyone, while the bombs they were making were. So I focused on the methodology; what the terrorists were doing to accomplish their criminal goals. I found the methodology is essentially the same for all terrorist groups, regardless of ideology. Hitler and Stalin had diametrically opposed ideologies, but the totalitarian regimes they established were remarkably similar in the methods they used to hold power. It is the same phenomena with terrorists.

Three universal truths about terrorists are: First, terrorists are unhappy with the status quo; second, terrorists lack the political power to alter the status quo through legitimate, peaceful means; and finally, terrorists lack the military power to force a change. A terrorist has a very black and white worldview that divides "us," the virtuous and pure, from "them," the corrupt and unclean. Terrorists see the world at a tipping point, and their goal is to devise an attack that will alter the status quo; that will throw the world into chaos, a cleansing war, a jihad. White supremacists call it RAHOWA, short for Racial Holy War.[6] Charles Manson called it Helter-Skelter. Whatever they call it, the terrorists believe that out of the chaos, their people will rise and dominate, either because God, or simply justice, is on their side.

They recruit in the places they find people who are similarly unhappy with the status quo: in prisons, among the unemployed. They seek idealistic young students eager to make a mark in the world. Typically there is a cleansing ritual to symbolize the separation of the group from the corrupt society; dress and dietary requirements are established; sexual taboos are either strictly enforced, or, as in the case of the Weather Underground, ceremonially violated. Sometimes there are physical manifestations of separation; neo-Nazi skinheads shave their heads, jihadists grow beards.

I have heard Richard Clarke, the former White House counterterrorism official, describe the jihadist movement as a series of concentric circles, with the smallest circle in the center representing hardcore al-Qaeda members and the outer circles representing varying levels of support for the movement.[7] I think this analogy is helpful, but my version is a little different in that it is generic to any terrorist group rather than specific to one. Imagine a series of concentric circles with the hardcore terrorist group at the center. In the next circle are supporters, who assist the group but do not participate directly in terrorist attacks. The third circle contains people who sympathize with the cause but who do not actively support the terrorists. In the fourth circle are people who the terrorists consider part of their "us" community, but who do not identify themselves as part of a community represented by the terrorist group. White supremacists refer to this group as "sheeple," whites who do not believe in a Jewish conspiracy to destroy their race. The fifth and final circle represents "them," the population of others that support the status quo and benefit from it. Outside the circle is the oppressive force; the government, the Jewish conspiracy, communism, capitalism, the New World Order, whatever the terrorists are against.

The core terrorist group must do something in order to gain influence among its supporters. This can be something positive, such as promoting sobriety or ridding a neighborhood of a criminal element that has been exploiting it, a further cleansing of the community. Getting attention from sympathizers in the next circle requires bolder action on behalf of the community, perhaps assassinating a corrupt police officer who has been shaking down the local businessmen. Now this is a critical stage for the terrorists because at this point they look very much like a gang of criminals and if the government can brand them as criminals, it will be very difficult for them to retain support among sympathizers and impossible to gain any support among the sheeple in the fourth circle. This is also a critical stage because moving to the next level of influence requires outside assistance, and that assistance can only come from one source: their enemy. To accomplish their goals, terrorists need to trigger a severe government reaction, one that will impact the innocent in the community as well as the guilty, to stir resentment and validate the terrorist's propaganda that "they" are persecuting "us." The overreaction will divide the population along the lines the terrorist wants them divided, driving the sheeple in the fourth circle to the cause of the terrorist. This strategy is laid out in Carlos Marighella's "Mini-manual of the Urban Guerilla," a virtual how-to guide for terrorists.[8] That a how-to guide for terrorists exists surprised me when I started working in counterterrorism, and I think it underscores what truly is an intelligence failure on the part of our government. Osama bin Laden has followed the how-to guide to a tee, and we fell far too easily into the role of the oppressor, just as it was scripted.

If you have seen Gillo Pontecorvo's film "The Battle of Algiers" lately, you might have noticed that my description of the development of a terrorist organization mirrors the first part of the movie in which the National Liberation Front, known by its French acronym FLN, starts a terrorist campaign against French colonial forces in Algiers.[9]

It is often dismissed as propaganda, but I think it has tremendous intelligence value because the original screenplay was actually written by an FLN terrorist, Yacef Saadi. In the film, as in real life, the security forces do overreact to the terrorist attacks, uniting the Algerian community behind the FLN. The French military resorts to torturing detainees to develop intelligence and they succeed in breaking the FLN, but the political fallout from the abuse energizes the Algerian resistance, undermines French support for the effort, and alienates the international community. France wins the battle of Algiers, but loses the war for Algeria. This is the crucial final stage of a terrorist campaign, when the people in the fifth circle start to believe their government is unjust and incapable of solving the terrorist problem. The film was made in 1967 but here, more than 40 years later, we find ourselves on the brink of that final stage, divided at home, alienated from allies abroad, fighting an enemy all over the globe that can strike when and where it wants.

Marighella's genius is that he understands that governments are compelled to overreact to terrorism: "The government has no alternative except to intensify its repression. The police networks, house searches, the arrest of suspects and innocent persons, and the closing off of streets makes life in the city unbearable." Written in 1969, is this applicable to our current situation? How about this quote from Osama bin Laden shortly after 9/11: "I tell you freedom and human rights in America are doomed. The U.S. Government will lead the American people—and the west in general—into an unbearable hell and a choking life."[10] Just as a terrorist's actions are designed to speak to his community, the government has an audience it must answer to as well. When a terrorist attack occurs, the victim population rightly questions why the government charged with protecting it has failed and the people demand more effective security. The easiest way for the government to satisfy this constituency, their own "us" in that fifth circle, is to take restrictive measures against "them" by expanding the powers of the security services.

Creating an effective security service is fairly easy. Militarize the police and consolidate military, intelligence, and law enforcement functions under one central authority. Make that authority accountable only to the executive branch of government. Authorize "emergency" powers that suspend traditional protections of personal liberties. Permit extrajudicial detentions and the use of coercive investigative techniques. Establish a tribunal system separate from the normal criminal justice system and allow the use of secret evidence. Ignore inconvenient international treaties and conventions. Restrict travel. Encourage people to inform on their neighbors, to report all suspicious activity, and then follow-up on every report to reinforce the perception that the government is in control. Gather and retain intelligence on the general population. Most importantly, give the security services the power to operate in secret so no one will know what the true security situation is, and so mistakes and abuses can be hidden. There are plenty of examples we can use as models; authoritarian regimes throughout history are defined by the effectiveness of their security services. But unchecked power and freedom from public accountability always lead to abuse, which undermines the legitimacy of the governing authority. The effectiveness of these security solutions tends to be short-lived and ultimately illusory.

This is Marighella's trap: measures we take to win each battle make it more likely we will lose the war. The good news is we can avoid the trap, not by increasing the power of the security services, but by increasing their efficiency. To be truly effective, a counterterrorism program must be efficient, not only in that its resources are used wisely, but in that all of the counterterrorism efforts are directed squarely at the terrorists. But increasing efficiency is much more difficult than simply increasing power. Governments by their very nature tend to be bureaucratic and inefficient. Luckily, our founding fathers created a mechanism that compels efficiency in government: the U.S. Constitution. We need to recognize that our Constitution and the freedoms it guarantees are not weaknesses, but rather the source of our strength. Nothing makes it more difficult for a terrorist to convince people that the government is oppressive and unjust than scrupulously protecting his rights in a public criminal trial.

First we need to take Sun-Tzu's advice and get to know ourselves a little better by being honest about why our counterterrorism efforts before 9/11 were ineffective. In the wake of the attacks, officials in the Bush administration denied the government had any forewarning of the plot. A lack of intelligence was cited as the cause of the failure, so Congress acted quickly, passing the U.S. Patriot Act to give the administration powers it said it needed to get the intelligence necessary to prevent another attack. Meanwhile, the administration resisted the investigations that ultimately revealed the true cause of the failure. It turned out that the government had a tremendous amount of intelligence and simply failed to respond to it, but by that time the idea that 9/11 was an intelligence failure had already taken root. The intelligence reform train had left the station.

The issue was further confused when the Justice Department and the FBI blamed their lapses on their overreliance on a criminal justice approach to counterterrorism,[11] which also was simply not true. In fact, while domestic terrorism cases such as mine were treated as criminal matters, the FBI has always handled international terrorism cases as counterintelligence matters. Each of the three FBI cases the 9/11 Commission cited as failed opportunities to prevent the attacks were intelligence investigations. FBI agents in New York actually were prevented from pursuing criminal investigations against two of the hijackers because managers at FBI headquarters misunderstood intelligence-sharing regulations.[12] FBI managers, who denied Minneapolis agents their request to get a Foreign Intelligence Surveillance Act (FISA) warrant in the case of Zacarias Moussaoui, later admitted in testimony before the Senate Judiciary Committee that they did not even know the standard of proof necessary to obtain a FISA warrant.[13] The Phoenix memo was never even read prior to 9/11.[14] Bureaucratic inefficiency and managerial incompetence were the true causes of the breakdown, not a lack of intelligence and certainly not an overreliance on criminal law enforcement.

In fact, proactive criminal investigations can be very effective in preventing terrorism, as my repeated success proves. That these cases are rare is not because the techniques are not effective, but because the FBI does not employ them effectively. A criminal law enforcement approach to terrorism has many inherent advantages that promote efficiency. By treating terrorists like criminals, we stigmatize them in their community, while simultaneously validating our own authority. Open and public trials allow the community to see the terrorist for the criminal he is, and successful prosecutions give them faith the government is protecting them. Judicial review ensures that the methods used are in accordance with the law, and juries enforce community standards of fairness. The adversarial process exposes improper or ineffective law enforcement techniques so they can be corrected. Checks and balances on government power and public accountability promote efficiency by ensuring that only the guilty are punished.

Finally, and this is perhaps counterintuitive, the exposure of proactive law enforcement techniques at trial is a force multiplier. Intelligence collectors focus on protecting sources and methods to ensure their continued availability, but this does not necessarily promote security as the three cases cited by the 9/11 Commission demonstrate. In each case, restrictions on intelligence-sharing caused the breakdown. If the presence of two al-Qaeda terrorists in the United States was broadcast to state and local law enforcement, or if the Phoenix memo was distributed to flight schools around the country, perhaps the outcome would have been different. Protecting this intelligence did not protect national security.

When I was undercover, I was present during the planning of dozens of terrorist attacks. In almost every case, the one thing that stopped the terrorists from following through on their plans was the fear they had been compromised by an infiltrator. If a terrorist knows that every new recruit is a possible agent; if every old friend might have been turned; if communications over the phone, or over the radio, or over the Internet are vulnerable to interception, his ability to operate effectively is greatly restricted. Certainly the terrorist will modify his behavior to try to avoid law enforcement detection, and this will require the government to constantly adapt and develop more effective techniques, but this is not a bad outcome.

Our security services do need to be improved. Congress needs to improve oversight and enact criminal laws to assist law enforcement in dealing with this threat, and some of the provisions in the Patriot Act and Intelligence Reform Bill are helpful. But overall, the reorganization and reform of the security services will fail because the real problems that led to 9/11 are not addressed, and bureaucratic inefficiency and managerial incompetence continue to hamper our counterterrorism efforts. After three years and 170 million dollars, the FBI still does not have a functioning computer system.

The worst part of these reforms, though, is that they increase the government's power to operate in secret, beyond judicial or congressional oversight, and beyond public accountability. After failing us once, the security services should be more accountable, not less.

We also need to better understand our enemy, and to do this, we need to use more efficiently the intelligence we already have. I spent over a year-and-a-half living undercover with right-wing extremists, but despite my many requests, I was never operationally debriefed by the Domestic Terrorism Unit. I recorded hundreds of hours of conversations with real terrorists, selecting targets, planning attacks, and discussing motives and methods. These tapes were used as evidence in public trials, but they have never been analyzed for their intelligence value. If someone had bothered to listen to these tapes in the early 1990s, they would have heard right-wing extremists discuss the possibility of crashing a passenger airliner into a military installation to start the race war.

Contrary to popular opinion, from the terrorists' perspective, 9/11 was a political disaster for the jihadist movement. The scale of the attack was so horrible, the world united in solidarity with the United States to stop terrorism. Even many jihadi supporters could not accept that Muslims did something so terrible, and they dreamed up conspiracy theories suggesting Israel planned the attack to frame Muslims. In Tehran, the heart of the most anti-American Muslim state, there was a spontaneous candlelight vigil in sympathy for the victims. Other Muslim countries with a history of antagonism toward the United States, such as Pakistan and Syria, agreed to assist us. When diplomatic efforts failed to convince the Taliban to arrest and extradite al-Qaeda criminals, the international community supported a military intervention to remove the Taliban from power and al-Qaeda, "the base" of the jihadist movement, was destroyed. But when we departed from the rule of law, both our own Constitution and our obligations under international conventions, when we antagonized and alienated the international community, we undercut our success and handed a victory to the terrorists.

What we have to realize is that this is not a struggle of ideologies; it is not Islam against Christianity or fundamentalism versus secularism. This is a battle for legitimacy, and as such, it is one that we should easily win. As an open and free democracy regulated by the rule of law, we offer a future of peace and prosperity that the jihadist movement does not. Its resort to terrorism is a sign of weakness, not of strength. We need to avoid the trap of demonizing our enemies, of dividing the world between "us" and "them" as the terrorist does. As former Weather Underground member Brian Flanagan said in a recent documentary, "if you think that you have the moral highground...you can do some really dreadful things."[15] That goes for both sides. Respect for the rule of law, international conventions, and treaty obligations will not make us weaker, it will engender international cooperation and goodwill that make it impossible for extremist movements to prosper. I have heard commentators suggest that we are losing the propaganda battle in the Middle East, but that misses the point entirely. The term "propaganda" connotes a fabrication or a spinning of facts to support one's position, and that is exactly what we must not do. In a battle for legitimacy, honesty and accountability are the most effective ammunition.

Terrorism will never go away, and free and open societies will always be especially vulnerable. But we do not win by becoming less free and less open. Ironically, al-Qaeda does not have the power to destroy the United States of America. But we do.

By playing into a script written by terrorists we have indeed squared the error.

NOTES

Michael German presented this lecture at a conference, "Beyond the U.S. War on Terrorism: Comparing Domestic Legal Remedies to an International

Dilemma," sponsored by the John Bassett Moore Society of International Law, University of Virginia School of Law, in cooperation with the Strategic Studies Institute, U.S. Army War College. It was held on February 25–26, 2005.

1. Sir Robert Thompson, "Squaring the Error," *Foreign Affairs*, 46 (April 1968): 442–453.

2. Sun-Tzu, *Art of War*, chapter III, pt. 14. "Hence the saying: If you know the enemy and know yourself, you need not fear the result of a hundred battles." Translated from the Chinese with Introduction and Critical Notes by Lionel Giles, MA, first published in 1910.

3. See Camille Jackson, "Terror, American Style," Southern Poverty Law Center Intelligence Report. 2005 (http://www.splcenter.org/intel/intelreport/article.jsp?aid=378).

4. See, e.g., Rita Katz and Josh Devon, "The End of Al-Qaeda?" *National Review Online*, March 21, 2003 (http://www.siteinstitute.org/bin/articles.cgi?ID=news8503&Category=news&Subcategory=0).

5. Louis Beam, "Leaderless Resistance," *The Seditionist*, February 12, 1992 (http://www.louisbeam.com/leaderless.htm).

6. Ben Klassen, *RAHOWA: This Planet is Ours*. Church of the Creator, 1987.

7. Richard Clarke, "Review of What We Owe Iraq," New America Foundation, November 21, 2004 (http://www.newamerica.net/index.cfm?pg=DocRelated&DocID=2255).

8. Carlos Marighella, "The Minimanual of the Urban Guerrilla," 1969 (http://www.latinamericanstudies.org/ marighella.htm).

9. Gillo Pontecorvo, *The Battle of Algiers*, 1967.

10. "Networks Row over Bin Laden tape." *BBC News*, February 1, 2002 (http://news.bbc.co.uk/1/hi/world/ middle_east/1795531.stm).

11. *The 9/11 Commission Report: The Final Report of the National Commission on Terrorist Attacks Upon the United States*. W.W. Norton & Co., 2004, 423.

12. Ibid., 271.

13. U.S. Congress, "Interim Report on FBI Oversight in the 107th Congress by the Senate Judiciary Committee: FISA Implementation Failures," Senator Patrick Leahy, Senator Charles Grassley, and Senator Arlen Specter, February 2003 (http://www.fas.org/irp/congress/2003_rpt/fisa.html).

14. *The 9/11 Commission Report*, 272.

15. Brian Flanagan, as featured in the documentary, *The Weather Underground: The Explosive Story of America's Most Notorious Revolutionaries*, Sam Green and Bill Siegel, dirs. 2003.

11

THE LIBERAL IDEOLOGY OF TORTURE: A CRITICAL EXAMINATION OF THE AMERICAN CASE

Lisa Hajjar

In November 2010, George W. Bush put American torture back in the news again as he promoted his new memoir, *Decision Points.*[1] On November 8, NBC interviewer Matt Lauer questioned Bush about authorizing waterboarding, to which the former president responded, "Damn right." Richard Falk characterized his admission of criminality as an "uncoerced confession." Waterboarding is torture, and torture is a crime. In fact, torture is not just a run-of-the-mill crime; it is a gross crime under international law, in the same company with war crimes, crimes against humanity, and genocide. What does it say about the state of American democracy when a former president can proudly and publicly admit to conspiring in the commission of a gross crime and face no risk of punitive consequences?

Dahlia Lithwick assessed the implications of Bush's uncoerced confession to the public: "We keep waiting breathlessly for someone, somewhere, to have a day of reckoning over the prisoners we tortured in the wake of 9/11, without recognizing that there is no bag man to be found and that therefore we are all the bag man."[2] There are three "wes" in Lithwick's quote: the first is "we" who advocate the rule of law and legal accountability for the crime of torture—whom I like to refer to as the "rule of law restoration" proponents. Perhaps "crowd" is an overstatement; it is a small but dedicated crowd of elite intellectuals and persons of conscience. The second "we" refers to our representative government, and the third—the bag men for torture—is we Americans.

In that NBC interview, Bush offered a variety of statements justifying the use of torture.[3] He said: "My job is to protect you . . . My job is to protect this country, man." "The American people need to know, we are using techniques within the law to protect them." And "I am confident the American people understand why we've done that." Bush was articulating a "liberal" rationale for torture by saying, in essence: In fulfilling our responsibility to protect you, we did what we did for you. PS, what we did wasn't "torture" because our lawyers said so. Torture is bad, we are good, and there haven't been any attacks on the United States since 9/11, thanks to the policies we instituted. You're welcome.

The liberal ideology of torture[4] is a nonsensical concept because torture is inherently illiberal. Yet just because it is nonsensical doesn't mean it's not real, as Bush so recently demonstrated. Let's begin with the concept of liberal ideology, which has three components: One is the representative state, of which political democracy is the idealized form—that is, state power derives from "the people." Two, the law regulates and limits the power of the liberal state; the alternative is tyranny and authoritarianism. Three, the liberal state is expected to act lawfully in devising policies to govern and protect its people. When it comes to foreign threats to national security, the applicable laws are international. Although the United States is an outlier among liberal democracies in terms of signing and ratifying international laws, it is a signatory—and thus is bound by—the Geneva Conventions of 1949 and the UN Convention on Torture.

Many states engage in torture. But only liberal states invoke liberal ideology to rationalize their torture as "necessary" for the "greater good."[5] The liberal ideological rationalization posits torture as a "lesser evil" to combat the dangers facing an innocent and vulnerable society; it is conceived and practiced as a means to an end, the end being the security of the nation. In this regard, torture in the context of war compares to other aspects of warfare, since both are forms of state violence directed at "enemy others." However, torture is a distinct kind of harm: it pertains explicitly and exclusively to the purposeful harming of a person who is in custody but has not been found guilty of a crime. (Painful lawful punishments are, legally, not "torture.")

The right not to be tortured is the most important right of all, not because torture is the worst thing that can happen to a person but because the prohibition of torture imposes a legal limit on the rights and discretion of the state in its treatment of human beings.[6] The right not to be tortured is foundational to the rise of modern liberal democracies. Three factors make the right not to be tortured unique. First, the prohibition is absolutely nonderogable because the law recognizes no exceptions, including in times of war or national emergency. There is no right to torture. Second, the prohibition of torture is a *jus cogens* norm under customary international law meaning that it is applicable everywhere in the world. Third, the right not to be tortured extends to all people regardless of their social status, political identity, or affiliations. Thus it is an unparalleled "ideal" right, comparable only to the universal right not to be enslaved. In contrast, the right to life is not comparably universal or absolute; there are many ways that people can lawfully be killed.

In the context of any kind of war, the universal baseline standard for "humane treatment" of prisoners is Common Article 3 (CA3) of the Geneva Conventions, which covers detained persons who do not have the status of prisoners-of-war or militarily occupied civilians. CA3 states that prisoners "shall in all circumstances be treated humanely," and that "to this end," certain specified acts "are and shall remain prohibited at any time and in any place whatsoever" including "cruel treatment and torture," and "outrages upon personal dignity, in particular humiliating and degrading treatment." To go below the baseline, as the Bush administration did—and justified doing—undermines the very concept of universal "humanity."

The Bush administration declared a "global war on terror" in response to the terrorist attacks of September 11, 2001. As is common in asymmetrical wars when states fight nonstate groups, the lack of—and the need for—information about al-Qaeda elevated the importance of gathering "actionable intelligence" through interrogation of captured enemies. However, the authorization and use of law-violating methods was a choice, not a necessity. Why did top officials make this choice?[7] Because they believed that violent and dehumanizing interrogation methods would be effective means of eliciting actionable intelligence—in other words, ignoring an abundance of contrary data and expert opinion, they chose to believe that torture can produce truth, and this truth would keep Americans safe.

Contrary to Bush's recent claims that "coercive interrogation" methods "worked" and that they were adopted as a last resort, in fact the torture policy was set in motion long before anyone had been taken into custody; it was the "torture works" myth that drove policymaking.[8] On September 17, 2001, Bush signed a memorandum of understanding granting the CIA authority to establish a secret detention and interrogation operation overseas. The Clinton-era rendition program was revamped as "extraordinary rendition" to permit the CIA to kidnap people from anywhere in the world and disappear them into secret prisons, euphemized as "black sites," where they could be held as "ghost detainees," or transferred extralegally to other states for interrogation. Contrary to Bush's claims that people disappeared by the CIA were "picked up on battlefields," in fact some were kidnapped from as far afield as The Gambia, Italy, Bosnia, and Macedonia.

Unlike the CIA, the U.S. military is subject to the Geneva Conventions, which are enshrined in the Uniform Code of Military Justice. Nevertheless, by December 2001, Pentagon officials were exploring how to "reverse engineer" SERE (survival, evasion, resistance, and extraction) techniques that had been developed during the Cold War to train U.S. soldiers to withstand torture in case they were captured by regimes that don't adhere to the Geneva Conventions.[9]

What distinguishes torture by liberal regimes from illiberal regimes is the energy devoted to frame government policies as "legal." Vice President Dick Cheney and his legal counsel David Addington took charge of interrogation and detention policies, which were varnished with opinions by lawyers in the Justice Department's Office of Legal Counsel (OLC), most prominently Berkeley law professor John Yoo who served in the OLC from 2001 to 2003. They devised a "new paradigm" for waging the "war on terror" based on a radical interpretation of Article 2 of the Constitution according to which the president, as commander-in-chief, has unfettered powers to wage war, and therefore efforts to constrain executive discretion in accordance with federal, military, or international law would be unconstitutional.[10]

On November 13, 2001, President Bush issued a military order declaring that captured terror suspects were "unlawful combatants," a heretofore nonexistent category conceived to place such prisoners outside of the law by claiming that they are neither combatants nor civilians and thus not privy to the standards of treatment of either. Anyone taken into U.S. custody could be designated an unlawful combatant by presidential fiat rather than on the basis of any status review by a tribunal, and could be held incommunicado indefinitely. In the same order, Bush declared that such detainees could be prosecuted in a new kind of military commission whose rules would admit coerced confessions, hearsay, and secret evidence.

On January 11, 2002, the first "unlawful combatants" were transported to the detention facility at the U.S. naval base in Guantánamo Bay (GTMO). They were denounced to the public as "the worst of the worst," and trophy photos of them bound and immobilized in physically straining positions and sensory deprivation gear were released for media publication. GTMO had been selected because it was far from the hot war zone of Afghanistan and, more importantly, according to the new paradigmers, it was beyond the reach of U.S. courts and lawyers.[11]

The coup de grace for the rule of law occurred secretly on February 7, 2002, when Bush issued a memorandum to his national security team endorsing the new paradigmers' claim that the Geneva Conventions are too "quaint" to apply to this novel form of global war against stateless enemies, and asserted that captured terror suspects have no legal rights but would be treated humanely as "a matter of policy," with the caveat that interrogation and detention policy would prioritize "military necessity." The State Department had sharply criticized the legal flaws and political dangers of this position, but their criticism was ignored and Secretary of State Colin Powell was cut out of the inner circle on prisoner policymaking.

The claim that everyone at GTMO was a terrorist is a lie that is still being peddled to the public. Intelligence officers who were instructed to fill out a one-page form on every detainee certifying the president's "reason to believe" that he was involved in terrorism began reporting almost immediately that interrogations were not producing the information needed to fill out the forms. Pentagon and White House officials assumed the problem was that these hardened terrorists had been trained to resist and dissemble. But in August 2002, a senior Arabic-speaking CIA analyst was dispatched to GTMO to do an assessment and concluded that at least half and probably more had no ties or meaningful information about al-Qaeda or the Taliban. He recommended a formal review process, and noted that continued imprisonment and interrogation of innocent people could constitute war crimes. The top lawyer with the National Security Agency scheduled a meeting to discuss the analyst's recommendations, but Addington canceled it, declaring: "No, there will be no review. The President has determined that they are ALL enemy combatants. We are not going to revisit it."[12]

In the division of interrogational labor, the CIA was vested with primary responsibility for "high value detainees" (HVDs)—people assumed to be terrorist leaders or planners of 9/11, or to have knowledge about terrorist operations and plots. On March 28, 2002, the first HVD, Abu Zubaydah, was captured in Pakistan and transported to a black site in Thailand. His interrogation led to a showdown between professional Arabic-speaking FBI interrogators who used conventional methods with success and unskilled CIA contractors who were inspired and authorized to use violence; the CIA won, and the FBI stopped cooperating in black-site interrogations. The escalating harshness of Abu Zubaydah's treatment was due to the amateur interrogators' frustration that he was not providing the actionable intelligence he was assumed to possess. But contrary to the initial claim that he was a "top al-Qaeda strategist," in fact he was more like a receptionist who had been responsible for moving people in and out of training camps in Afghanistan. The brutal and dehumanizing methods authorized for Abu Zubaydah, which included waterboarding him 83 times and placing him in a coffin-like "confinement box," set the stage for the CIA's secret interrogation program.

By mid-summer 2002, some CIA agents were growing anxious about their vulnerability to future prosecution under federal antitorture laws. In response to the Agency's questions about legal liability, the OLC produced two memos dated August 1, 2002. One interpreted the applicable definition of physical torture to exclude anything less than "the pain accompanying serious physical injury, such as organ failure, impairment of bodily function, or even death," and opined that cruel, inhuman, or degrading treatment would not constitute mental torture unless it caused effects that lasted "months or even years." The second memo provided legal cover for tactics already in use. Although these OLC memos were written for the CIA, the White House forwarded them to the Pentagon, which was seeking a solution to military interrogators' frustrated efforts to get actionable intelligence out of GTMO detainees.[13]

This confluence of radical legal reasoning and the ideologically driven presumptions that all detainees are terrorists and that torture is effective in obtaining actionable intelligence meant that U.S. military interrogators, CIA agents, and government-hired contractors were, in effect, licensed by the Bush administration to utilize methods that were no longer regulated by the laws of this nation or the world. But the Bush administration never officially authorized "torture." Rather, "torture" became the euphemism for anything that was not authorized by the U.S. government. What was authorized included stripping prisoners naked, short-shackling them to the floor for protracted periods of time, forcing them to defecate and urinate on themselves; subjecting prisoners to days or weeks of sleep deprivation by bombarding them with constant light, excruciatingly loud music or grating sounds, or extremes in temperature; weeks, months, or even years of isolation; stress positions such as "long time standing," sometimes with arms extended outward, and "wall hanging" prisoners from hooks on the wall or ceiling; "walling," which referred to bashing prisoners into walls; and waterboarding to induce the feeling and fear of death by drowning.

The Bush administration's decision to take the "war on terror" to Iraq had to be sold to the American public and skeptical allies. In early 2003, CIA and military interrogators were under intense pressure to produce evidence that the regime of Saddam Hussein had an active weapons of mass destruction (WMD) program, and that there was a link between Iraq and 9/11.[14] The "actionable intelligence" that the administration presented to make the case for war included a statement by a Libyan prisoner named Ibn al-Shaykh al-Libi that Iraq had provided training in chemical weapons to members of al-Qaeda. However, al-Libi subsequently recanted the false claim, which he had made to stop the torture. By the late summer of 2003, the failure to find the (nonexistent) WMD, and the escalation of antioccupation insurgency had made a mockery of Bush's claim in May that the Iraq mission had been "accomplished." In August the Pentagon sent GTMO commander General Geoffrey Miller to Iraq to provide advice on how to "set the conditions" to get actionable intelligence from the thousands of people—including women and children—who were being taken into custody. The commander of the Iraq theater of operations General Ricardo Sanchez signed off on a policy to "GTMO-ize" Iraqi prisons, a euphemization for the use of dogs, sexual humiliation, stress positions, protracted sleep deprivation and isolation, and other forms of torture and cruel treatment, despite the fact that up to 90 percent of detainees were picked up in military sweeps or as a result of intra-Iraqi score-settling and had no connection to the insurgency, let alone to al-Qaeda.

On April 28, 2004, shocking photos of naked, abused, humiliated, bloodied, and dead prisoners from the Abu Ghraib prison in Iraq were published on CBS's 60 Minutes II. The context was provided by the online version of Seymour Hersh's *New Yorker* exposé on the leaked ("not meant for public release") report by Maj. Gen. Antonio Taguba, which concluded that prisoner abuse was "systematic" and "wanton," and that unlawful interrogation tactics linked Iraq to Afghanistan and Guantánamo.[15] The Bush administration's initial reaction to the Abu Ghraib scandal was to blame "bad apples" ostensibly acting autonomously. In other words, officials knowingly lied to the public.

The Abu Ghraib scandal created political pressure for information about prisoner policies. In June 2004, the first batch of legal memos and policy documents was declassified or leaked.[16] These "torture memos" were, in their own way, at least as shocking as the photos because they exposed a pervasive disregard for the law. But there was no official denunciation of "the program." On the contrary, top officials asserted the prerogative to continue the use of "coercive" tactics as necessary and effective means of combating terror. Although

Republicans lost control of the Senate in 2006, the combination of continuing executive secrecy and political partisanship enabled the torture policy to endure to the end of Bush's second term.

The torture policy was a failure in its ostensible mission of eliciting valuable intelligence. By subjecting thousands of prisoners to violent and dehumanizing treatment, the quest for information and cooperation in critically important communities was as damned as America's reputation abroad. Under torture some people revealed some information about al-Qaeda's structure and operations, but there is abundant evidence that many tortured statements were false. Indeed, the American experience has verified the ageless truism that many people will say anything to make the torture stop; a worst case example is al-Libi's false claims about a Saddam-al-Qaeda connection, a tortured lie that has cost tens of thousands of lives and a trillion of dollars. David Rose, an investigative journalist who interviewed numerous counterterrorism officials from the United States and elsewhere, reported that their conclusions were unanimous: "Not only have coercive methods failed to generate significant and actionable intelligence, they have also caused the squandering of resources on a massive scale..., chimerical plots, and unnecessary safety alerts."[17] The 2008 report by the bipartisan Senate Armed Services Committee rendered its own harsh judgment that the use of aggressive techniques "damaged our ability to collect accurate intelligence that could save lives, strengthened the hand of our enemies, and compromised our moral authority."

What toll did the American people exact for revelations about the vast and ineffective use of torture? During the 2008 campaign season, the issue barely registered. But to their credit, both presidential candidates—Republican John McCain and Democrat Barack Obama—vaunted their antitorture credentials on occasion. While Obama promised to end torture, increase governmental transparency, and restore the rule of law, to demonstrate his aspirational postpartisanship he skirted questions about accountability for the authors of the torture policy with the rhetoric of wanting to "look forward, not backward."

Obama's victory provided a hopeful moment for the rule of law restoration crowd. On his second day in office, he signed executive orders requiring the CIA to adhere to the 2006-revised *Army Field Manual for Human Intelligence Collector Operations* and shuttering their black sites, canceling the discredited military commissions, and promising to close GTMO within one year. But the administration quickly buckled because every initiative became fodder for partisan attacks that Obama was pandering to "the far left." Influential advisors (notably Obama's first White House chief of staff Rahm Emmanuel) regarded the devotion of political capital to press the president's rule of law restoration promises as a loser for Democrats.

Cheney, renowned for his secretive silence, became uncharacteristically voluble after he was out of office. In numerous interviews in 2009, he admonished the Obama administration for sacrificing security by relinquishing methods that "work." Cheney's fact-free protorture offensive found a receptive audience among America's chattering class, who seized the opportunity to engage in woolly speculations about the efficacy of torture and treated partisan historical revisionism as legitimate critique. Obama defensively asserted a postpartisan posture by contending that officials who had made the policy decisions and those who had followed orders had acted in "good faith," and conceded to right-wing arguments that any type of meaningful accountability—even a nonprosecutorial truth commission—would constitute a "criminalization of policy differences."

By the end of his first year in office, Obama had resurrected the military commissions, abandoned the promise to close GTMO, authorized indefinite detention without trial for dozens of GTMO prisoners, and asserted that people who were captured abroad and transported to the Bagram facility in Afghanistan have no habeas corpus rights and could be held incommunicado indefinitely (earning the facility the nickname "Obama's GTMO"). The administration stepped into the defendant role in domestic lawsuits brought by victims of U.S. torture, and replicated the stance of its predecessor by invoking "state secrets" to shut them down. The ongoing national debate about torture, terror, and the law intensified following the 2009 Christmas Day attempt by Umar Farouk Abdulmutallab to detonate a bomb in his underwear while traveling on a transatlantic flight bound for Detroit. Right-wing critics excoriated Attorney General Eric Holder for allowing Abdulmutallab to be read his Miranda rights and for not subjecting him to "enhanced" interrogation or shipping him off to GTMO, despite the fact that the Bush administration had followed an identical course of action with Richard Reid, the "shoe bomber," and despite the fact that Abdulmutallab readily provided information to FBI interrogators who used conventional methods. In May 2010, following a failed attempt to detonate a bomb in Times Square, again Holder was condemned for providing constitutional protections to (nonwhite) terrorists arrested within the United States. That these events could be treated by so many officials and commentators as evidence of the "need" to subject suspects to torture should be unsurprising for a country that has failed to face the truth about the actual record of torture's inefficacy.

The Obama administration's "looking forward" posture functions as a form of denial, and has led, inevitably, to a need to rely on heavy-handed classification to block public access to information deleterious or embarrassing to the U.S. government. When the CIA's Office of the Inspector General report was finally released in August 2009, excessive redactions made it impossible to glean how the torture program had grown and spread. The report by the Justice Department's Office of Professional Responsibility (OPR) into the role that OLC lawyers played in formulating the torture policy—which was withheld (without explanation) until February 2010—contained substantial evidence that lawyers had colluded with the White House to "legalize" unlawful tactics. But David Margulies, the DOJ official who Holder had authorized to make the final determination, concluded that the lawyers had merely exercised "poor judgment."

And what of Obama's promises to end torture and close black sites? In April 2010, the BBC reported testimonies of prisoners who said they had been subjected to beatings, sexual humiliation, sleep deprivation, isolation, and other stress and duress tactics at a secret facility in Kabul. The facility is run not by the CIA but by the Defense Intelligence Agency, which has secret authorization to use "special" interrogation methods detailed in the classified Appendix M to the Army Field Manual. When this news broke, Defense Department officials initially denied the existence of a secret facility. Later, they acknowledged that the black jail is an "interrogation facility," not a "detention site," and therefore neither does the ICRC have a right to access those held there nor do the regular interrogation rules apply.

Who cares about torture? Human rights and legal organizations have been at the forefront of investigating and condemning the systematic abuse of prisoners, including the ACLU which expanded its mandate after 9/11 to address international law violations by the U.S. government abroad. Protest activism by civil society groups such as Witness against Torture and the ecumenical National Religious Campaign against Torture has been determined but demographically marginal. However, nothing resembling an antitorture social movement emerged. The American public has neither exacted a political price for torture nor demonstrated any serious investment in the issue. Because those subjected to "enhanced interrogation" and incommunicado detention are foreigner Muslims abroad—with a few nonwhite exceptions at home, no domestic constituency has been directly affected or immediately imperiled, which helps explain the nonemergence of an antitorture social movement. But equally important is the fact that the general public is too ignorant to formulate intelligent opinions, and their ignorance has been nourished by coverage in the mainstream media of specious "torture works" and "worst of the worst" arguments propounded by Bush, Cheney, and other torture advocates.

When it comes to American torture, the American people have failed to exercise their vaunted and fearsome democratic rights responsibly by demanding that their state rules "right." Worse than that, the vast majority have bought into the liberal ideology of torture's necessity defense, and subscribe to or accept the notion that torture critics are "far leftists," "un-American," or "apologists for terror." Passivity, apathy, or ignorance about the rights violating practices of a state is common in many societies and has many causes, some unavoidable (state secrecy being a prime example), but it is not normatively acceptable as long as democracy invests people with a right and a responsibility to determine how states rule. The more representative a state claims to be, and the more people believe themselves to be represented by the state that rules them, the greater their responsibility for the state's rights-violating practices. Torture by a military regime is deplorable, but torture by a democracy is inexcusable.

NOTES

1. George W. Bush, *Decision Points* (New York: Crown, 2010).
2. Dahlia Lithwick, "Interrogation Nation," *Slate*, November 10, 2010.
3. See "Matt Lauer Corners Bush on Torture" (http://www.youtube .com/watch?v=Mp4vLBvU1bA).
4. See David Luban, "Liberalism, Torture, and the Ticking Bomb," *Virginia Law Review* 91 (2005): 1425–1461.
5. See Mirko Bagaric and Julie Clarke, *Torture: When the Unthinkable is Morally Permissible* (Albany: State University of New York Press, 2007); Anat Biletzki, "The Judicial Rhetoric of Morality: Israel's High Court of Justice on the Legality of Torture," School of Social Science Occasional Paper No. 9 (2001); Stanley Cohen, "Talking about Torture in Israel," *Tikkun* 6 (1991): 23–30; Colin Dayan, *The Story of Cruel and Unusual* (Boston: Boston Review Press, 2007); Alan Dershowitz, *Why Terrorism Works: Understanding the Threat, Responding to the Challenge* (New Haven, CT: Yale University Press, 2003); Jean Elshtain, *Just War against Terror: The Burden of American Power in a Violent World* (New York: Basic Books, 2004); Karen Greenberg, ed., *The Torture Debate in America* (New York: Cambridge University Press, 2005); Lisa Hajjar, "Sovereign Bodies, Sovereign States and the Problem of Torture," *Studies in Law,*

Politics and Society 21 (2000): 101–34; Jennifer Harbury, *Truth, Torture and the American Way: The History and Consequences of US Involvement in Torture* (Boston: Beacon, 2005); Scott Horton, "State of Exception: Bush's War on the Rule of Law," *Harper's Magazine*, July 2007, 74–81; Michael Ignatieff, *The Lesser Evil: Political Ethics in an Age of Terror* (Princeton: Princeton University Press, 2004); John Parry, "Torture Nation, Torture Law," *Georgetown Law Journal* 97 (2009): 1001–1056; Eric Posner and Adrien Vermeule, *Terror in the Balance: Security, Liberty and the Courts* (New York: Oxford University Press, 2007); Darius Rejali, *Torture and Democracy* (Princeton: Princeton University Press, 2007); Stuart Streichler, "Mad about Yoo, or Why Worry about the Next Unconstitutional War?" *Journal of Law and Politics* 24 (2008): 93–128; Jeremy Waldron, "Torture and Positive Law: Jurisprudence for the White House," *Columbia Law Review* 105 (2005): 1681–1750.

6. Lisa Hajjar, "Rights at Risk: Why the Right Not To Be Tortured Is Important to *You*," *Studies in Law, Politics and Society* 48 (2009): 93–120.

7. See Jane Mayer, *The Dark Side: The Inside Story of How the War on Terror Turned into a War on American Ideals* (New York: Doubleday, 2008); Ron Suskind, *The One Percent Doctrine: Deep Inside America's Pursuit of Its Enemies since 9/11* (New York: Simon and Schuster, 2006).

8. See Lisa Hajjar, "Does Torture Work? A Sociolegal Assessment of the Practice in Historical and Global Perspective," *Annual Review of Law and Social Science* 5 (2009): 311–345.

9. Phillipe Sands, *Torture Team: Rumsfeld's Memo and the Betrayal of American Values* (Hampshire, UK: Palgrave Macmillan, 2008).

10. See John Yoo, *War by Other Means: An Insider's Account of the War on Terror* (New York: Atlantic Monthly, 2006).

11. See Joseph Margulies, *Guantanamo and the Abuse of Presidential Power* (New York: Simon and Schuster, 2006).

12. Mayer, *The Dark Side*.

13. See Jameel Jaffer and Amrit Singh, *The Administration of Torture: From Washington to Abu Ghraib and Beyond* (New York: Columbia University Press, 2007).

14. See Seymour Hersh, *Chain of Command: The Road from 9/11 to Abu Ghraib* (New York: Harper Collins, 2004).

15. Seymour Hersh, "Torture at Abu Ghraib," *New Yorker*, May 10, 2004.

16. See Mark Danner, ed., *Torture and Truth: America, Abu Ghraib and the War on Terror* (New York: New York Review of Books, 2004); Karen Greenberg and Joshua Dratel, eds., *The Torture Papers: The Road to Abu Ghraib* (New York: Cambridge University Press, 2005).

17. David Rose, "Tortured Reasoning," *Vanity Fair*, December 16, 2008.

12

UNETHICAL ALLIANCE? THE UNITED STATES, PAKISTAN, AND THE "WAR ON TERRORISM"

Cris Toffolo

INTRODUCTION

One of the United States' most important relationships in its "war on terror" ("WOT") has been with Pakistan, the world's second largest Muslim democracy and a staunch ally of the United States for most of the years since its formation in 1947. This essay studies how the United States' "WOT" has impacted Pakistan and it examines ethical questions raised by the nature of that impact, especially given that Pakistan is a close ally. It concludes with suggestions for an alternative way for the United States to engage with Pakistan and other states, in order to stem terrorism.

CURRENT U.S. POLICY TOWARD PAKISTAN

After the 9/11 events—as in the 1980s when the Soviet occupation of Afghanistan led to the *mujahedeen* resistance—the United States has sent supplies through Pakistan. Again, as in the past, the U.S. military has worked very closely with Pakistan's government and military, particularly it's Inter-Service Intelligence (ISI), on the conduct of operations inside Afghanistan. Also like before, the United States supported a military dictator rather than encouraging democratic processes in Pakistan (i.e., General Zia ul-Haq in the 1980s, and after 9/11, General Musharraf, until his own people removed him in 2009).

The major difference between U.S. policy then and now is that during the 1980s the United States and Pakistan were both supporters of the mujahedeen. In the case of the United States, that support amounted to around six billion dollars in aid. Today, many of the mujahedeen (most famously, Osama bin Laden) are members of the Taliban and al-Qaeda, and are now the people whom the United States sees as its main enemies.

Despite the fact that the United States and Pakistan in the past both supported the mujahedeen, they have very different historic—and likely future—connections to these groups, especially the Taliban. Whereas the United States had a short-term utilitarian interest in their predecessor in the 1980s, Pakistan, of necessity, has an ongoing relationship, because Afghanistan is Pakistan's closest neighbor, and one with whom it's population shares ethnic and kinship ties. Just as the United States understands its neighbor Canada to be a necessary ally, and hence develops a stronger relationship with that country than with most others, so Pakistan regards Afghanistan, but with more urgency because of Pakistan's hostile relationship with India, its large eastern neighbor. Given those hostilities, Pakistan feels a great need to have peaceful relations with its western neighbor, Afghanistan. This, Pakistani's believe, would be easy to achieve if not for repeated superpower involvement in Afghanistan. This is the larger context within which ordinary Pakistanis judge their government's collaboration with the United States.

This collaboration is made more controversial by the fact that in order to pursue objectives the United States considers vital to its national interest, it has pressured the government of Pakistan to pursue policies that are not always seen by Pakistanis to be in their national interest. This is because U.S. policy has resulted in the disappearance, and sometimes death, of over a thousand people, and to the internal displacement, at one point in 2009, of over two million Pakistani citizens, according to Human Rights Watch and the United Nations High Commission for Refugees.

Two U.S. policies in particular raise troubling ethical concerns. The first is the use of "forced disappearance" and "extraordinary rendition," which are extrajudicial (outside of the law) practices that often include torture of the detained persons. The second is the use of missiles launched from unmanned drones inside Pakistan's territory, as well as other covert counterinsurgency operations, ostensibly without the Pakistani government's permission. Such actions violate international law and frequently result in the killing of innocent civilians.

FORCED DISAPPEARANCE AND
EXTRAORDINARY RENDITION

Rendition is a legal procedure the United States has used since the 1800s, to "render" suspects from other countries for criminal prosecution. Traditional rendition involves surrendering a person to a foreign jurisdiction, in accordance with procedures stipulated by treaty.

After the first World Trade Center bombing in 1993, the Clinton administration expanded its counterterrorism operations. This included expanding rendition to embrace rendering people to non-judicial authorities, outside the legal process, which typically is accomplished by kidnapping and transferring persons against their will to other countries, usually in order to circumvent their rights. These "ghost detainees," as they are called, often are tortured. After 9/11 President Bush substantially expanded both the scale and purpose of this practice by signing a secret presidential order authorizing the CIA to capture, kill, or detain al-Qaeda members anywhere in the world. According to one expert at New York University's School of Law, obtaining information through the use of torture "became a primary goal, and not merely a collateral consequence, of rendition to third countries."[1]

How extensively is extraordinary rendition used, particularly in Pakistan? To date Russia, Sweden, and the United States have orchestrated extraordinary renditions, and more than 17 other countries, including Pakistan, have participated in some way.[2] According to Sangitha Millar, by late 2001, as a result of prisoners captured in Afghanistan during Operation Enduring Freedom, the CIA and other U.S. intelligence agencies had "up to 100 high-value detainees being held 'off the books' in unknown locations."[3] Of these, 39 remained unaccounted for in 2008.[4] In 2008 the New America Foundation released a paper that reviewed the reports of Human Rights Watch, Amnesty International, the American Civil Liberties Union, and the Center for Human Rights and Global Justice at New York University's law school, among other sources. From this they concluded there were 67 known cases of extraordinary rendition by the United States between 1995 and 2008 of which 53 occurred after 9/11 and included sending these people to countries criticized in the U.S. Department of State's annual Country Reports on Human Rights for using torture. Of the cases surveyed in this article, 4 were Pakistani citizens, 3 were rendered to Pakistan, and 23 were rendered from Pakistan. Of the last group, 8 were never heard from again; this is the only country named in the report for which this was the case.[5]

These numbers for Pakistan only reflect the people known to have been handed over to the United States under extraordinary rendition. The full impact of this policy is much larger, however, for it is estimated by Amnesty International that "hundreds, if not thousands" of Pakistanis and foreign nationals have been forcibly disappeared in Pakistan,[6] and that many "if not most...have been tortured or otherwise ill-treated."[7]

Since Pakistan joined the "WOT" in late 2001, it began to take advantage of the more permissive attitude in Washington toward human rights violations. With the United States now demanding Pakistan's assistance in extraordinary rendition, and given the United States' own human rights violations of terror suspects, the Pakistani government feels freer to act in a similar manner toward its own internal critics, including activists from Sindh and Baluchistan who are agitating for more development resources to be directed to these provinces and for greater rights.

A sense of the scope of the problem can be gained from examining petitions filed with Pakistan's highest court. Beginning in December 2005, with the disappearance of Masood Janjua, the court began asking the government about "disappeared" persons. Encouraged by this, in August 2006, Masood's wife, Amina Masood Janjua, and another woman founded the group Defense of Human Rights and filed a petition with the supreme court seeking information about 16 disappeared persons. The court immediately began hearings and by October 2006 had found 186 people mentioned in 458 cases brought before them. These individuals had by then either been released or placed in official detention centers.

In February 2007 the Human Rights Commission of Pakistan (HRCP), a nongovernmental group, filed another petition on behalf of 148 missing persons. The court demanded the government provide information about these cases. Partly in response to this, as well as due to other sensitive political issues, General Musharraf suspended the court's chief justice, Iftikhar Muhammad Chaudhry, on March 9, 2007. Lawyers throughout the country then boycotted the courts and began the "lawyers' movement" that led to Chaudhry's reinstatement on July 20. By then the HRCP's petition list had grown to 198 persons. In October 2007, Chaudhry summoned the heads of the intelligence agencies to explain their role in forcibly disappearing hundreds of people, and stated he would initiate legal action against those responsible.

Facing this and other tough issues, on November 3, President Musharraf issued a state of emergency and suspended the bulk of

Pakistan's constitution. He did this despite the fact that such power is not given to anyone by the constitution. He then prohibited all courts from issuing any orders against the president or any other governmental official, and he ordered all high court judges to take a new oath stipulating the constitution was "in abeyance," and that the president "shall be deemed always to have had the power to amend the Constitution" and that they would discharge their duties in accordance with provisional orders he was now issuing.[8] Three weeks later, Musharraf reinstated the constitution, but not before adding a new provision, Article 270AAA, that stipulated the emergency and all of his other orders were "declared to have been validly made by the competent authority and notwithstanding anything contained in the Constitution shall not be called in question in any court."[9]

These dramatic events were followed by the tragic assassination of former Prime Minister Benazir Bhutto in December 2007. The February election then produced a coalition government led by her widower, Asif Ali Zardari, of the Pakistan People's Party (PPP). This government was formed in March 2008, and shortly thereafter Pakistan signed the international Covenant on Civil and Political Rights, and the international Convention against Torture. At that time the new government pledged to restore the 1973 Constitution, to resolve the status of disappeared people, and to reinstate the deposed judges. While judges were reinstated in March 2009, and parliament finished passing the amendments necessary to bring the Constitution back to its original 1973 form in spring 2010, by October 2010 more than 70 disappeared persons were still missing and numerous cases were still pending before the Supreme Court. Further, violence may be escalating in that over 40 people in Baluchistan have been assassinated in "kill and dump" operations between July and October 2010.[10]

One of the most disturbing aspects of forced disappearance and extraordinary rendition is that very young children have been among those victimized. According to Amnesty International, in September 2002 Yusuf al-Khalid, age nine, and Abed al-Khalid, age seven, in violation of international law, were apprehended by Pakistani security forces during an attempt to capture their father, Khalid Sheikh Mohammed. After Mohammed's arrest in March 2003, his sons reportedly were transferred to the United States and used as leverage to force their father to cooperate. In a press report from March 10, 2003, one U.S. official explained: "We are handling them with kid gloves...but we need to know as much about their father's recent activities as possible."[11] Also in March 2003, in Karachi, several other children in Mohammed's family were detained in unknown locations.[12]

This practice has continued beyond the immediate aftermath of 9/11. In May 2006 in Pakistan a ten-year-old was disappeared along with his father. The boy was reportedly tortured to make him confess that his father had links with al-Qaeda. Amnesty International also reports the case of another nine-year-old boy, Asad Usman, who was only released in April 2007, after the Supreme Court got involved. There are also other cases of children being held in secret detention in Pakistan.[13]

In summary, in Pakistan the U.S. policy of extraordinary rendition has contributed to a weakening of the rule of law and to a dramatic upsurge in domestic disappearances. All of these facts decrease the desire of ordinary Pakistanis to maintain an alliance with the United States. Other allies are also increasingly uneasy about the United States in the wake of its use of extraordinary rendition. Germany has issued arrest warrants for 13 U.S. intelligence officers, Italy has indicted 26 Americans for their role in just one extraordinary rendition of an Egyptian cleric, and Great Britain has issued a report stating that the practice has serious implications for future intelligence collaboration with the United States. In other words, "circumventing legal channels weakens international judicial and prosecutorial cooperation, which makes the rule of law [more unstable]."[14] The practice also contributes to undermining the growth of democracy by setting a bad precedent and strengthening internal security forces, typically the least law-abiding parts of any government. Now Sudan, Zimbabwe, and Egypt justify disappearing their political foes by referring to the U.S. practice.[15] Additionally, this practice undercuts other counterterrorism efforts, by providing al-Qaeda and other terrorist organizations with a powerful recruiting tool.

Given these facts, it is easy to understand why Vice President Joseph Biden (while he was a senator serving as chairman of the Senate Committee on Foreign Relations) stated, "rendition, as currently practiced, is undermining our moral credibility and standing abroad and weakening the coalitions with foreign governments that we need to effectively combat international terrorism."[16] He went on to argue, "In our long-term effort to stem the tide of international terrorism, our commitments to the rule of law and to individual rights and civil liberties are among our most formidable weapons." This point of view is consistent with the 9/11 Commission, which emphasized the need for the United States to "offer an example of moral leadership in the world, committed to treat people humanely, abide by the rule of law, and be generous and caring to our neighbors."[17]

THE VIOLATION OF PAKISTANI SOVEREIGNTY BY THE USE OF UNMANNED DRONES

The other U.S. policy that deeply angers Pakistanis is the pursuit of al-Qaeda and the Taliban inside Pakistani territory, in violation of Pakistani sovereignty, using missile strikes from both unmanned drones and piloted aircraft, as well as counterinsurgency forces. According to the most recent study of the New America Foundation, between the beginning of 2004 and October 2010 there have been a 188 drone strikes reported in northwest Pakistan, 92 of which occurred in 2010. These strikes have killed somewhere between 1,218 and 1,879 people, of which between 897 and 1,344 likely were militants, making the civilian fatality rate since 2004 about 28 percent. Of the total deaths, between 869 and 1,474 have occurred since President Obama came into office, though it is estimated that in 2010 the civilian casualty rate has dropped to 8 percent.[18]

Such use of drones is illegal under international law. For instance, Article 51 of the UN Charter allows for preemptive attacks only to repel an *imminent* attack. Further, any such attack must be proportionate and not punitive.[19] U.S. drone attacks are not done to repel imminent attacks, and when conducted in Pakistan, they are done within the territory controlled not by an enemy but by an ally. Given the illegality of drone attacks under international law, the Bush administration, in order to justify such attacks, relied on the U.S. domestic law concept of "hot pursuit"[20] even though domestic law has no force in the international arena, and the doctrine itself only applies to certain exigent circumstances when obtaining a search warrant can be foregone in order to apprehend a suspect or obtain evidence in order to save lives. By contrast cross-border *killings* are of a completely different nature and negate all due process and preclude all accountability, which even the doctrine of hot pursuit maintains.

Sometimes the use of drones and secret counterinsurgency forces are applied together. An especially troubling case in point is that of Hayatullah Khan, a Pakistani journalist who reportedly had photographic evidence that contradicted official accounts of a December 1, 2005, U.S. drone attack.[21] He was abducted on December 5, 2005, while on his way to cover a rally organized to protest that attack. Following his abduction, Pakistani officials made contradictory statements about his whereabouts. In May 2006 his brother was told by a government official that the family would get "good news" by June 20. But on June 16 Hayatullah's emaciated body was found handcuffed and riddled with bullet wounds. In August 2006, after countrywide protests by journalists, the Peshawar High Court submitted a report of its inquiry to the federal government; however no one has been arrested. Then in September 2006, his 14-year-old brother was shot dead by unknown attackers. A year later, in November, Hayatullah's widow, who had vigorously pursued her husband's case, was killed when a bomb was thrown into her house.[22]

In addition to being ethically troubling and illegal, the use of drones is self-defeating in terms of the "main goal" of this counter-insurgency operation, which according to General Petraeus, former U.S. commander in Afghanistan, is to win over the local population.[23] That this is the case was made very apparent by the first ever opinion poll conducted in mid-2010 by the New American Foundation in the Federally Administered Tribal Areas (FATA) where most of the drone attacks have occurred. It found nearly 90 percent of the population intensely opposes U.S. military operations in the region, with much of their anger due to drone attacks which, 83 percent believe don't accurately target only militants.[24]

WHAT IS OWED TO ALLIES?

An alliance is a formal relationship typically specified by a treaty. Because an alliance is an especially close and formal bond and one that sets up a community of common interest and expectations about future behavior, what is owed to an ally is much more than what is due to other members of the international community. This is because each state has made a formal and public pledge of assistance, and because the relationship is ongoing. In the case of Pakistan, this ally has made considerable sacrifices in support of U.S. policy, including standing by while its own citizens have been killed by the U.S. military in pursuit of U.S. (but not necessarily Pakistani) national interests. At the very least, the United States should consult with Pakistan's government as it devises strategies that will involve Pakistani personnel, resources, and territory and put Pakistani civilian lives and infrastructure at risk. Further, given that the norm of all ethical systems is that members of the community are understood as having claims and rights against all other members, when devising strategies of engagement with Pakistan, the United States needs to begin with the commitment that Pakistanis are just as important as Americans, and that Pakistan's national security needs are just as relevant to consider as America's when designing policy.

In short, American policymakers need to take seriously the way Pakistan understands its own security needs, which typically are framed by its complex and hostile relationship with India. This is central to Pakistan's identity. So beyond the particular policy issues discussed earlier, about how the United States has conducted its military strategy in Pakistan, there is the broader issue of how the alliance with the United States skews Pakistan's own national security policy. American policymakers sometimes argue that Pakistanis misunderstand their own security needs—that due to historic and parochial biases they are obsessed with India, to their own detriment. While this analysis could be true—as some Pakistanis believe—it is also true that the United States makes this argument mainly because it wants Pakistan to shift its resources to better assist the United States' own agenda, which logically could be as parochial and misconceived as that of Pakistan.

A Blueprint for a More Ethical Response to Terrorism

From the earlier discussion it is clear that U.S policies of extraordinary rendition and unmanned drone attacks pose very high costs to Pakistan. In addition these policies have contributed to thwarting the development of democracy and undermining the rule of law in Pakistan. We have also discussed how these policies violate and undermine international law. Finally, these policies are contrary to the norms for relationships with allies, and hence make other allies less likely to trust the United States. Finally, these policies also violate America's public norms for human rights and justice, as stipulated in the U.S. constitution.

Is there a different set of policies that would constitute an ethical response to terrorism, specifically as related to Pakistan? Yes. At the broadest level, forming a new and more ethical response should begin by changing the paradigm through which terrorism is understood. Instead of seeing it as a military problem, it should be understood fundamentally as a political problem. Although terrorism is a horrifically violent and unethical tactic, it is one that is chosen "rationally" under certain conditions, by both states and nonstate actors. Usually nonstate actors resort to terrorist tactics because they have exhausted other means, or because they lack any access to the arenas of power where the groups' core concerns can be addressed. Understood in this light, terrorism is a very deadly form of political theater, elaborately and symbolically staged to grab the attention of the parties who have the power to change the situation.[25] As a theatrical tactic, terrorism is a *politics* of "threat magnification." It is a way for the weak to expose the weaknesses of the militarily strong. Al-Qaeda illustrates this point well, as its main weapon is the spread of psychological terror that is disproportionately greater than the death and destruction its actions actually cause.[26]

Approaching terrorism politically would bring the United States back into line with the rest of the world, both philosophically and in terms of adherence to law. Presently even the United States' closest allies do not view 9/11 in the same Manichean way that the Bush administration did (i.e., as a long-term global war of good vs. the axis of evil, in which tactics such as preemptive unilateral military action and regime change are warranted). Most other nations view the attacks of 9/11 as a crime and, thus, as a policing problem. From this point of view, one should deal with the terrorist perpetrators of death and destruction as violent criminals, using the extensive bodies of domestic and international criminal laws to punish them. This requires patient police work, intelligence sharing, coordinated international apprehension strategies, and legal proceedings. The Obama administration has taken some steps in this direction, by redefining the current conflicts the United States remains embroiled in not as a global war on terrorism (which is a tactic), nor as a war against Islam (a religion), but as a war against al-Qaeda and its violent affiliates (i.e., a specific political network that uses illegal terrorist tactics).

In terms of prevention, it is necessary to address the social, political, and economic roots of terrorism. This requires the United States to take a long-term view of both its past and future actions. Knowledge of history is critical because those whom we have supported as "freedom fighters" in the past later transformed into terrorist foes, in part as a result of the United States suddenly cutting off patronage to these groups. A prime example of this was the termination of U.S. support of the mujahedeen in 1989 at the end of the Cold War when Afghanistan was still in ruins after a decade of warfare. This was viewed as a serious betrayal of a staunch ally, and it directly contributed to the current hostility with which these groups view the United States. It was found that 15 of the 19 who were involved in the 9/11 attacks were citizens of Saudi Arabia angered mainly by the United States' staunch support for that country's undemocratic regime, which many Saudis view as unjust, but which cannot be challenged as long as the United States continues to back the monarchy. Understood from this long-term and broad political perspective the central remedies for terrorism are political, economic, diplomatic, and criminal. Efforts in these areas must address the roots of the phenomenon in a sustained and consistent way.[27]

Terrorism is also a function of state weakness; therefore, in Pakistan (and Afghanistan), the United States should consider providing ordinary citizens what al-Qaeda and the Taliban provide, and what their own governments do not (i.e., access to education, jobs, local security, and justice). In addition, making sure ordinary people have access to water, electricity, and long-term national development is also essential to making sure people see the existing system as beneficial to them. History has demonstrated that the Pakistani population is very pragmatic; they have voted for religious parties when mainstream parties have failed to keep their promises, but they just as quickly have thrown religious parties out when similarly they have failed. For example, in the elections of October 2002 religious parties won 12 percent of the votes cast, and 63 of the national parliament's 272 seats, and were able to dominate two provincial governments; however, in the next election of 2008, these same parties only garnered 1.5 percent of the votes cast and only 6 seats in the national parliament (Pakistan Election Commission). This decline—in one election cycle—is an incredible statement about this pragmatism of Pakistan's electorate. If Pakistan's political parties where strengthened so they were more internally democratic and less reliant on a small circle of elites, these institutions could function to provide what ordinary citizens need. The Pakistani state likewise needs to be strengthened, not weakened, in the process of working to end terrorism aimed at both the United States and Pakistan.

CONCLUSION

The logic of U.S. actions since 9/11 has coalesced around the "Bush doctrine," which is no longer just a strategy for how the United States combats terrorism, but has become the new paradigm for organizing all of the United States' foreign policy.[28] It is centered on a new and more aggressive national security principle that appears to have been embraced by the Obama administration. For the first time in its history, and in opposition to much settled international law, under the Bush doctrine the United States has embraced taking offensive action. Now prior armed attack against the United States is no longer considered necessary for the United States to strike. The Bush administration's justification for breaking with existing U.S. strategic policy, tradition, and international law, and allowing preemptive strikes was that the nature of warfare has changed, and this necessitates a different type of response. This "new kind of war" is fought "by a new kind of enemy"—nonstate actors whose capacity to operate has been greatly enhanced by globalization, networking, and new communications and weapons technologies.[29] They employ stealth and deception to attack in unconventional and asymmetrical ways. Their operations are directed against political, cultural, and population targets with the goal of killing as many as possible.[30] Thus, as former secretary of defense Donald Rumsfeld stated, "this will be a war like none other our nation has faced."[31]

The problem with this argument, however, is that terrorism is *not* a new or exceptional form of political activity and hence the premise that justifies this new approach is false. In the months immediately following 9/11, fear caused by the events of that day led large numbers of Americans to accept the new premise uncritically, because they saw 9/11 as "exceptional." Interesting, however, is the fact that the first use to which this doctrine was put was to justify attacking Iraq, a *country* (not a "new kind of enemy") that was not planning to strike at the United States. Before 9/11 the administration faced stiff opposition both abroad and at home (including from within the military) to using a more aggressive approach to deal with its outstanding problems with Iraq. The events of 9/11 and the use of the war paradigm, as is often the case, permitted the administration to rally support for programs and policies that would have otherwise encountered stiff opposition. In this case, the "new kind of warfare" argument justified going to war under new rules of engagement against an old and very traditional enemy.[32]

Behind this whole new foreign policy edifice lays another set of assumptions that have very important ethical consequences. They run something like this: terrorists who use direct violence again civilians to intimidate and get their way act outside the law and the norms of civilized society, therefore, we are morally justified in responding to them outside the law and our usual moral norms. Admittedly, this "eye for an eye" morality doesn't live up to the standards of Christian virtue, but it is the only type of morality terrorists understand. The argument continues that since Muslims use such a primitive morality, they have no right to complain when we apply that same standard of justice to them. Second, people who engage in terrorist acts have no real morality or rationality to appeal to; in doing horrific violence to innocent civilians they demonstrate they do not follow natural law. As such, they aren't really fully human, for the mark of a human being is reason, which allows us to make moral calculations and to follow laws. These "creatures" are lawless and amoral, outside the rules that govern normal human conduct and accountability. This frees us to perpetrate violence upon them just as we might do to other nonhuman species for our own needs (e.g., we kill rats and cockroaches to protect ourselves from the spread of disease, we kill cattle for food to sustain ourselves, and we kill rabid doges and other predatory species because they are dangerous). If terrorists are not really or fully human, but merely animals, then only the law of the jungle (i.e., force) can be used to respond to them, either as a way to teach them a lesson, or to protect ourselves by deterring or eliminating them.

The problem with this way of thinking is that it suffers from a very central paradox: in our use of preemptive and overwhelming violence against terrorists, especially when it causes the loss of innocent civilian life or suffering—which is acknowledged when we use such terms as "collateral damage" or "extraordinary" rendition to link an illegal practice to accepted moral and legal norms—we too are guilty of killing innocent civilians. Further, in using violence that results in the death of noncombatants, we go against the norms that we claim to hold our own behavior to, and the norms that we use to judge others (as to whether they are civilized). In doing acts that result in the deaths of innocent people we are no different from "the terrorists." We also violate the norms that are at the very center of our public morality, as articulated in our most sacred public document, the Constitution. In addition, we propel a dynamic in which we change the trajectory of human behavior, from that of bringing our actions more into line with internationally recognized norms of morality and law, to undertaking actions that break down the credibility of such standards and regimes. So instead of advancing the development and practice of moral and legal norms we are effectively promoting the law of the jungle over the rule of law. In our use of force we legitimate the use of violence, and the right of the powerful to rule (simply because they are powerful). This comes at the expense of the idea that legitimate rule derives from the rule of law and morality, and the consent of the governed. For law and morality rest not on the force that imposes them but upon people's voluntary acquiescence—that is, people follow them because they are considered valid, legitimate, useful, and effective. Every violation of the law and moral codes therefore lowers their force and power, and thus when we too use force we also contribute to the problem. Hence the ethical response to terrorism is not to outdo a terrorist opponent by using even greater displays of violence and "shock and awe." That is to play into their game of using violence to provoke enough fear to achieve their objective by force. Instead, the ethical way to respond to terrorism is to insist on a different game that maintains standards of ethics and political arrangements that rest on genuine popular legitimacy.

NOTES

1. Aziz Z. Huq, "Extraordinary Rendition and the Wages of Hypocrisy," *World Policy Journal* (Spring 2006), 2.

2. David Weissbrodt and Amy Bergquist, "Extraordinary Rendition: A Human Rights Analysis," *Harvard Human Rights Journal* 19 (Spring 2006): 128.
3. Sangitha McKenzie Millar, "Extraordinary Rendition, Extraordinary Mistake," *Foreign Policy in Focus*, August 29, 2008 (http://www.fpif.org/fpiftxt/5502).
4. Ibid., 2.
5. Peter Bergen and Katherine Tiedemann, *Extraordinary Rendition by the Numbers: Terrorism and Counterinsurgency Initiative* (Washington, D.C.: New America Foundation, March 2008).
6. Amnesty International, "Take Action on Enforced Disappearances in Pakistan on International Day of the Disappeared—30 August 2010," August 2, 2010, AI Index: ASA 33/007/2010.
7. Carlotta Gall, "Picture of Secret Detentions Emerges in Pakistan," *The New York Times*, December 19, 2007.
8. "Oath of Office (Judges) Order 2007," November 3, 2007: www.pakistani.org/pakistan/constitution.
9. Constitution (Amendment) Order, President's Order No. 5 of 2007, November 21, 2007: http://www.comparativeconstitutionsproject.org/files/Pakistan_2007.pdf.
10. Amnesty International, "Pakistan: Investigate Murder and Torture of Baloch Activists," Press Release, October 26, 2010.
11. Olga Craig, "CIA Holds Young Sons of Captured al-Qaeda Chief," *Sunday Telegraph* (U.K.), March 9, 2003: http://www.telegraph.co.uk/news/main.jhtml?xml=%2Fnews%2F2003%2F03%2F09%2Fwalqa09.xml.
12. Amnesty International, *Pakistan: Human Rights Ignored in the "War on Terror,"* September 2006, AI Index: ASA 33/036/2006, 29.
13. Ibid.
14. Millar, "Extraordinary Rendition," 6.
15. Ibid.
16. Ibid.
17. Ibid.
18. Peter Bergen and Katherine Tiedemann, *The Year of the Drone: An Analysis of U.S. Drone Strikes in Pakistan, 2004–2010* (Washington, D.C.: New America Foundation, February 24, 2010): http://counterterrorism.newamerica.net/sites/newamerica.net/files/policydocs/bergentiedemann2.pdf.
19. Tariq Hassan, "The Illegality of Drones," *The Dawn* (Leading English Newspaper of Pakistan), June 2, 2009: http://www.dawn.com/wps/wcm/connect/dawn-content-library/dawn/news/pakisatn/16-the-i.
20. Ibid., 2.
21. Amnesty International, *Pakistan: Human Rights Ignored in the "War on Terror,"* 40.
22. "Slain tribal area journalist's widow murdered." Reporters Without Borders. November 17, 2007. http://www.rsf.org/article.php3?id_article=24417 (retrieved August 10, 2011).

23. Christian Science Monitor, "Drone Aircraft in a Stepped-up War in Afghanistan and Pakistan," December 11, 2009 (http://www.csmonitgor.com/layout/set/pring/conent/view/print/268420).

24. Opposition to the use of drones drops dramatically if they could be operated by Pakistanis, and in general, 70 percent of FATA residents want the Pakistani military—without America's help—to pursue the militants living among them. Another interesting finding of the poll is that fewer than 10 percent of FATA residents support al-Qaeda and fewer than 20 percent support the Pakistani Taliban. If either group were on an election ballot they would not get 1 percent of the vote. Peter Bergen, Patrick C. Doherty, and Ken Ballen, "U.S.-Led Drone War is Self-Defeating: New Poll, First of Its Kind, Shows Widespread Opposition to U.S. Drone Attacks in Pakistan," CNN.Com, September 30, 2010. The New American Foundation (http://security.newamerica.net/publications/articles/2010/us_led_drone_war_is_self_defeating_37742).

25. Hence the choice of the 9/11 targets were the centers of U.S. power: the Twin Towers of the World Trade Center, representing the U.S. financial system, and the Pentagon, and either the White House or Congress, representing global U.S. political and military domination.

26. Peter J. Katzenstein, "Same War, Different Views: Germany, Japan and the War on Terrorism," *Current History* (December 2002): 427–435; reprinted as Article 27 in *Annual Editions: Violence and Terrorism 06/07*, 9th ed., Thomas J. Badey, ed. (Dubuque, IA: McGraw Hill, 2006), 194.

27. Ibid., 193.

28. As the new organizing principle of U.S. foreign policy, counterterrorism now defines the parameters of everything from alliances, to the use of aid money, to military doctrine, force structures, and domestic law. In this way it is very much like the Truman Doctrine and the adoption of the strategy of containment in the late 1940s [James Steinberg, "Counterterrorism: A New organizing Principle for American National Security?" *Brookings Review* (Summer 2002): 4–7. Reprinted as Article 26 in *Annual Editions: Violence and Terrorism 06/07*, 9th ed., Thomas J. Badey, ed. (Dubuque, IA: McGraw Hill, 2006), 189]. And it could not have come at a better time for foreign policy hawks who had been at sea after the end of the Cold War made their bipolar and Manichean worldview obsolete, at least as defined as a fight against communism. Al-Qaeda and the specter of international terrorism provided a new lease of life for foreign policy framed in biopolar terms.

29. At the time there was much gnashing of teeth about the fact that al-Qaeda had no "hard targets" to attack, which is the normal way in which military operations are used to punish an enemy. U.S. military strategy for decades has been designed around fighting wars with other countries, not small mobile groups, and so we fought the kind of war we knew how to fight, rather than the type of conflict al-Qaeda used,, which meant finding *countries* to hit.

30. Richard H. Shultz and Andreas Vogt, "The Real Intelligence Failure of 9/11 and the Case for a Doctrine of Striking First," in *Terrorism and Counterterrorism: Understanding the New Security Environment: Readings and Interpretations*, ed. Russell D. Howard and Reid L Sawyer (Guilford CT: McGraw Hill, 2003), 385.
31. Ibid.
32. Katzenstein, "Same War, Different Views," 198.

BIBLIOGRAPHY

Amnesty International. *Pakistan: Working to Stop Human Rights Violations in the "War on Terror"* (December 2006), AI Index: ASA 33/051/2006.

————. "South Asia: 'War on Terror' Spawns New Patterns of Enforced Disappearance," AI Press Release (August 30, 2006), AI Index: ASA 04/001/2006. News Service No. 221.

————. "Pakistan: Authorities Must Investigate Killings of Baloch Leaders." Press Release (April 9, 2009).

Bergen, Peter, and Katherine Tiedemann. *Revenge of the Drones: An Analysis of Drone Strikes in Pakistan.* Summary Report of a Study Conducted by the New America Foundation (October 19, 2009) (http://www.newamerica.net/publications/policy/revenge_of_the_drones).

Central Intelligence Agency of the United States. *The World Fact Book* (August 2009) (https://www.cia.govt/librar/publications/the-world-factbook/geos/xx.html#People).

Election Commission of Pakistan. http://www.ecp.gov.pk/.

Human Rights Watch. *Pakistan: Events of 2009.* http://www.hrw.org/en/node/87399.

Huysmans, Jef. "The Question of the Limit: Desecuritisation and the Aesthetics of Horror in Political Realism." *Journal of International Studies* 27.3 (1998): 569–589.

Majidia, Mazda. "'Pakistan Cedes to Mass Protest's Main Demand' Party for Socialism and Liberation" (Mar 17, 2009) (http://www.pslweb.org/site/News2/159233817?page=NewsArticle&id-11545&news_iv_)

Raghavan, V. R. "The Double-Edged Effect in South Asia," taken from the *Washington Quarterly* (Autumn 2004): 147–155. Reprinted as Article 30 in *Annual Editions: Violence and Terrorism 07/08*, 10th ed., Thomas J. Badey, ed. (Dubuque, IA: McGraw Hill, 2007), 198–201.

Rohde, David. "Pakistani Sets Emergency Rule, Defying the US." *New York Times,* November 4, 2007.

Satterthwaite, Margaret. "Extraordinary Rendition and Disappearances in the 'War on Terror.'" *Gonzaga Journal of International Law* (July 17, 2009) (http://www.gonzagajil.org/content/view/141/26/).

United Nations High Commissioner for Refugees. "Civilians Still Need Help in Swat, a Year after Conflict Engulfed the Area." *News Stories,* April 3, 2010 (http://www.unhcr.org/4bdaeb646.html).

13

THE AGENT

Mark Arax

Before the wins and losses get tallied up and the war on terror finally goes down in the books as either wisdom or folly, it may be useful to recall what took place on a spring day in 2006 on the thirteenth floor of the federal courthouse in Sacramento. There, in a perfectly digni-fied room, in front of prosecutors, defense attorneys, and a judge, a tall gaunt man named James Wedick Jr. was fighting for a chance to testify, to tell jurors about the 35 years he had spent with the FBI and how it came to be that he was standing before them not on the side of the U.S. government but next to two Pakistani Muslims, son and father, whose scrapbooks and prayers and immigrant dreams were now being picked over in the first terrorism trial in California.

From his seat at the defense table, Wedick stared straight ahead as the prosecutor from Washington, a stocky guy with a little too much bounce in his step, called him a hired gun for the terrorists, argu-ing that any criticisms the former FBI agent had about the investiga-tion would only confuse the jury and waste the court's time. Wedick might have stood up and shouted that he was the most decorated FBI agent ever to work out of the state capital, that for years prosecutors, judges, and juries had nothing but time to consider the way he busted dirty state senators and cracked open the biggest health care scam in California history. But now he could only sit and listen as the judge ruled that the highlights in his career—Abscam, Operation Fountain Pen, Shrimpscam, Bonanno—were no reason to believe he had any-thing of value to offer about the FBI's conduct in the age of terror or, more to the point, about the government's case against Hamid Hayat, the cherry packer, and his father, Umer, the neighborhood ice cream man. By order of the court, Wedick was muzzled.

In eight weeks of trial, fifteen witnesses for the prosecution and seven witnesses for the defense took the stand, yet the one witness whose testimony might have struck a devastating blow to the claims of the U.S. government never got to tell his story. He never got to trace his metamorphosis from agent's agent to turncoat to a Sunday morning in June 2005, when he woke up thinking he had seen all the absurdities that a life of crime fighting had to offer only to find the FBI videotape—the confession that would lie at the heart of the case—on his doorstep.

It had arrived with no small hype. Down the road on Highway 99, the feds had busted up an al-Qaeda sleeper cell in the farming burg of Lodi, population 60,000, the apparent inspiration for Credence Clearwater's "Stuck in Lodi Again." The town sits at the far northern edge of the San Joaquin Valley and has gone from the "watermelon capital of the world" in the 1880s to the "Tokay grape capital of the world" in the 1920s to the "Zinfandel capital of the world" today. The community boasts 60 wineries, 36 tasting rooms, a Zinfest in May, and its own appellation: Lodi-Woodbridge. Somehow burrowed into the 90,000 acres of grape fields that pleat the rich flat loam of the Mokelumne River basin was a radical young Muslim carrying a prayer of jihad in his wallet.

Hamid Hayat had just returned home to Lodi from a terrorist camp in the hills of his ancestral Pakistan. He had been trained there with Kalishnikov rifles and curved swords and target dummies wearing the faces of Bush and Rumsfeld. He was awaiting instructions, via a letter in his mailbox, to bomb hospitals and supermarkets in California's heartland. In the meantime, he was processing Bing cherries on the outskirts of town. The two imams at the small marigold mosque across the street from the Lodi Boys and Girls Club directed the cell at the behest of Osama bin Laden. They were building a multimillion dollar school to spread the seeds of Islamic holy war to Pakistani immigrant children up and down the farm belt. If the story sounded too bizarre to be true, the 22-year-old cherry packer and his 47-year-old father, Umer Hayat, the ice cream man known to the kids of Lodi as "Mike," had confessed to everything on camera.

At home in the Gold River suburbs of Sacramento, Jim Wedick agreed to study the FBI video as a favor to one of the defense attorneys. He fully expected that he would be calling the attorney back and advising him that son and father, guilty as charged, needed to strike a quick plea deal. After all, it is hard to trump a confession, and in this instance the feds were holding not one confession but two. As Wedick stuck the video in his player and sat back on the couch to watch the grainy images, he recognized the setting right off. It was the old polygraph room at the FBI's regional headquarters on the north side of the capital. Despite the blanked-out faces, he recognized several of the agents too. They had come a long way, he thought, from the days when he ran the white-collar crime squad and they handled $1,000 thefts by bank tellers. In the year since his retirement, after the office had been completely reorganized in the wake of 9/11, these same agents had become experts on counterterrorism. Now, two at a time, they began the five-hour interrogation that would crack a Muslim suicide bomber in the making.

Wedick could see that Hamid Hayat was cold and scared. To keep from fidgeting, he locked his hands between his legs like a kid trying not to pee. He was rail thin with sunken eyes and eyebrows so wonderfully arched that he had the gaze of perpetual befuddlement. Even with his long black beard, he looked more teenager than man.

The agents gave him a blanket and pulled their chairs closer. We're here to listen, not judge. Whatever you tell us about the training camp won't come as a surprise. We have spy satellites over Pakistan, so if you're thinking about lying, you may want to think again. Wedick knew all too well the game they were playing, the back-and-forth between trust and fear. It might take hours, but if trust and fear were maneuvered the right way, the whole room suddenly would turn. One moment the suspect was way up here—seeing the world his way. And the next moment he was way down here—seeing it your way. The free fall, Wedick called it, the release that came from finally shedding the weight of lies. It happened with even the most cunning of crooks.

Hayat shifted in his chair, and his voice grew submissive. One hour, two hours, yawns, cigarette break, yawns, candy break, exhaustion. The free fall never came. Instead, each revelation, each new dramatic turn in his story, was coming from the mouths of the agents first. Rather than ask Hayat to describe what happened, they were describing what happened for him and then taking his "uh-uhs" and "uh-hmms" as solemn declarations. The kid was so open to suggestion that the camp itself went from being a village of mud huts to a building the size of the ARCO basketball arena. His fellow trainees numbered 35, 40, 50, how about 200? The camp was run by a political group, a religious school, maybe his uncle, maybe his grandfather, yes, it was al-Qaeda. The camp's location was all over the map too, from Afghanistan to Kashmir to a village in Pakistan called Balakot. As for weapons training, the camp owned one pistol, two rifles, and a knife to cut vegetables.

Deep into the confession, as the agents kept trying to pin down the contours of one believable story, they succeeded only in betraying

their own ignorance. They didn't seem to know the terrain of Pakistan
or the month of Ramadan. They didn't seem to fully appreciate that
they were dealing with an immigrant kid from a lowly Pashtun tribe
whose sixth-grade education and poor command of the English language ("Martyred? What does that mean, sir?") demanded a more
skeptical approach. And then there was the matter of the father's
confession, which veered wildly from his son's account. Umer Hayat
described visiting the camp and finding a thousand men wearing
black Ninja Turtle masks and performing "pole vaulting" exercises in
huge basement rooms. The camp wasn't located in Balakot but 100
miles in the other direction. Even so, the agents going back and forth
between the two interrogations never attempted to reconcile the stark
differences in the confessions.

Maybe it couldn't be helped, Wedick thought. Maybe the Hayats'
ties to terrorism had popped up out of nowhere and the agents were
scrambling to catch up. Yet Wedick would soon find out that this
wasn't the first night the agents had encountered the Hayats. They
had been tracking them, recording them for three years in an operation launched just weeks after 9/11. It began when a Pakistani undercover informant, fresh from working at McDonald's and Taco Bell,
passed on an incredible tip: Dr. Ayman Zawahiri, one of the world's
most wanted terrorists, Osama bin Laden's number two man, had
been living and praying in Lodi.

The video ended and Wedick picked up the phone and called
defense attorney Johnny Griffin. Whatever hesitation he had about
taking on the FBI office that he, more than anyone, had put on the
map—the office where his wife still worked as an agent—was now
gone.

"Johnny, it's the sorriest interrogation, the sorriest confession, I've
ever seen."

They speculated that the government had its best evidence still
tucked away. "There's got to be a silver bullet, Johnny. Because without it, I just can't see the bureau or the U.S. attorney going forward
with this case."

It would take Wedick another year to fully appreciate that this was
a different Justice Department, charged with a more righteous task,
than the one he had sworn his allegiance to.

Whether the terrorist in our midst is Timothy McVeigh or
Mohammed Atta, we, the citizens of the United States, expect the
FBI to catch him and his cohorts before they strike. The national
conversation about vigilance rarely concedes that no amount of vigilance could ever be enough. No politician dares say that we are too

vast a land, too diverse a people blessed with too many freedoms to
ferret out every madman. So whenever a madman does strike, we go
into overdrive to turn the FBI into something it isn't. From the start,
it was more accountant than cop, a bureaucracy (the Bureau) whose
turf wars and play-it-safe culture made it tough on any risk taker. For
every Melvin Purvis, the G-man who ran down John Dillinger and
Baby Face Nelson and earned the jealous wrath of J. Edgar Hoover,
there were a dozen agents who sat in the corner and worked nine to
five, answering phones and pushing paper.

Jim Wedick had no intention of being one of those faceless agents.
Even as a kid growing up in the Bronx in the 1950s, he could tell
you the stories that make up FBI lore. Out there was a new "public
enemy no. 1," and he wrote the bureau saying he'd like to join. A
month later, an agent from New York was on the phone, wonder-
ing if he would come in for an interview. Wedick paused and stam-
mered. He must have forgotten to mention in his letter that he was
barely fourteen years old. Nine years later, an accounting degree from
Fordham University in his back pocket, he was standing inside the
FBI Academy when he received his first posting: Indiana. "How in
the hell did that happen?" his fellow graduates wanted to know. All
through training, as the other rookies set their sights on San Diego or
Miami Beach, Wedick kept telling them about his dream job in Gary,
Indiana. That's where Purvis worked. That's where Dillinger carved
the gun out of soap to escape from prison. That's where the Lady in
Red who fingered Dillinger ran her brothels.

Within a week of landing in Gary, Wedick was trailing a ring of
thieves who were hijacking big rigs loaded with steel. He leaned so
hard on one crook that the local mob assumed the guy was blabbing
to the new agent with the blue eyes. As a favor to the guy, Wedick
faked a late-night confrontation in an underworld bar to show that
the crook hadn't sold out to the feds. The crook was so pleased to
have his loyalty to the mob restored that he agreed to turn informant.
The next day, he led Wedick to a sprawling industrial yard outside of
town where a chop shop was hidden inside a giant silo. The hijacked
trucks and all their cargo were being cut up like cattle for market.

Wedick's hustle had caught the eye of Jack Brennan, the star of the
office who had grown up in Alabama as the son and grandson of FBI
agents. Brennan asked Wedick to join him in an undercover operation
known as Fountain Pen that was exploring the growing ties between
white-collar executives and the mafia. The investigation had begun
to focus on a brilliant Minnesota swindler named Phil Kitzer who
was using paper banks to sell phony lines of credit to businessmen,

looking to bilk real banks out of millions of dollars in loans. Posing as a pair of young cons, Wedick and Brennan slowly worked themselves into the role of Kitzer's protégés, meeting clients in Germany, Pakistan, Japan, and the Bahamas before flying back to New York City where the flamboyant swindler wined and dined them at the fanciest restaurants, ordering without the benefit of menus. "Give us one of every item you serve," Kitzer would tell the waiters.

Operation Fountain Pen ended with the conviction of dozens of con men and mafioso across the country. Kitzer himself did six years in a federal penitentiary, but his loyalty to Wedick never wavered. "Jimmy, you and I can talk forever," he'd say. Freed from prison, Kitzer would go on to become one of the FBI's best cooperating witnesses, mailing Christmas cards to Wedick from wherever the bureau had posted him. The mafia boys, though, never got over their grudge. Fearing reprisal, the FBI decided to ship Wedick all the way out west—to the safety (slumber) of Sacramento.

He arrived in the summer of 1978. The regional headquarters and its satellite offices covered the largest federal beat in the country—from Bakersfield to the Oregon border—with fewer than 100 agents. It had a reputation, as far back as Prohibition, as a graveyard for federal agents who wanted no part of the front lines. Soon after settling in, Wedick created a splash by snaring Joseph Bonanno Jr. for wire fraud and the chairman of the state teachers retirement system for stealing $1.5 million from the pension fund. As he made his way around town, he kept hearing the same rumor from Sacramento insiders: the state legislature was rife with corruption; $30,000 passed to the right politicians could buy you any law.

Even the most committed undercover agents, working a new angle, took off now and then to relax with their families. Wedick was so obsessed with finding a way to infiltrate the statehouse that he began skipping meals and sleep. During one long stretch, he came home only long enough to watch his first wife leave him. "I was so lost in work I didn't even see it happening. She was packing her bags right in front of me, and it didn't sink in. She ran off with somebody else, and it nearly destroyed me. I kept the house exactly the way she left it for almost two years. Same pictures, same calendars, same notes affixed to the refrigerator."

One day, driving by a Sacramento fish market, the perfect setup struck him. Why not create a dummy business that would import gourmet shrimp from the Gulf of Mexico to Northern California? The company—phony papers, phony home office in Alabama, phony president Jack E. Gordon (a.k.a. FBI agent Jack Brennan)—would require the passage of special legislation to qualify for state loans. If lawmakers and their staff were corrupt and payoffs were needed, the FBI would write the checks. And so it began, Wedick's most brazen sting. From start to finish, Shrimpscam took a decade and became the most ambitious political corruption investigation in California history, netting 17 convictions and ending the political careers of 4 state senators and an Assembly leader. When it was over in 1994, Wedick was flown out to Washington, D.C., to receive the Director's Award as the criminal investigator of the year. He shook hands with FBI chief Louis Freeh and then rushed back to Sacramento, where a grand jury was about to hear his next case.

All through the 1990s, as he headed the public corruption squad, Wedick and his team continued to break big cases and make national headlines. They caught developers in Fresno and Clovis buying zoning votes from city councilmen for a pittance: a set of tires, a brake job, a new blue suit. They caught hundreds of medical care providers defrauding the state out of $228 million in health care payments. Prosecutors in the local U.S. attorney's office lined up for a chance to take one of Wedick's cases to court. "Jim brought a New York City pugnacity and abrasiveness to Sacramento and changed the culture of the office," recalled Matt Jacobs, a prosecutor in Shrimpscam. "That detective on TV always in trouble with his supervisors—that was Jim. He didn't go to the shooting range like he was supposed to. He didn't get his physical when he was supposed to. All he did was make big cases."

Wedick's run, like so much else, came to an abrupt end on September 11, 2001. He was in Europe with his wife, Nancy, riding bicycles through the Scottish highlands when the hijacked planes struck the World Trade Center. His first thought was his deceased father, James, who had been a New York City firefighter for 35 years, retiring as battalion chief. He recalled the long campaign his father had waged to keep the Twin Towers from being built. Hours and hours he spent on the phone warning city leaders that the skyscrapers, if hit by a plane, would be a deathtrap for firefighters. "What would Dad think now?" he kept muttering.

He came home to a different imperative. The war on white-collar crime, his bread and butter, was suddenly an indulgence. In FBI offices across the country, the shift to counterterrorism was swift and unmistakable. In Sacramento alone, dozens of agents from public corruption and other squads were now working foreign intelligence, domestic terrorism, and international terrorism. Federal prosecutions of white-collar crimes would drop by one-third over the next five years. "With everyone looking for bin Laden," Wedick told friends outside the Bureau, "there's no better time for the good old-fashioned American crooks to steal from the people."

Twice he had voted for George W. Bush, but he couldn't help but wonder if the entire war on terror was overblown, based on the false premise of a threat that never went away. He was struck by how willingly people surrendered their civil liberties in a vain experiment to calm themselves, and how they naturally assumed that the federal government must be right when it targeted Muslim communities with moles and wiretaps. Hauling off Arab and Pakistani immigrants to prisons here and abroad without a charge or even a public show of the slightest evidence reminded him of our treatment of Japanese Americans a half century before. What was happening to the Muslims, of course, was less sweeping than the way fear had been used to wrench Japanese families from their farms and ship them off to internment camps in the desert. Even so, Wedick wondered how a country still haunted by the memory of that injustice could allow these new injustices to take root so casually.

As the Bureau's charge shifted, he felt himself becoming more and more an outcast, until one spring day in 2004 when federal agents, prosecutors, and judges gathered at a restaurant on the grounds of McClellan Air Force Base to pay him tribute. They read a letter from Attorney General John Ashcroft praising his outstanding career and calling his cases "models for other agents to emulate." Then they shook his hand and wished him luck in his new life as a private eye. Whether they realized it or not, they were saying goodbye to the old FBI, as well.

In a cramped little room off the tenth floor of the federal courthouse in downtown Sacramento, a trio of federal officials gathered on the morning of June 8, 2005, to tell the public about the terrorist nest found across the river and down the field in Lodi. The day before, the government officials had leaked word of the arrests to a few trusted reporters at the *Los Angeles Times* and *Sacramento Bee,* who then broke the news in front-page stories that, while careful with the right qualifiers, had the huff and puff of hyperventilation. Now McGregor W. Scott, the tall, handsome son of a Eureka lawyer who had risen from Shasta County district attorney to the top prosecutor in the Eastern District of California, was standing front and center before a bank of TV news cameras. "I wish to emphasize that this investigation is evolving literally by the moment. Every step we have taken—and will take— is examined, reexamined, and vetted by the highest levels of the Justice Department."

The joint terrorism task force, more than a dozen federal, state, and local agencies, was working around the clock with the Department of Homeland Security to pursue all aspects of a Lodi sleeper cell intended to "kill Americans." Agents had searched the residences of the Hayats and two local Muslim clerics, Muhammed Adil Khan and Shabbir Ahmed, who were suspected of leading the plot. The imams were safely tucked away in the arms of U.S. Immigration and Customs. "I would also like to make a statement to the Muslim community in Lodi and elsewhere," Scott said in closing. "We have the greatest respect for the Muslim faith and Muslim members of our community. These are criminal charges and immigration charges against certain individuals, not a religion or people in a community."

By the second day, the feds already were backing away from some of the more damning details they had leaked to the press. In a revised affidavit, the U.S. attorney's office had removed any mention of hospitals and supermarkets as potential targets. Also deleted was the assertion that Hayat's grandfather in Pakistan, a prominent Muslim cleric, was friendly with a man who ran a terrorist camp in Afghanistan. As it turned out, his friend was actually a different man who shared the same last name—Rehman—with the terrorist. It was the Pakistani equivalent of Jones or Johnson.

"Bureaucratic errors," the Justice Department called them, though it hardly mattered to the cable news crews stampeding into Lodi and chasing down everything Muslim: S. Khan's auto repair shop, the Pak India market, the Jehovah's Witnesses kingdom hall turned mosque, and, finally, the terrorist's lair on the side of a wood shed where Hamid Hayat had fed his growing hatred of America.

"Hi everybody. This is *The Big Story*. I'm John Gibson. Fox News has live team coverage and expert analysis of these terror arrests. We begin with Claudia Cowan in Lodi, California."

"Hi John. Well, news crews and a number of curious neighbors have descended on the home of Umer Hayat here in Lodi. He and his twenty-four-year-old son have been arrested on charges of lying to the FBI. But federal agents really believe that this father-son team has been secretly helping America's biggest enemy, Al Qaeda."

Gibson: "The Patriot Act was created to help keep America safe following the terror attacks of 9/11. Does this particular bust prove that the Patriot Act is working or was this a case of being lucky? Joining us now, the former undersecretary of the Department of Homeland Security, Asa Hutchinson."

Hutchinson: "Well, I don't think they just got lucky...It is of great
concern that a camp in '03, '04 would exist in Pakistan."
Gibson: "Asa Hutchinson, sorry to interrupt. This is a Fox News
alert. We have news coming from Santa Maria, California. Trace
Gallagher is out there. Trace, we all assume it's a verdict. Yes or
no?"

And thus with a seamless tilt of the satellite dish, the "big story"
shifted from a suicide bomber in the California vineyards to singer
Michael Jackson in a California court on charges of molesting a little
boy. The curious among Fox's audience would have to wait another
day to learn why the FBI had chosen to target Lodi or how it came
to be that a few thousand Pakistani immigrants found themselves
living amid "the Grape American Dream," a town built by German
Russian wheat farmers from the Dakotas whose descendants still lived
in neat brick and stucco houses lined with oak trees and azaleas and
every Tuesday still grabbed a bowl of creamy borscht soup for $2.89
at Richmaid's.

It was a familiar story, really. Like the Chinese and Japanese
and Mexicans before them, the peasant farmers of the great Indus
valley—Hindu, Muslim, and Sikh—had migrated to California in the
early 1900s to work the land. They had grown cotton, wheat, sugar
cane, and row crops back home and though the soil was fertile and
the water plentiful, they were caught at the bottom of a strict caste
system. They had traveled thousands of miles only to land smack dab
on the same old line of latitude. The Punjab sun was the valley sun.
And they had come to a new land only to find the old land's caste, a
system where each immigrant group was pitted against the other to
keep wages in the fields low. By the 1960s, a few dozen Pakistanis
had congregated on Lodi's east side, living and working in the cor-
rugated shadows of the packinghouses and canneries. As long as they
were productive and didn't carouse at night, townsfolk looked past
the pajama-like pants and long shirts they wore and the goats they
brought home to slaughter. They had kept their end of the bargain,
until now.

Umer Hayat was 18 years old, a village boy with few prospects,
when he left Pakistan in 1976. He had nothing to show a future wife.
No family farm. No schooling beyond the eighth grade. He might
have been expected to marry a girl from the village like his father and
grandfather, but he had a different idea. He would migrate to Lodi,
become a naturalized U.S. citizen, and use his paper status to attract

a city girl back in Pakistan. His scheme worked in a way he could have never imagined. The young woman was the daughter of Qari Saeed-ur-Rehman, the revered Muslim scholar who operated a religious school or madrassa in Rawalpindi. The marriage was arranged, and to the surprise of Hayat's entire village, her father had said yes. The citizenship paper clutched by the young suitor—the chance for future generations of Hayats and Rehmans to prosper in the United States—was all the assurance the old cleric needed.

That Umer Hayat ended up squandering this opportunity may have been his one true crime. The problem wasn't so much what he had chosen to do with own life. After all, he had found a job outside the fields and the canneries, driving a beige ice cream van with Homer Simpson painted on the back, learning Spanish to better serve the neighborhood kids. And it wasn't so much the strong ties he kept to Pakistan. He was like so many other immigrants who made their way to America as adults, never quite accepting the country as their own, still looking backward and intending one day to return home. Rather, the problem was his insistence that his four children, each one born in the United States, follow the same path.

Keeping America outside the door of the little yellow frame house proved a monumental task. Because the public schools didn't segregate boys from girls and there were no classrooms at the mosque for his daughters, he insisted that they drop out at 13 and marry young. He fretted most about his oldest boy, Hamid, and wanted badly for him to become a Muslim scholar like his father-in-law. Toward that goal, he yanked him out of school in the sixth grade and sent him back to Pakistan to live with his grandparents. The boy was there for more than a decade and memorized the entire Koran. Once he returned home, though, he was too lazy to even take the $800 a month job as a cleric in training at the Lodi mosque. So he lived with his father and sick mother and 11 other relatives, sleeping all day and waking up to eat six McDonald's fish sandwiches and watch big-time wrestling and the Pakistani national cricket team on satellite TV. Late at night, all by himself, he'd head down Highway 99 to nowhere. "I'm a speeder," he boasted. "Seventy miles per hour, man."

Caught between two lands, the kid kept a scrapbook in his room with articles he clipped from a Pakistani newspaper that harangued against the United States and "Bush the Worm." He had no friends to speak of, and he whined that no Pakistani girls in the United States would give him a second look. His nose would bleed at the most inopportune times, and he was convinced that a black magic curse by an enemy had jinxed his love life. Maybe things would change, he told himself, if he could ever quit smoking and drink less tea and save more money from his job packing cherries.

Then in the summer of 2002, a real friend walked into his world, a man ten years his senior, a clean-cut guy with neatly pressed pants and shirt always tucked in and wavy black hair brushed back. He had a fancy job at a computer company and drove a shiny SUV and spoke perfect English and fluent Pashto and Urdu, two of the main languages of Pakistan. His name was Naseem Khan, and he had come to the United States with his mother in the late 1980s, living for a time in Lodi.

Umer Hayat wasn't sure about his son's new friend that first day he found him eating beef curry in the living room. Hamid assured him there was no cause for worry. Khan had arrived in town several months earlier and already befriended the two imams, spending the night at their homes and working on the website for the planned Farooqia Islamic Center. This new friend was, above all, a passionate Muslim who believed "we are from God and to God we return."

For Hamid, it quickly became something more than that. Khan was the first friend who actually wanted to see his scrapbook and hear his stories about the mujahedeen fighters who attended his grand-father's religious school before heading off to Afghanistan to fight the Soviets. This was jihad in its truest, most righteous sense, Hamid insisted, defending a Muslim country from an invading army.

"Have you watched the news?" his friend Khan asked, referring to the arrest of one of bin Laden's highest-ranking deputies in March 2003.

"No. About what? The Al Qaeda thing?" Hamid asked. "Al Qaeda is a tough group, man. They're even smarter than the FBI, friend."

"Huh?"

"Smarter than the FBI."

Khan laughed. "Yeah, better than the FBI, huh?"

Whether in Urdu or English, Khan wasn't much of a talker. That he was considerably more comfortable asking questions might have been Hamid's first clue. Yet the kid was so desperate for someone to take him seriously that he didn't seem to notice how every time he talked about the girl who turned down his marriage proposal or his uncle who was the "king of Pakistan," Khan steered their conversation to the same place. Jihad.

"I'm going to fight jihad," Khan declared. "You don't believe, huh?"

"No, man, these days there's no use in doing that," Hamid replied. "Listen, these days we can't go into Afghanistan...the American CIA is there."

As for the training camps, Hamid said he had seen one on a video, and it demanded far too much out of its students. Forty days of training. Guard vigil all night. Push-ups in the cold morning. Bazooka practice. "Man, if I had a gun, friend, I wouldn't be able to shoot it," he said.

Over the next six months, Khan would record more than 40 hours of conversations with Hamid and his father, mostly in the privacy of their home. As a job, working as a confidential witness for the FBI's war on terror paid considerably better than Taco Bell—more than $225,000 when it was all said and done—and Khan threw himself into the part with such ardor that he looked more FBI than the agents themselves. Still, it wasn't easy doing this to your own people, especially to a kid who had the mental capacity of a nine-year-old and kept referring to him as his "older brother" and to a father who had gotten over his initial distrust and now called Khan his "other son." Khan replied in kind: "If you've accorded me the position of a son, then you're no less than my honored father."

The FBI had come calling on Khan in the weeks after 9/11. He was living in Oregon, working double duty at McDonald's and a convenience store, bringing home $7 an hour to an American girl who was falling in love with him. He did his best to impress the two agents. Yes, he was familiar with the Pakistani community in Lodi. A few years earlier, he had seen al-Qaeda's number two man, Zawahiri, going in and out of the small mosque on Poplar Street. And not only him. Among the men on their hands and knees praying were the main suspects in the 1998 bombings of the U.S. embassies in Kenya and Tanzania and the 1996 bombing of the Khobar Towers military housing complex in Saudi Arabia.

The FBI would later concede that Khan's sightings were almost certainly false. Yet such flights of fancy didn't deter the Bureau from opening the case and giving him the code name Wildcat and sending him back to Lodi in a new Dodge Durango. The two imams would eventually grow uncomfortable with his jihad talk and warn students to steer clear of him. Inside the yellow house, though, he would have no trouble getting Hamid Hayat to pour out his heart.

"I have a friend in Pakistan who starts talking to me over the phone," Hamid confided to Khan. "He cusses America, right? He tells me, 'My friend, don't you get offended? I'm abusing your country.' I said, 'Man, this country is mine in name only, understand? My heart is in Pakistan.'"

Hamid began to cover up his impotence with a tough guy persona that found comfort in Khan's caricature of slickster jihadist. During one visit, Hamid wondered if Khan had read the news about the murder of Daniel Pearl, the *Wall Street Journal* reporter, in Pakistan. "They killed him. So I'm pleased about that. They cut him into pieces and sent him back. That was a good job they did. Now they can't send one Jewish person to Pakistan."

If Hamid felt that strongly, Khan wondered, why was he hesitating to return to Pakistan for more religious training and possibly a camp. "You told me, 'I'm going for jihad,'" Khan said. "What happened?"

"I'm ready, I swear. My father tells me, 'Man, what a better task than this. But when does my mother permit it? Where is a mother's heart? She said, 'I kept you separated for ten years. I won't let you be separated from me again.'"

In the summer of 2003, with his mother's apparent blessing, Hamid did go to Pakistan to meet the girl his parents had arranged for him to marry and bring back an herbal medicine to cure his mother's diseased liver. But the bride-to-be rejected him, and his mother was forced to fly in and go door-to-door in the village until she found another father willing to marry his daughter to Hamid. Two months into his stay in Pakistan, the phone rang and he heard the stern voice of his friend Khan calling from the United States.

"You're just sitting around doing nothing," Khan said.

"I do one thing. I pray. That's it."

"Don't lie to me. Don't talk bullshit."

"Why would I lie to you?" Hamid pleaded. "There's nothing of note regarding our area of interest. Understand?"

"There's nothing at all, eh?" Khan asked.

"Nothing. Absolutely nothing."

"The plan to go. What happened about that?"

"The plan to go where?"

"To the camp."

"That can't be done these days, man. It's too difficult. Strict restrictions have been imposed on the madrassas. There are lots of spies."

"So what kind of Muslims are these, then? Here in the U.S., they're all afraid, too."

"Well, see, my friend, Naseem Khan, what strange times these are!"

To Khan, this sounded like the student lecturing the professor, and he grew angry.

"You told me, 'I'm going to a camp. I'll do this. I'll do that.' You're sitting idle. You're wasting time."

"No choice."

"You fucking sleep for half the day. You wake up. You light a fucking cigarette. You eat. You sleep again. That's all you do. You're just walking around like a loafer. A loafer guy."

"What else am I going to do?"

"Yeah. Fuck you in the ass…You sound like a fucking broken bitch. Come on. Be a man. Do something."

"Whatever I can do, I'll do that, man."

"When I come to Pakistan and I see you, I'm going to fucking force you, get you from your throat and fucking throw in you in the madrassa."

"I'm not going to go."

"Oh yeah, you will go."

In the months after the arrests and before the trial, even as President Bush congratulated the FBI for a job well done in Lodi and the nation's intelligence czar John Negroponte, in his annual threat assessment, cited a network of "Islamic extremists" in the farm town, it became more and more clear that no case existed beyond the Hayats. The two imams, the so-called big fish who allegedly formed the sleeper cell, were found to have uttered anti-American remarks years earlier during a clamorous time in Pakistan but nothing more. In the end, citing minor immigration violations, the government deported them. "We have gone and will continue to go wherever the evidence takes us," U.S. Attorney Scott pledged a few weeks later. "We have detected, we have disrupted and we have deterred, and whatever was taking shape in Lodi isn't going to happen now."

On an overcast day in mid-February 2006, Jim Wedick strode down the long, polished hall of the thirteenth floor in the U.S. district courthouse and swung open the heavy door to the courtroom of Judge Garland Burrell, the former Marine from south-central Los Angeles who had presided over the Unabomber case. During his FBI years, Wedick had been an overweight agent whose courtroom attire aspired to drab. Now he was bone thin from a thyroid condition and dressed in a blue pinstriped suit and red Windsor-knotted tie, his gray beard and mustache shaved tight. He scooted past defense attorneys Johnny Griffin and Wazhma Mojaddidi and took a seat next to the two defendants. For the last eight months, he had tried to down-play this moment, telling friends that it was all part of the routine of crossing over. He was joining a long line of old FBI agents who retired one day only to hang out their private eye shingle the next. Because of his reputation, he knew that sooner or later he would land a high-stakes case pitting him against his former colleagues, but the Bureau and the U.S. attorney's office would surely understand he was only doing his job. Besides, the only person he owed an explanation to was his wife, Nancy, also an FBI agent. She was the one who had to go to work each day with the same agents who had targeted the Hayats. Yes, she would be in a tough spot, but she told him not to worry about it. As the case headed to trial, Wedick knew where he stood with the government. He wouldn't be sharing old war stories with prosecutors and agents in the halls outside the courtroom, but neither did he expect to encounter outwardly hostile feelings. His former cohorts, he figured, were pros who knew how the system of justice worked.

Anyone watching Wedick find his place that first morning could see that he had underestimated the situation. This wasn't your garden-variety betrayal. If the Hayats greeted his arrival like a good luck charm, the trio of young prosecutors, S. Robert Tice-Raskin, Laura L. Ferris, and David Deitch, went out of their way to ignore his presence. He tried not to make eye contact with the FBI supervisors and agents huddled around the government's table, and they pretended not to see him. In the days to come, his wife would drive home from work in tears, telling Jim that fellow agents were calling him a "traitor." The regional boss would sit her down in his office and remark that Jim would be wise not to attend a retirement luncheon for an old FBI colleague. Some of the more angry agents, the boss suggested, might go after him. Wedick understood that it wasn't simply a matter of bad blood inside the Sacramento office. The entire bureaucracy of the Justice Department, already evangelized by Attorney General John Ashcroft, was being shoved even further to the right by his successor, Alberto Gonzales. Job candidates from Ivy League schools or Stanford—those who spoke Arabic or did volunteer work to clean up the environment or once posted a cartoon on a MySpace page poking fun at President Bush—would be deemed too elitist, too liberal, too soft for the mission at hand. The same sort of quality control was being used to decide which assistant U.S. attorneys would stay or be fired. Even the silliest cases had become worthy of pursuit if they happened to involve a Muslim shooting off his mouth about blowing up a tower in Chicago or, better yet, a Palestinian on American soil sending humanitarian funds to the Holy Land. This was a war of wholesale battlefronts, and Jim Wedick had crossed the line to join sides with the enemy combatant. "I guess I was naive to think that it could be some other way between me and them," he would say later. "But I honestly didn't expect the boss of the FBI office in Sacramento to lean on Nancy the way he did. I didn't expect that they'd actually retrieve my old personnel file to see if they could find some dirt on me. But that's how badly they wanted to keep me off the stand and win this prosecution."

Wedick felt so strongly about the case that he had performed almost all of his duties for free, deconstructing the confessions of father and son and poring over every piece of paper the FBI had handed over. The way he saw it, the trial boiled down to a few basic questions: Why, if this case was so important, did the FBI entrust the investigation to a rookie agent? Why didn't the Bureau use its considerable manpower in Pakistan to follow Hamid and determine if he actually attended a terrorist camp? Hamid had vowed in his last recorded conversation with Khan that he would attend not a camp but a madrassa. "After Ramadan, God willing, I'll study and become a religious scholar," he promised. Khan had booked a flight to Pakistan to see for himself what kind of camp, if any, Hamid had decided to attend. Why, at the last minute, did the FBI scuttle that trip? Why, if Hamid was such a threat to national security, did the FBI take him off a no-fly list and let him reenter the United States? And why, if he was truly confessing, did the agents find it necessary to spend all night spoon-feeding him the answers?

Now Wedick turned a sharp eye on the female prosecutor addressing the jury of six men and six women who had come from one of the most conservative regions in California (it could have been a jury in Texas or Oklahoma, for that matter) to decide Hamid's fate. Ferris, a fit woman with short dark hair and small features, told jurors that Hamid kept a "jihadist" scrapbook and immersed himself in extremist Muslim views before heading off to Pakistan. There he attended an al-Qaeda training camp and returned home to do harm to Americans. "He talked about training camps. He talked about acts of violence," she said. "He talked about jihad, jihad, jihad."

The young man with a fresh haircut and hip goatee and new black sports jacket with matching slacks and tie made no expression as the prosecutor's words came to him, via earphones, in Urdu. "Hamid

Hayat had three faces. One when he was lying to law enforcement. One when he was confessing to law enforcement. And one when he was talking and didn't know law enforcement was listening."

Hamid's attorney, Mojaddidi, had come to court for her first criminal trial and first federal trial wearing a dark pantsuit with a hot pink blouse and hot pink shoes. Color, she would explain later, was the way a middle child got attention in a large family that escaped war-torn Afghanistan and came to the United States as refugees. Her father, a Kabul banker, had worked at a pizza parlor in Washington to send his children to medical school and law school. She and the Hayats came from the same Pashtun tribe, only they were from the village and her family was from the city. The difference explained everything.

"The government cannot prove that he actually attended a camp," she told jurors in her opening. "It's a crucial missing link." Instead, his time in Pakistan was spent playing cricket and getting married and taking religious classes at a madrassa. As for the confession, Hamid merely uttered "the words the FBI wanted to hear," she said. It was nothing more than garbage in and garbage out.

Then the witnesses began to take the stand.

There was Lawrence Futa, an FBI agent in Japan who testified that on May 30, 2005, a Korean Air Lines flight to San Francisco was diverted to Tokyo because it carried a passenger who appeared on a no-fly list. Futa interviewed Hamid Hayat and found a pleasant young man who denied any links to terrorism. His thin build made it seem unlikely he had recently undergone rigorous training, and Futa permitted him to board a later flight.

There was Pedro Tenoch Aguilar, the rookie agent who headed the government's case and conceded that he could never corroborate whether Hamid had attended a camp or not. "Minus his statement, no," Aguilar said. There was Naseem "Wildcat" Khan, the bureau's mole, who also testified that Hayat expressed a desire to go to camp but never told him that he'd done so.

There was Hassan Abbas, a former high-ranking police official in Pakistan who testified that religious schools in the predominantly Muslim country were centers of terrorist recruitment. When the defense got its chance to cross-examine Abbas, prosecutor Tice-Raskin kept objecting to the questions. After each objection was overruled, Abbas, as if on cue, sidestepped the question with a vague answer. It turned out that he was following a script that the government had laid out for him. In the prosecutor's notes, which were inadvertently turned over to the defense, Abbas was coached to play dumb whenever Tice-Raskin objected to a defense question. It was an eye-opener into the tricks the federal government was willing to pull to win the case, but Judge Burrell let the tactic pass without ever admonishing the government.

There was the professor of Islamic studies who testified that the verse Hamid kept in his wallet—"Oh Allah, we place you at their throats, and we seek refuge in you from their evil"—may have been the prayer of a traveler seeking divine protection. More likely, though, it was the supplication carried by "fanatics and extremists." Finally, there was the Defense Department analyst who testified that satellite pictures taken in northeastern Pakistan revealed a camp near Balakot that "likely" matched one of the camps described by Hamid.

It was all rather murky, and son and father weren't about to testify to clear things up. The trial, it seemed, would turn on the confession that really didn't become a confession until the early morning hours of June 5, 2005. That's when agent Tim Harrison replaced agent Gary Schaaf as Hamid's main inquisitor.

"The thing I want to talk about, most importantly, is the camp where you went."

"Uh-huh."

"Did they teach you how to read maps?"

"No."

"Did you get to play with GPS...global positioning?"

"What's that?"

"Satellite."

"No, no."

"All right. So you came to the United States. They sent you off. 'Allah Ahkbar. You've got to go to jihad.'"

"Uh-huh."

"And you left with marching orders."

"What's that?"

"You know. 'Here's what your mission is. Here's what you do with all this training. You're training to be a good jihadi.'"

"Uh-huh."

"What did they want you to do?"

"They didn't tell me nothing."

"I'm trying to get to the truth here. Because we're going to try to make an argument for you. That you are not one of the big players. So they sent you to the U.S. after you've done your training. You're ready for jihad."

"No. I'm not ready for jihad."

"You're here to take orders."

"No, I didn't take orders from them. They will give me the orders to fight. But they didn't give me no orders right now."

"Who's going tell you?"

"Maybe, uh, send a letter."

"I don't think they're going to send a letter. I think you're going to have to talk to somebody here in Lodi."

"Yeah, maybe."

"Give me an example of a target. A building?"

"I'll say no buildings. I'll say people."

"Okay, people. Yeah. Fair enough. People in buildings...Whatever looks like a person, shoot?"

"Yeah."

"I'm trying to get some details about plans over here."

"They didn't give us no plans."

"Did they give you money?"

"No money."

"Guns?"

"Nope."

"Targets in the U.S.?" the agent asked again.

"I'll say they're going to tell us big buildings. I'll say that for sure."

"Here in Sacramento or San Francisco?"

"I'll say maybe in L.A. Maybe, ah, San Francisco."

"Your goal is to do jihad here?"

"Yeah."

"You have to go to America to fight jihad?"

"Yeah."

"Who was in charge of the camp? We're talking about someone you know very well."

"Maybe it's my uncle."

"Maybe it's your uncle?"

"Maybe my grandfather."

"Maybe your grandfather? You can't play dumb with me. It insults me and it..."

"Hurts me and hurts you. Yeah, I get that."

"Is Al Qaeda tied to this camp that you went to?"

"I'll say...they are."

"Al Qaeda? Al Qaeda runs?"

"I'll say they run the camp."

"Ah, all right," said the agent. "They're the supporters. You mean they provide instructors."

"Yeah, that's what I'll say."

"Yes, clearly, they want to do damage to us, the United States. Whether it is overseas or here."

"Anywhere."

"So a big part of your training was against the U.S.?"

"Um-hmm."

"Bush, Colin Powell, Rumsfeld. They put their faces on the dummies. Do you remember that?"

"Um-hmm."

"You're being trained to act against targets. What kind of buildings? Financial buildings? Private buildings? Commercial buildings?"

"I'll say finance and things like that."

"Hospitals? Did they say hospitals."

"Maybe. I'm sure."

"They plant ideas in your head?"

"Uh-huh."

What were the jurors thinking, Wedick wondered. If he wouldn't be able to tell them exactly what he thought—that this was the "most derelict and juvenile investigation" he had ever seen the FBI put its name to—he could at least take the stand and point out the gibberish in the interrogation. He could at least tell them about the care he took in Shrimpscam, how he had prepared a single year for one interview and got an informant to cooperate after he meticulously lined the interrogation room with giant surveillance photos of the guy accepting a sizable campaign check. Or how he brought in an FBI behavioral scientist from Washington to help him design a set of questions that fit the particular language and style of one of the suspects—all in the name of eliciting an accurate confession.

It was far from certain, though, that the court would agree to Wedick serving as an expert witness. Up until now, Judge Burrell had shown something akin to belligerence when it came to any requests from the defense side of the table. A small, frenetic man, Burrell gave the impression of feeling uneasy in his robes, and he seemed to compensate for this insecurity by playing bully. Ironically, he found his most convenient target in defense attorney Griffin, a black man like himself. Each time Burrell ruled against Griffin, he did so with an impatience that bordered on browbeating. On the matter of Wedick testifying, Assistant U.S. Attorney Deitch had filed nearly 100 pages of motions to keep the former agent off the stand. He argued that Wedick had "grossly overstated" his experience in counterterrorism and that his musings would prejudice the jury and amount to "needless" cumulative evidence, the legal equivalent of piling on.

Griffin stood up to offer several reasons why Wedick's testimony was needed to illuminate serious flaws in the government's case, but he appeared intimidated, his articulations reduced to mutterings. Burrell ordered him to sit back down. "I know his proposed testimony," he snarled at Griffin. "You can go on to the next issue." To no one's surprise, the judge sided with the government and put a muzzle on Wedick.

Outside the courtroom, a dazed Wedick tried to fathom the ruling. He wondered how the prosecutors and agents could muster the gall to dismiss his credentials as if he had never worked for the FBI, much less achieved star status. These were the same prosecutors and agents who had failed to produce a single piece of corroborating evidence in four years of sleuthing that cost taxpayers millions of dollars and unearthed not bin Laden's right hand but a pair of immigrants, father and son, who canvassed the town of Lodi blaring "Pop Goes the Weasel." "To see the government's power from this side of the fence is a strange thing for me," Wedick conceded. "What we're doing to these Muslims is along the same lines of what we did to the Japanese in the 1940s. It comes from the same fear and the same overreaction. Instead of camps in the desert, we're deporting them on trumped up charges or sending them to prisons in Cuba or the Middle East." With Wedick silenced, the defense put on its final witness, a university scholar who testified that madrassas typically focused on teaching an orthodox brand of Islam, not churning out suicide bombers. Then both sides closed and the case went to two separate juries that had sat side by side for two months.

The Pakistani Muslims of Lodi watched and waited, old men huddled in the shade of the marigold mosque, young men with heads bowed down as they wheeled out 40-pound boxes of fresh kosher chicken from the Pak India market—the same store that the government's informant had placed at the center of a ring delivering funds to al-Qaeda. "This little place can't even support one goddamn family," storekeeper Mumtaz Khan said. "How can it support Al Qaeda?" He motioned to the 15 brands of tea, the basmati rice from the Punjab, the red lentils, pickled mango, Islamic prayer clocks, and the small stick tree filled with Tootsie Rolls. "We are trying to raise our children to live in America but still keep a little faith and not become fully westernized." The storekeeper said a Muslim American no longer had the freedom to criticize the United States. So if asked his opinion, he would criticize his own. "Osama bin Laden has done more harm to the Muslim people throughout the world than anyone else in history," he said. "Everybody is scared. Everybody is scared."

At the yellow house, the kids were shooting hoops along a driveway lined with pomegranate, fig, and loquat trees, one child in traditional garb driving to the basket and his cousin in jeans trying to block him. They stopped playing as soon as they spotted the strange SUV parked across the street, not sure if the driver wearing sunglasses and taking notes, a journalist, might be a government agent. The ice cream truck sat idle, and the coop where father and son used to tend to their birds was empty. Hamid Hayat's uncle shuffled outside in his leather sandals and stood beneath a row of the freshly washed purple and gold cotton garments hanging from a cord strung across the porch. He lit a Marlboro cigarette and sighed. "We are sitting and waiting. We have been sitting and waiting for a year." Then a young man, a dead ringer for Hamid Hayat, only he was wearing a Tupac Shakir cap turned backward, baggy jeans slung low, and Air Jordans, walked up the steps and into the house. This was Arslan Hayat, Hamid's teenage brother. "It's a lie," he said. "The whole world's a lie." He emerged a few minutes later pushing a wheelchair that carried his dying grandfather. He and four other relatives loaded the old man into a small truck to take him to the doctor. As they backed out of the driveway, the new ice cream man, also a Pakistani but playing a different tune on his musical box, made a left turn and blocked their path. They waited patiently as he sold popsicles in the colors of the U.S. flag to a gaggle of kids.

The verdicts came a day later. The jury deciding the fate of Umer Hayat was deadlocked, and the judge declared a mistrial, though the government vowed that it would try him again. As for young Hamid, he was found guilty on two counts of making false statements to the FBI and one count of providing "material support" to terrorists. He faced up to 39 years in prison. "I hope it gets the message out," said juror Starr Scaccia, explaining why she and the others voted guilty. "Don't mess with the United States. It's not worth it."

Wedick had a difficult time looking the son in the eye. He had pledged to him months earlier that he was going to do everything he could to see injustice righted, even if it meant turning his back on the bureaucracy he had served for 35 years. "This kid could be my kid. My sons boasts. My son does all sorts of things that drive me nuts. Hamid is a hapless character, but my God he isn't a terrorist. The government counted on hysteria, the thousand-pound gorilla, to be in the room. And it worked. Damn, it worked."

He saw one juror holding back tears, and the next day he tracked her down to an apartment in downtown Sacramento. She wouldn't let him in, preferring to talk through a crack in the door. For four hours, he stood on her front porch and tried to calm her fears. When she finally relented and opened the door, it took only a few minutes to tell him what he suspected. No, she didn't believe the kid was guilty. The pressure to convict him from fellow jurors was so intense that she had to check herself into the hospital a few days earlier. Throughout the trial, she said, the foreman kept making the gesture of a noose hanging. "Lynch the Muslim," she took it to mean. Another juror, she said, had prepared a six-page analysis on her home computer to persuade the others to vote guilty—a direct violation of the judge's instructions. Wedick asked her to write it all down and sign it. Then he filed the affidavit with the federal court, hoping it might lead to a new trial.

The next day, he drove out to a field at the edge of a vineyard alongside Highway 99 and gazed down a long entrance road to a spot where 400 men in skull caps and flowing robes had gathered after work. He drew close enough to see their faces burned by the sun and hands worn to the bone, the faces and hands of fruit pickers and truck drivers and machine operators who had left Pakistan years before to try a new life in California. He watched them unload a plain wood box from the back of a hearse and carry it over the graves of the other Muslims. Then they broke into 20 lines, side by side, facing east, toward Mecca, and began praying. They prayed the same supplication—"May Allah protect us from evil. May Allah destroy our enemies"—that the holy warrior prayed. Then in the distance, as the sun was setting, a half dozen men removed the body of Hamid Hayat's grandfather from the casket and placed it directly into the ground. What was left of the old immigrant had been wrapped in three linen sheets, all that would separate him from the earth of this unaccustomed land.

NOTE

Based on "The Agent Who Might Have Saved Hamid Hayat," *Los Angeles Times*, May 28, 2006 (http://articles.latimes.com/2006/may/28/magazine /tm-wedick22). Also published in *West of the West* (New York: PublicAffairs, Perseus Books, 2009).

CONCLUSION

THE WAR OF THE WORLD? IS THERE A VIABLE NONVIOLENT ALTERNATIVE TO THE GLOBAL WAR ON TERRORISM?

Charles P. Webel

> If we assume that humankind has a right to survive, then we must find an alternative to war and destruction...The choice today is no longer between violence or nonviolence. It is between nonviolence or nonexistence.
>
> —Martin Luther King Jr.

> The term "terrorism" means premeditated, politically motivated violence perpetrated against noncombatant targets by sub-national groups or clandestine agents, usually intended to influence an audience.
>
> —CIA and U.S. State Department.

The "Global War on Terror" (GWOT) has entered its second decade, and may continue indefinitely. Since September 11, 2001, the world in general and the American and British publics in particular have become acutely aware of international terrorism and its devastating effects on the bodies, minds, and hearts of its victims. But while great attention has been paid to the military and geopolitical dimensions of terrorism and counterterrorism, relatively little effort has been made to understand the historical, cultural, and ideological roots of terrorism. And almost no one appearing in Western mass media has proposed a nonviolent, or less violent—an ethically defensible, sustainable, and effective—alternative to the current GWOT, and to the "resource wars" over water and energy that are becoming an increasing threat to global and regional peace and security.

What is increasingly becoming a war without end—a conflict that may escalate to a war of the world involving weapons of mass destruction—must cease. In its place should be an effective and ethical plan for the prevention of terrorism from above and below, as well as for reconciliation between the adversaries. But how can this be accomplished?

It is widely assumed in much of the Anglophonic world that the only alternatives are either to "stay the course" until "the terrorists are defeated," or to "cut and run," that is, to withdraw "prematurely" from such "frontlines" of the GWOT as Afghanistan and Iraq. Accordingly, it is incumbent on critics of this "war" to pose a viable alternative to this false dilemma. This would achieve such demonstrable results as reducing the incidence and lethality of "terrorist" attacks globally and locally, and minimizing casualties.

As figure C.1 from the RAND reports illustrates, the number of terrorist attacks attributed to al-Qaeda went up dramatically between 2002 and 2007, even after excluding such attacks in Iraq and Afghanistan. This trend does not seem to have been reversed since then, casting into doubt the efficacy of the military means used in attempting to achieve a key goal of the "War on Terror."

Clearly, the GWOT is not succeeding as a primarily military effort to defeat al-Qaeda or to subdue the Taliban and other insurgents. Here we hope to pose one possibly effective alternative to the continuation

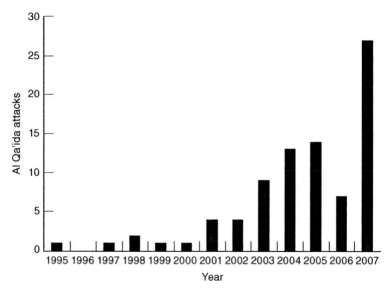

Figure C.1 Attacks attributed to al-Qaeda: 1995–2007. From RAND document MG-741-1-RC, How Terrorist Groups End. Reprinted with permission.

and expansion of the GWOT on the one hand, while more effectively pursuing the laudable goal of defending the public against political violence on the other hand.

In considering possible "endgames" for the current wars in the Muslim world in particular and against what is labeled as "terrorism" in general, it is imperative to assess how subnational terrorist groups end. It is also necessary to examine past and prospective possibilities for negotiations between deadly adversaries.[1] Accordingly, in making our overall assessment and recommendations, we will rely on three relatively recent systematic investigations of what Noam Chomsky in this volume has called "the evil scourge of terrorism."

In 2008, at the request of the U.S. House Armed Services Committee, researchers for the RAND Corporation presented the results of a comprehensive study for "Defeating Terrorist Groups."[2] In 2009, Audrey Kurth Cronin published *How Terrorism Ends*.[3] And in early 2011, an international task force, organized by The Century Foundation and led by Ambassadors Lakhdar Brahimi and Thomas Pickering, published its findings and recommendations for determining the kind of political path that might end the war.[4] These empirically oriented studies are useful for examining possible "outcomes" for the GWOT and in proposing viable nonviolent alternatives to a conflict that seems not to have met its stated goals in defeating al-Qaeda and in diminishing the lethality and incidence of terrorist and insurgent attacks in the Middle East and more globally. For reasons of space, we will focus on the RAND study.

The RAND researchers examined 648 U.S.-designated terrorist groups[5] between 1968 and 2006. They provide many examples of former terrorist groups who, by cooperating with governments on collective or individual agreements, ceasefires, and peace settlements, have been more successful in achieving their political goals than through the use of force alone. Governments are much more likely to reduce terrorist violence and eliminate insurgencies by reaching political accommodations with their adversaries than by counterterrorist and counterinsurgency military and paramilitary operations. *Politicization and policing are how governments usually succeed in ending violent opposition to their rule, and negotiations and accommodation are how terrorist and insurgent groups are most likely to achieve some if not all of their goals. Military force unaccompanied by dialogue is almost always a losing strategy for both sides,* as figure C.2 indicates.

The RAND researchers found that "terrorist groups end for two major reasons: They decide to adopt nonviolent tactics and join the

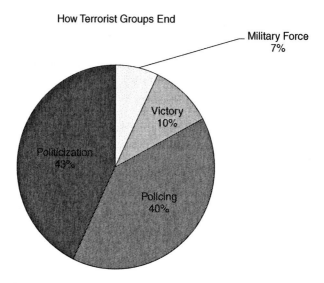

How Terrorist Groups End

Military Force
7%

Victory
10%

Politicization
43%

Policing
40%

Figure C.2 How terrorist groups end: The RAND findings. Based on figures from RAND document MG-741-1-RC, How Terrorist Groups End. Recreated with permission.

political process, or local law-enforcement agencies arrest or kill key members of the group. "Military force has rarely been the primary reason that terrorist groups end, and few groups have ended by achieving victory."[6] The study accordingly concluded that:

1. "[The U.S. military] should generally resist being drawn into combat operations in Muslim countries where its presence is likely to increase terrorist recruitment because the use of military force as a primary tool in the 'global war on terrorism' against al Qa'ida (and related Islamist terrorist groups) has not worked and should be replaced with a counterterrorist strategy that perceives terrorists as criminals not as holy warriors."

2. Since "by far the most effective strategy against religious groups has been the use of local police and intelligence services, which were responsible for the end of 73 percent of [terrorist] groups since 1968," policing and intelligence efforts, including cutting off terrorist financing, providing foreign assistance, sharing information with other governments, and engaging in diplomacy, should be the backbone of U.S./Western counterterrorist effort.

3. The study argued that "ending the notion of a 'war' on terrorism" and "moving away from military references would indicate

that there was no battlefield solution to countering terrorism." Accordingly, "negotiations and dialogue between Western and Islamic adversaries should replace bombing as the core of a multi-dimensional approach to reducing and eventually eliminating the threats to the planet posed by terrorism and counter-terrorism."

There is no battlefield solution to terrorism, and, citing Peter Bergen, Jones and Libicki argue that "making a world of enemies is never a winning strategy." But "terrorist groups typically end due to a combination of strategies."

The GWOT has not made the world safer. Many scholars and ethicists concur.[7] On the contrary, it has increased the number and lethality of officially designated terrorist attacks since September 12, 2001, and threatens to become a war of the world in which weapons of mass destruction are deployed by and against terrorist groups or terrorist states that may harbor them. So what are the alternatives to fighting the lesser fire of nonstate terrorism with the more incendiary violence of state "counter"-terrorism?

A NONVIOLENT ALTERNATIVE TO A GLOBAL WAR OF TERROR

Whenever the conditions are present that would give what Joan Bondurant calls "the process of creative conflict" a chance of successes, it should be favored. The Gandhian method of winning over one's opponents through nonviolent pressure may well be more effective than violence in undermining people's attachment to mistaken views...if the massive violence of war can be justified, which is dubious, terrorist acts can also be, if they have certain characteristics...as limited terrorism is better than war, less violent alternatives to terrorism are better than terrorism, and nonviolent pressures are better than violent ones. It is indeed the case that violence leads to more violence. Rather than trying to "wipe out once and for all the enemies that threaten us," which is impossible, the more successful, as well as more justifiable, approach to violence is to lessen its appeal.

—Virginia Held, *How Terrorism is Wrong*

The realpolitik strategy of negative peacemaking, put into effect in September 2001—almost a decade ago—has not defeated radical Islamism, has resulted in many thousands of casualties, has led to a global clash between Western and Islamist civilizations, and threatens to escalate to a war of the world in which nonstate terrorists and state counterterrorists may both employ weapons of mass destruction. If the incorporation of official terrorist groups in the political process combined with the efforts of police and intelligence services to prevent terrorist attacks result in a success rate (ending terrorist actions) greater than other strategies, why shouldn't this strategy replace the GWOT with its associated counterterrorist strategy?

This is part of a more general *antiterrorist* strategy. Antiterrorism is an ethical and possibly effective alternative to the largely unethical and ineffective "war on terrorism." According to Haig Khatchadourian, antiterrorism refers to

> the "administrative, police, psychological resources, tactics, equip-ments, security, judicial, and political measures" employed by gov-ernments...designed to prevent terrorist attacks...Antiterrorist measures include the use of judicial and penal systems as a whole to bring terrorists to justice. Thus antiterrorism has both a deter-rent and a punitive aspect: to deter and so to prevent terrorism, to apprehend and bring to justice suspected terrorists, and to punish convicted terrorists...Therefore, antiterrorist measures and strate-gies are, ideally speaking, nonviolent and in accord...with extant international law.[8]

But antiterrorism is only the "negative" component of a long-term process. It must be combined with the *prevention* of terrorism, both from above and from below, which requires the development of a global strategy of peacemaking and peace-building. Sustainable peace and conflict resolution involves the development and imple-mentation of effective strategies and policies that de-escalate the cycles of violence and institutionalize effective nonviolent methods of conflict prevention and transformation. International efforts will be needed to increase "peace literacy" (understanding of these concepts and how they can be applied) in decision-makers and the public. Additionally, efforts to encourage best practices in journal-ism and to promote and protect freedom of the press will provide essential support for nonviolent conflict prevention, conflict resolu-tion, and peace-building policies and practices. A strong, free press dedicated to communicating vital information to the public remains one of the best safeguards against the violence of terrorism and tyranny.

Instead of fighting fire with fire, of combating terror with greater terror, why not try the force of dialogue and negotiation instead of the force of arms? What do we have to lose?

NOTES

1. See James Dao, "The Endgame in Afghanistan," *New York Times Week in Review,* March 27, 2011: 1 and 4; Alissa J. Rubin, "Afghan and Pakistani Leaders Meet in Peace Bid," *New York Times,* April 17, 2011: A9; Rod Nordland, "Talks on U.S. Presence in Afghanistan after Pullout Unnerve Region," *New York Times,* April 19, 2011: A4 and A8.

2. Seth Jones and Martin C. Libick, *How Terrorist Groups End: Lessons for Countering al Qa'ida* (Rand Corporation: Santa Monica, 2008) (www .rand.org).

3. Audrey Kurth Cronin, *How Terrorism Ends: Understanding the Decline and Demise of Terrorist Campaigns* (Princeton and Oxford: Princeton University Press, 2009).

4. Lakhdar Brahimi and Thomas Pickering, *Afghanistan: Negotiating Peace* (New York: The Century Foundation Press, 2011) (http://tcf.org /publications/2011/3/afghanistan-negotiating-peace).

5. For the Rand researchers Jones and Libicki, "A terrorist group is defined as a collection of individuals belonging to a nonstate entity that uses terrorism to achieve its objectives. Such an entity has at least some command and control apparatus that, no matter how loose or flexible, provides an overall organizational structure" (*How Terrorist Groups End,* 3–4).

6. Ibid., 9.

7. Some examples: "the chief problem is that the WOT is not like any other kind of war. The enemy, Terrorism, is not a territorial state or nation or government. There is no opposite number to negotiate with. There is no one on the other side to call a truce or declare a ceasefire, no one among the enemy authorized to surrender ... In the WOT, no capitulation is possible. That means the real aim of the war is ... to kill or capture all the terrorists—to keep killing and killing, capturing and capturing, until they are all gone ... (but) Of course, no one expects that terrorism will ever completely disappear" [David Luban, "The War on Terrorism and the End of Human Rights," in *War After September 11,* ed. Verna V. Gehring (Plymouth, UK: 2003), 59]. "The effort to destroy 'every terrorist group of global reach' quickly became a much larger effort to leverage U.S. military power to long-term economic and political advantage, something that had been advocated by many neoconservatives even before Bush was elected. This larger effort has nothing to do with preventing further terrorist attacks ... There are powerful vested interests in the perpetuation of a terrorist threat from which we need to be protected, and in the control of political activity that might alter or challenge this situation" [George Leman, "Iraq, American Empire, and the War on Terrorism," in *The Philosophical Challenge of September 11,* ed. Tom Rockmore, Joseph Margolis, and Armen T. Marsoobian (Oxford: Blackwell Publishing, 2005), 10–11]. "*The U.S. is losing to terrorism* ... In large measure, this is because of incentives and dynamics built into our policy processes and

deeply rooted popular beliefs" [David B. Bobrow, "Losing to Terrorism," in *The Philosophical Challenges of Sept. 11*, 156]. *"Terrorism may not be fought by terrorism.* Nor may it be fought by means of a strategy that does not amount to terrorism, but must be condemned on the ground of the same moral values and principles that provide the strongest reasons for our rejection of terrorism. In this respect, so far the record of 'the w.o.t.' has been very poor indeed" [Igor Primoratz, "State Terrorism and Counterterrorism," in *Ethics of Terrorism and Counterterrorism,* ed. G. Meggle (Frankfurt: Ontos Verlag, 2005), 80].

8. Haig Khatchadourian, *The Morality of Terrorism* (New York: Peter Lang, 1998), 113–114.

Appendix

Eight Steps toward Ending the Global Clash of Terrorisms and Initiating a Process of Understanding and Reconciliation

1. Recognize that the conflicts in Iraq, Afghanistan, and the rest of the Middle East and Southwest Asia are regional in nature, with global reach, and therefore require multilateral solutions, with the active participation of all the nations and subnational groups involved, as well as the United States, the United Kingdom, Russia, China, and the European Union (EU).
2. Accordingly, immediately convene a UN-sponsored fact-finding and solution-oriented conference, with the participation of all the nations, subnational groups, and international/regional organizations affected by these conflicts. These include the United States, the United Kingdom, Iraq (all major factions, including insurgent representatives), Afghanistan (all major factions, including Taliban representatives), Iran, Syria, Jordan, Turkey, Pakistan, India, Israel and Palestine, Egypt, Saudi Arabia, the Gulf States, the EU, the Arab League, and the Organization of Islamic Countries (OIC). The conference would have as its mission the design and implementation of an action plan for confidence-building and conflict-reducing measures among the actors most at odds with each other.
3. Initiate a multilateral GRIT (graduated and reciprocated initiatives in tension reduction) model of small steps to reduce armed conflict and reprisals and increase recognition of the legitimate

security needs of each party, especially those engaged in escalating cycles of violence.

4. Gradually withdraw coalition forces from Iraq and Afghanistan, concomitant with gradual deployment of UN/OIC peacemaking and peacekeeping forces. Coalition forces are redeployed offshore to naval facilities to guarantee safe passage of ships in and near the Persian Gulf, and peacemaking and peacekeeping forces assume the responsibility for maintaining security inside Iraq and Afghanistan and the flow of oil. Later, if tensions ebb, Western forces could also be moved offshore from the Saudi Peninsula and Gulf States.

5. Gradual resettlement of Israelis on the West Bank and a series of measures to accelerate a final settlement of the Israeli-Palestinian conflict with the aim of resolving the status of Jerusalem, Palestinian refugees, water and other natural resource allocation, and creation of an economically and politically viable Palestinian state.

6. Diplomats and conflict-resolution specialists from the United States, the United Kingdom, the EU, Russia, India, Pakistan, Israel, Turkey, the Arab states, and China to begin a series of informal and formal, UN- and OIC-mediated, confidence-building workshops with representatives of and from subnational insurgent and "terrorist" groups. While these are being conducted, a truce is to be declared among the antagonists, including the United States and the al-Qaeda, which is to be monitored by UN and OIC peacekeepers. Intelligence-gathering, security measures to protect ports, power facilities, and transportation, as well as the policing and interdiction of violent subnational groups would be brought under independent, multilateral control and supervision of the UN and OIC.

7. Decision-makers from all sides of the global conflict would engage in continuing small-group workshops and training facilitated by social scientists and independent conflict-reduction specialists. The goal would be to gradually increase awareness of prejudices, biases, perceptions, and misperceptions of "antagonists," and to promote attitudinal awareness and behavioral change. Concrete nonviolent alternatives to terrifying violence would be modeled at the interpersonal, small group, organizational, ethnic, religious, and international levels.

8. Make UN-sponsored global conferences and specialized training opportunities available to all journalists, with the goal of improving best practices in professional journalism. Areas of interest

would include professional ethics in journalism (including con-flicts of interests and universal responsibility to inform the public); deconstruction of information warfare (including rhetorical narra-tives, framing, and propaganda); investigative reporting; conflict resolution; and peace journalism.

CONTRIBUTORS

Mark Arax is a journalist and author of three books: *West of the West, The King of California* (a *Los Angeles Times* bestseller and Best Book of the Year), and *In My Father's Name*. He teaches nonfiction writing at California State University, Fresno, and is working on his first novel.

John A. Arnaldi is a educator, photographer, and life coach. As an instructor at the University of South Florida, he has taught ethics of war and peace in the Honors College and graduate counseling courses. He is coauthor of "Teaching the Applied Ethics of War and Peace" (2009) with James Hudson and "Future Trends in Selected Settings," with Steve Simon in Dixon and Emener, eds., *Professional Counseling: Transitioning into the Next Millennium* (1999).

Scott Atran is presidential scholar at the John Jay College of Criminal Justice in New York City, visiting professor of psychology and public policy at the University of Michigan, and research director in anthropology at the National Center for Scientific Research in Paris. His recent books include *In Gods We Trust: The Evolutionary Landscape of Religion, The Native Mind and the Cultural Construction of Nature,* and *Talking to the Enemy: Faith, Brotherhood, and the (Un)Making of Terrorists*.

Molly Bingham is a filmmaker, journalist, and photographer who has covered conflict, including the war in Iraq. Bingham codirected the award-winning documentary *Meeting Resistance* (2007), about the Iraqi resistance. She wrote "Ordinary Warriors" (*Vanity Fair*, July 2004), among other articles and her photographs have been published in a wide array of publications including the *New York Times* and the *Guardian* of London.

Laurie L. Calhoun is research fellow at the Independent Institute and advisory editor of *Transition: An International Review*. She has served as director of publications at the Du Bois Institute at Harvard

University, as executive editor of *Transition: An International Review*, and as managing editor of the *Du Bois Review: Social Science Research on Race*. She has taught philosophy at St. Cloud State University; SUNY College, Fredonia; and the University of South Florida, St. Petersburg. Calhoun is the author of *Philosophy Unmasked: A Skeptic's Critique* (1997) and her essays have appeared in *Politics, New Politics, Peace Review, New Political Science, Dissent, Peace & Change, International Journal of Human Rights, Peace and Conflict Studies*, and *Ethical Theory and Moral Practice*, among other journals.

Noam Chomsky is institute professor emeritus in the MIT Department of Linguistics and Philosophy. He is the author of numerous best-selling political works. His latest books are a new edition of *Power and Terror, The Essential Chomsky* (edited by Anthony Arnove), a collection of his writings on politics and on language from the 1950s to the present, *Gaza in Crisis*, with Ilan Pappé, and *Hopes and Prospects*.

William A. Cohn, an attorney and constitutional law scholar, has practiced and taught law since 1993, working with clients, judges, international organizations, bar associations, and scholars, lecturing and publishing extensively on law and policy, particularly on international jurisprudence and rule of law principles. An antiwar activist and member of the State Bar of California, he received his law degree from the University of California and his BA degree in international relations from Stanford University. He currently lectures on law, ethics, and critical thinking in the undergraduate and graduate programs at the University of New York in Prague.

Michael German is senior policy counsel for the American Civil Liberties Union (ACLU). He has served as a special agent for the FBI, taught counterterrorism at the FBI National Academy, and worked as undercover agent against white supremacist and militia groups. His first book, *Thinking Like a Terrorist*, was published in 2007.

Lisa Hajjar teaches sociology at the University of California at Santa Barbara. Her research and writing focus on law and legality, war and conflict, human rights, and torture. She is author of *Courting Conflict: The Israeli Military Court System in the West Bank and Gaza*, and coeditor with Richard Falk and Hilal Elver of *Human Rights: Critical Concepts in Political Science*, Vols 1–5. She is a coeditor of the e-zine *Jadaliyya*, and serves on the editorial committees of *Middle East Report, Journal of Palestine Studies*, and *Societies without Borders*. She is currently working on a book about antitorture lawyering in the United States.

Jørgen Johansen is editor of *Resistance Studies* Magazine, a regular lecturer at Syracuse University, Gothenburg University, and the World Peace Academy, a visiting scholar at Coventry University, and course director in nonviolence at Transcend Peace University. Johansen has published six books and hundreds of articles on nonviolence, peace, democracy, and terrorism. He is coeditor of the book *Experiments with Peace, Celebrating Peace on Johan Galtung's 80th Birthday.*

Seth C. Lewis is assistant professor, School of Journalism and Mass Communication at the University of Minnesota—Twin Cities. His research focuses on media sociology, digital technology, and innovation in journalism, and his work has appeared in a number of academic journals. He earned a PhD from the University of Texas at Austin, and previously was an editor at the *Miami Herald* and a Fulbright scholar in Spain.

Stephen D. Reese is Jesse H. Jones Professor and associate dean for academic affairs in the College of Communication, University of Texas, where previously he was director of the School of Journalism. He was editor for the "Media Production and Content" subfield in the recent *International Encyclopedia of Communication*, and his research interests include the sociology of news, framing, and the impact of globalization on journalism.

Cris Toffolo is professor and chair, Justice Studies Department, Northeastern Illinois University in Chicago. Her publications include: *The Arab League* (2007) and *Emancipating Cultural Pluralism* (ed., 2003). She has worked and taught in organizations around the world and currently serves as the cochair of the Peace and Justice Studies Association (PJSA). Since 1991 she has served as Amnesty International's (United States) Pakistan country specialist. Her research and teaching areas include: human right, theories of justice, social movements, and Third World politics. She received her PhD from the University of Notre Dame.

Charles P. Webel is a three-time Fulbright scholar who teaches at the University of California at Berkeley, the University of South Florida, and the University of New York in Prague. He is the author of *Terror, Terrorism, and the Human Condition*; the coauthor (with David Barash) of *Peace and Conflict Studies*; and the coeditor (with Johan Galtung) of the *Handbook of Peace and Conflict Studies,* and (with Jorgen Johansen) of the forthcoming *Reader in Peace and Conflict Studies.*

INDEX